Destroyer Down

Destroyer Down

An Account of HM Destroyer Losses
1939–1945

A. S. Evans

Pen & Sword
MARITIME

First published in Great Britain in 2010 by
Pen & Sword Maritime
an imprint of
Pen & Sword Books Ltd
47 Church Street
Barnsley
South Yorkshire
S70 2AS

Copyright © A. S. Evans 2010

ISBN 978-1-84884-270-0

The right of A. S. Evans to be identified as Author of this Work has been
asserted by him in accordance with the Copyright, Designs and Patents Act
1988.

A CIP catalogue record for this book is available from the British Library.

Typeset in 11pt Ehrhardt by
Mac Style, Beverley, E. Yorkshire

Printed and bound in the UK by the MPG Books Group

Pen & Sword Books Ltd incorporates the imprints of Pen & Sword Aviation,
Pen & Sword Maritime, Pen & Sword Military, Wharncliffe Local History,
Pen and Sword Select, Pen and Sword Military Classics and Leo Cooper.

For a complete list of Pen & Sword titles please contact
PEN & SWORD BOOKS LIMITED
47 Church Street, Barnsley, South Yorkshire, S70 2AS, England
E-mail: enquiries@pen-and-sword.co.uk
Website: www.pen-and-sword.co.uk

Contents

Publishers Note

The manuscript for this book came to light as a result of a visit to the late author's widow, Joan Evans, in connection with the republication of his much acclaimed record of wartime submarine losses entitled 'Beneath the Waves'. This book follows the same theme but as applied to World War II Destroyers of the Royal Navy. Pen & Sword have made every effort to ensure the accuracy of the information within this volume, but without the author to consult, every minute detail cannot be checked. The publishers would be pleased to note any factual modifications readers may wish to offer.

Chapter One

1939

At sea there was no such thing as a Phoney War. In the four months from the outbreak of hostilities until the end of 1939, thirty Royal Navy vessels were sunk. Three of His Majesty's destroyers featured among the casualties.

HMS *Blanche*

The first was the *Blanche*, captained by Lieutenant-Commander Robert Aubrey. The cruiser-minelayer *Adventure*, under the command of Captain Arthur Halfhide, was being escorted from the Humber to Portsmouth by *Blanche* and the destroyer *Basilisk* when shortly after 0500 on 13 November the *Adventure*, by then in the vicinity of the Thames estuary, exploded a mine port side and just before the bridge. Correctly assuming that his ship had been mined and not torpedoed, Captain Halfhide ordered *Basilisk* alongside *Adventure* to transfer the wounded, which numbered about sixty. After lowering boats *Blanche* proceeded to carry out an anti-submarine sweep. Although severely damaged, *Adventure* was in no danger of sinking and by 0715 was again underway. *Basilisk* was ordered to lead the cruiser into the Edinburgh Channel, one of three deep-water channels in the Thames estuary. Speed was gradually built up to 8 knots and all appeared to be going as well as could be expected when at 0745 sea-water was found to have mixed with *Adventure's* oil fuel. While *Basilisk* was making preparations to take the cruiser in tow, good work by *Adventure's* crew enabled her once more to proceed under her own power.

The improved situation had given cause for optimism when disaster once more befell the group. *Blanche* was in station on *Adventure's* starboard bow when at 0810 the destroyer's after end detonated a mine. Heavily damaged, and rapidly losing steam, *Blanche* quickly came to a halt. Able Seaman William Eldridge was in charge of the bridge searchlight and had gone below for a cup of tea when, says Eldridge:

The explosion aft shook the cup right out of my hand. The bows of the ship seemed to leap right out of the water. We were thrown all over the place. There was no panic. We made everything safe, shutting doors and so on, took our places on the upper deck, and then put on our life-jackets. Two hours later our ship rolled over and sank. Some of us had already jumped into the water, which was thick with oil; others were thrown in as the ship turned over for the last time. We were picked up wonderfully quickly. From Leading Stoker John Mutton I heard how a number of the ship's company, instead of bothering about their own safety, searched the ship high and low for 'Black Em', the ship's mascot, a tiny black cat. But it appears that 'Black Em' had taken fright from the explosion and had stowed away and, presumably, was lost. Two officers standing on the deck only a few feet from the seat of the explosion escaped unhurt. Another officer was in his bath, but managed to crawl to safety.

The officer taking a bath was Sub-Lieutenant Dudley Davenport. Davenport reports:

Having been up most of the night, Lieutenant Patrick Graham and I tossed a coin to decide who should remain on watch and who should go below first for a bath and a breakfast. I won. I was in the bathroom at the fore-end of the after superstructure when we hit a mine in the same minefield. The explosion, just forward of the after superstructure, knocked me out and I imagine that it was the shattered mirror and basin which cut me about the head and feet, hence the origin of the report 'Bloody Officer Found in Bath.' I came to lying on the upper deck by the torpedo tubes. I soon felt well enough to walk forward towards the bridge to find out what was going on. After the effort of climbing the forecastle ladder I felt the need of a rest and sat down on the deck with Midshipman Byrne, who had also been injured.

A tug came alongside to tow us. Shortly after she took the strain, the ship's back broke and she slowly rolled over to port and sank. Mr Byrne and I were able to slide down the starboard side of the forecastle and were soon picked up by one of the tugs. After drying our clothes in the tug's boiler room, we were landed on Ramsgate pier. At Ramsgate there was a large assembly of ambulances (military, civil, and volunteer) all keen to collect their first casualties of the war!

Another survivor was Able Seaman Hoyle:

I was on deck when a terrific explosion shook the ship. I saw a man blown right past me over the side of the ship into the water. At the same moment the mast snapped and crashed down. A lifeboat was lowered to rescue the man; the ship was already listing badly. Our first thought was for the men trapped below near the explosion. We forced our way through the wreckage to rescue them. The injured men were brought up and laid on the deck while we tended to their injuries.

We were sinking by the stern, but there was no order to abandon ship. Every man was eager to save her. They worked hard shoring up the bulkheads and manning the pumps. By this time the quarter-deck was awash. Some of the men were so badly injured that they had to be tied to the stretchers. We carried them to the other side of the ship, away from the list. Then a tug arrived on the scene, and actually got a line to us and began to tow us. The ship had practically righted herself and everybody thought she would hold, but a few minutes later she turned quickly over to port and lay on her side. One again we were concerned for the injured. I saw the captain, who had no lifebelt himself, unstrapping one of the injured from the stretchers. We put lifebelts on the injured and as the ship was sinking slid them into the water. The captain swam around encouraging the men. Gradually the tug picked up most of us, and then a trawler and a little pleasure boat came out and picked up the rest.

Skipper Jack Pocock, owner of a trawler that came to assist, reports:

We were within a quarter of a mile of the destroyer when we saw her heel over and go down stern first. Men were pouring over the side, and the sea seemed full of swimming sailors and oil. I shall never forget the courage of those men. One swam round singing 'Even Hitler had a Mother'[1]. And another man I tried to pick out of the water refused my hand, saying there were other men in a worse plight. I saw one sailor push a piece of wreckage into the hands of a boy and swim away.

Time for *Blanche* ran out at 0950 when she heeled hard to port and failed to righten. Fortunately casualties were light: one rating killed and three officers and twelve ratings wounded.

HMS *Gipsy*

The dubious distinction of being the first destroyer loss of the war had almost gone to *Gipsy*, as within days of *Blanche's* loss she too had been mined and sunk.

On Tuesday 21 November a German seaplane was seen to fly low over the harbour entrance of Harwich. Two unidentified objects were observed to fall from the plane and into the sea. The approximate position in which the mines fell, for that was what they were, was charted and the matter reported to the C-in-C Nore. During late evening of the same day it was necessary for a merchant ship and two destroyers to put to sea. These vessels were instructed to keep well to port of the suspected position of the mines. The merchantman and *Griffin* passed safely to sea but the *Gipsy*, at 2120, struck a mine. Her captain, Lieutenant-Commander Nigel Crossly, sustained fatal injuries (he died less than a week later) when he was hurled off the bridge and onto the gun deck, and from there onto the forecastle deck.

The explosion had broken *Gipsy's* back. She sagged until her midship section grounded in 30 feet of water. Her fore and after ends remained buoyant for some considerable time, and then settled quite slowly. Eight ratings had been lost outright and a further twenty-one were missing. Several others were wounded.

HMS *Duchess*

The west coast of Scotland was the scene of the third and last destroyer loss of 1939. The battleship *Barham* sailed from Gibraltar on 6 December screened by the destroyers *Duchess* and *Duncan*. She was *en route* to join the Home Fleet in place of *Nelson*. On 11 December *Barham's* screen was augmented by the destroyers *Exmouth* and *Eclipse,* and later the *Echo.* The following morning the force was to the west of Scotland and Islay was in sight. At 0427 a change of course was ordered by *Barham.*

Shortly after this the *Barham* and *Duchess* were in collision with tragic results. *Barham* had struck *Duchess* between the forward funnel and the gallery flat. The collision turned *Duchess* over completely, leading many of those in the battleship, who had rushed on deck from below, into believing, at first, that a submarine had been struck.

The cold water quickly took to their death many of the destroyer's crew who were able to escape before she had turned over. Once she had turned turtle escape was almost impossible. In the early days of the war no escape scuttles had been incorporated in ships' hulls. This omission of some extra large scuttles resulted in almost every scuttle in the upturned *Duchess* having a crewman frantically, but with no success, trying to pass through. It was one of the saddest sights of the war at sea. About 20 minutes after the collision the destroyer's depth charges exploded and sent her to the bottom.

The fact that *Duchess* had quickly turned turtle, plus the darkness and exploding depth charges, was against there being many survivors. Her captain, Lieutenant-Commander Robin White, and five officers were lost with the ship. Of the ratings, 123 did not survive. The collision is believed to have been the cause of *Duchess* confusing *Barham's* manoeuvring signals.[2] When the signal to change course was given by *Barham* the *Duchess* appears to have responded at once instead of waiting for the executive signal, thus she crossed the track of *Barham.*

Notes
1. This song had been banned during the years of appeasement (Author).
2. Manoeuvring signals did not order the manoeuvre indicated to take place immediately, but only warned that it would shortly take place.

Chapter Two

1940

HMS *Grenville*

Captain (later Admiral of the Fleet Sir) George Creasy was thirty-two when he succeeded Captain C. M. Blackman as Captain D1 in *Grenville* in June 1938. He was still Captain D when at 1245 on 19 January 1940 *Grenville* was sunk to the east of Harwich while on an A/S sweep.

With *Grenade* a mile to her north and *Griffin* a mile to the south, *Grenville* was making the sweep on a course of 250 degrees at 20 knots when she set off a mine. *Grenville* immediately started to sink, the bow and stern rising out of the water. She settled on the bottom with about 60 feet of her bow and about 12 feet of her stern showing. As will be seen from the experience of Able Seamen J. Walton and S. G. Bromfield, there was little time to launch the ship's boats. Able Seaman Walton:

> *I was buying some chocolate in the canteen when there was a terrific explosion. I tried to reach a lifeboat but it was impossible, and I followed the rest into the icy seas. The bridge and superstructure collapsed and many men were trapped underneath. I was lucky to grab hold of a spar. After being tossed about for 2 hours I was rescued by another warship. One of my shipmates had to release his grip and drowned. In a few minutes more he could have been saved. Many men were clinging to all kinds of wreckage, though the survivors were becoming fewer as each minute passed. One man was holding onto part of the foremast with one hand while in the other he had a piece of toast which he was eating! Captain Creasy, while in the water, shouted messages to cheer us up. We responded with an effort to sing Beer Barrel Polka, but the water went into my mouth every time I opened it.*

Twenty-six years old Sidney Bromfield was the last to leave *Grenville*. When her bow went down Bromfield held onto one of the port scuttles:

> *I had just come off watch after being up all night, and was snugly bunked down when the explosion happened. At first I thought we were dropping a few depth charges, and turned over to have another snooze. But suddenly the ships started to*

list over. My mates ran towards the gangway. I sat up, rubbing the sleep out of my eyes, and decided, 'The hatchway for me.' When I got on deck there was a terrific list, and I wondered what to do. You see, I couldn't swim, and that made it a bit difficult. I decided I'd hold on to anything solid, so long as there was anything solid to hold on to. As the ship listed I squatted on the seat of my pants and slithered with her, trying to keep an even keel. But there was a sudden plunge and I found myself in the water holding onto one of the porthole bars. By using these as a ladder I swung myself from porthole to porthole until I reached the top. While I was clinging there I saw two ships circling round trying to pick up survivors. Two lifeboats, both seemed to be overloaded, passed me. The whole sea beneath me was dotted with the bobbing heads of sailors swimming for their lives.

After half an hour balancing on the porthole Able Seaman Bromfield felt that he was unable to hang on any longer:

But when I thought of those poor devils swimming about, I told myself 'You have got a cushy billet, what are you grumbling about?' Then came the most heartening sound I've ever heard. It was the voice of our captain, Captain Creasy, in the water himself, cheering his men. And you can bet it cheered me. Somehow it sent my blood tingling and gave me the strength to hang on until the rescue boat arrived about a quarter of an hour later. I'd been stranded on that bow for only an hour, but it seemed more like a month.

Grenade and *Griffin* rescued survivors until 1430, by which time no more could be seen. Both destroyers returned safely to harbour.

HMS *Exmouth*
The first U-boat captain to sink a Royal Navy destroyer was Kapitanleutnant Karl-Heinrich Jenisch in U22 and his target was the *Exmouth*. U22 sailed from Kiel on 16 January. Her area of operations for the nine days patrol was to the east of Kinnaird Head. In the early hours of Tuesday 21st the bridge party of U22 sighted a merchantman in company with a destroyer. Jenisch closed to 1,500 metres and at 0435 fired a torpedo, which he estimated hit the destroyer forward. He did not wait around to see his victim sink, being more interested in pursuing the merchant ship.

The *Exmouth* had gone down to the east of Hemlsdale with the loss of all hands: fifteen officers and 173 ratings. But three months after her loss the U22 was mined in the Skagerrak. There were no survivors.

HMS *Daring*
A patrolling U-boat (U23) to the east of the Orkneys also accounted for the loss of *Daring*. Around 0250 on 18 February convoy HN12 (Bergan-Methil) was in

position 54.40'N/01.40'W steering 178 degrees at 7 knots. HM destroyers *Inglefield, Daring, Delight, Ilex,* and the submarine *Thistle* were the convoy escort. U23 fired two torpedoes that hit *Daring* to starboard. Less than 30 seconds after being hit *Daring,* captained by Commander Sydney Cooper, turned turtle, and then broke in two. The captain of *Thistle* relates his part in the events of the night:

> *Daring had been in view most of the night, but at this time only occasionally visible, being in the dark sector. Being below, at 0256 I heard two loud explosions about five seconds apart which gave me the impression that depth charges had been dropped a mile or two away. On reaching the bridge the officer of the watch informed me that a column of black smoke about 150 feet high had risen with the first explosion approximately where* Daring *had last been sighted. On approaching the spot an object could be seen, which I later believed to have been* Daring's *forecastle pointing upwards at an angle, with the top of the bridge visible abaft this; at the time, however, it appeared to be equally like a U-boat's bow and conning tower in a sinking condition, although this seemed gradually less probable as no destroyer could be seen. I circled near the position trying to identify the wreck and also to look for survivors and a possible U-boat. As the depth of water was 60 fathoms it appeared that a U-boat was a more likely cause of the sinking than a mine and consequently I considered it advisable then to stop for a closer examination. Asdic watch was set but nothing was heard. I also expected at every moment to see the port bow destroyer of the escort, who was normally not far ahead of* Daring, *drop back and lower a boat to search, but as no ship appeared I tried again to make contact with one of the escorts by lamp.*
>
> *At about 0320 I was in touch with* Ilex, *the starboard wing destroyer, and I told her to close me, informing her of the situation.* Ilex *passed the wreck at about 0335 and signaled to* Thistle *to pick up survivors while she provided cover. By the time I had realized that she had not left a boat to assist me, I had lost touch with her and could not ask for this assistance.*
>
> *Three survivors were found: one disappeared soon after* Thistle's *arrival, one was on* Daring's *stern which was floating separately, and another was clinging to a small raft. The latter shouted that he could not swim as his arm was broken, so* Thistle's *stern was placed as near to him as possible and Lieutenant Ennor, RNR, swam to him with a line and tried to bring raft and man alongside together; however, the man had misunderstood his intentions and, letting go the raft, clung to the officer. Both went under and Lieutenant Ennor had to push the man off, grasping him again when both came back up. Owing to the man being covered with oil fuel, he slipped through Lieutenant Ennor's hands when they were practically alongside. He sank and did not reappear.*
>
> *During this time touch had been regained with* Ilex. *Boats were asked for and at about 0430 two whalers were lowered.* Ilex *again opened to carry on the hunt*

and provide cover. One of Ilex*'s boats picked up the man from the floating piece of* Daring*'s stern and, as he was only semi-conscious, came alongside* Thistle. *The man was got inboard, a difficult operation in the prevailing conditions. The man, William McBride, soon recovered, except for the discomfort due to having swallowed a good deal of oil fuel.*

At about 0545 *Daring's* bows lifted to the vertical and slowly sank. Her captain, Commander Sydney Cooper, was not among the twenty or so survivors. The U-boat ace Otto Kretschmer had made the attack on *Daring*. In March 1941 he was taken prisoner when his U-boat was sunk by HMS *Walker*.

HMS *Glowworm*

Fearful that the British might occupy Norway, and thus at a single stroke cut not only Germany's vital iron-ore supply but also her outlets to the Atlantic, Hitler gave approval for Operation *Weserbung*, the invasion of Norway. Denmark would be seized at the same time. On 1 April Hitler signed the order that would place Norway and Denmark under Nazi occupation. Zero hour was timed as 0515 9 April.

At the same time as the German invasion forces were heading for their respective destinations a small Royal Navy Force, unaware that *Weserubung* was in progress, was also making for Norwegian waters to lay mines in several locations with the intention of forcing German ore ships away from the safety of Norwegian coastal waters. Screened by the destroyers *Greyhound*, *Glowworm*, *Hero*, and *Hyperion*, the battle cruiser *Renown* sailed from Scapa Flow as a protecting force for the minelayers.

On 8 April *Renown* and her destroyers were battling against heavy seas. The weather grew worse as each storm-tossed hour merged with the next. *Glowworm*, captained by Lieutenant Commander Gerard Roope and having lost a man overboard, left the screen to make a search. Sometime later she was endeavouring to regain contact with *Renown* when shortly after daybreak a destroyer was sighted to the north. This ship, the German *Paul Jakobi*, identified herself as Swedish but she then opened fire. *Glowworm's* 4.7s returned the fire. A second German destroyer, the *Bernd von Arnim*, was then observed. The mess decks of *Bernd von Arnim* were crammed with invasion troops. Her captain was understandably keen to put the troops safely ashore as quickly as possible, and so attempted to evade *Glowworm*. Lieutenant-Commander Gerard Roope, *Glowworm's* captain, believed the Germans were trying to lure him on to a more powerful force, but decided to follow in hope of gaining details of what ships the Germans had at sea. By this time *Glowworm's* gun-director tower had been flooded by heavy seas, two hands had been washed overboard, and several ratings injured by the ship's violent rolling.

Bound for Trondheim with troops was the German heavy cruiser *Admiral Hipper*. At 0935 she had received a signal from the *Bernd von Arnim* stating that she was engaging an enemy destroyer. *Hipper* had then proceeded towards the scene of the action. At 0950 *Hipper* sighted the Bernd von *Arnim* and *Glowworm*. At 0957 the cruiser opened fire, hitting *Glowworm* with her first salvo. The heavy weather made successful escape or evasive shadowing unlikely, so Roope sent off an enemy sighting report and then closed *Hipper*. A shell tore through *Glowworm's* wheelhouse. This was speedily followed by another, which burst in the radio office. Another shell entered *Glowworm* under the torpedo tubes and traversed the width of the ship before exploding against a bulkhead of Roope's cabin, in use as a medical station, and killed or wounded all present. Yet another shell brought down part of the foremast and W/T aerials, which fouled the siren on the funnel, and so *Glowworm* went into action with her siren wailing loudly. *Glowworm* fired a spread of five torpedoes. All missed the target. She was again hit forward, and in her engine room where fire broke out. *Glowworm* made smoke and prepared to make another torpedo attack. She emerged from the smoke-screen, crossing *Hipper's* bows from port to starboard, and fired a spread of five torpedoes, four of which ran wide and the fifth narrowly missing. Lieutenant Commander Roope had already made up his mind to ram. At about 20 Knots he turned sharply to starboard and made towards *Hipper's* starboard side. Vice-Admiral Helmuth Heye, in command of *Hipper*, tried to turn to starboard and ram *Glowworm*. But the cruiser was slower under helm than *Glowworm*. With a grinding crash she smashed into *Hipper's* starboard side, tearing away about 130 feet of the cruiser's armoured belt. Drawing clear, and even though her decks were being swept by fire from *Hipper's* 4.1-inch and 37mm close-range weapons, *Glowworm's* guns fired another salvo. With his ship settling by the bows and a fire raging amidships, and all steam lost, Roope ordered abandon ship. *Glowworm* capsized soon after.

In the sea Roope was observed helping men put on their life jackets. He was also seen to grasp one of the lines thrown to survivors. After hauling himself up the cruiser's side almost to deck level, Roope's strength gave out and he fell into the sea and perished. Out of *Glowworm's* 149 crew only thirty-one survived. Admiral Heye was later to comment: '*In our opinion the bearing of the commander and the crew of Glowworm was excellent*'.

For his fight against hopeless odds Lieutenant Commander Gerard Roope was awarded the Victoria Cross.

HMS *Gurkha*

By the early hours of 8 April it had become evident that the Germans had launched a full-scale invasion of Norway. In the confused situation the British considered that Bergen may have already fallen. It was therefore proposed that a naval force attack Herman shipping therein. The home fleet was at that time on a southerly course 90 miles south-west of Bergen. At 1130 Vice-Admiral Geoffrey Layton's 18th Cruiser Squadron (*Manchester, Southampton, Glasgow*, and seven destroyers), which had joined the home fleet at 0630, was detached with orders that the destroyers be sent up fjord to Bergen while the cruisers patrolled the fjord's entrance. However soon after 1400 the plan was cancelled. The home fleet had by then turned about and was heading north. With the destroyers screening the cruisers, Vice-Admiral Layton steamed to rejoin the fleet. It was during this period that one of the destroyers, the tribal class *Gurkha*, was sunk.

The cruisers became the target of enemy aircraft but a very rough sea considerably affected the accuracy of the ships' gunners in beating off attacks. Frustrated by his ship's lack of success against the aircraft, Commander Sir Anthony Buzzard, *Gurkha's* CO, at about 1430, took his ship out of the screen and to a more comfortable course in the hope that a more stable platform would profit his gunners. As soon as *Gurkha* became separated from the group she was singled out by the aircraft for special attention.

A *Gurkha* petty officer observed:

In the fourth attack a bomb struck the ship. All the other bombs fell into the sea, but the plane dived and machine-gunned us. Our wireless aerials were smashed early in the fight but despite this we managed to rig up temporary aerials. Down below, the ship was plunged into darkness; plates and pipes were falling from above. After we were hit the ship began to list to starboard. This gradually increased and we battened down and started pumping. Ship's stores and everything moveable went overboard. Our guns were going all the time and we definitely accounted for one plane. Hit by a shell it went straight down into the sea. Another plane was hit and when last seen was wobbling away.

Eric Hagon, a nineteen years old stoker, recalls:

I was down below when the bomb that sank us exploded. The stern was lifted out of the water and the lights went out. One of the stokers was injured: I believe his back was broken. Everyone went on with his work until we had orders to shut down the boilers. We went on deck, which was awash, and helped to throw gear and surplus ammunition overboard. The guns of the Gurkha *were still firing as many planes came over. When the order came to abandon ship I tried to get one of the* Gurkha *knives in the after part of the ship as a souvenir, but was unable to reach it. I saw the lieutenant-commander and the chief stoker on a Carley float rescuing a number of men from the water, while three or four wounded men were strapped to tables and lowered over the destroyer's side.*

The bomb had struck the ship aft, blasting a 40 feet hole in the starboard side. A fire in the after end necessitated flooding the after magazine and the stern became awash. *Gurkha's* lights having failed, it was only with considerable difficulty that the wounded were brought up and laid on the fo'c'sle. The 45 degree starboard list taken by *Gurkha* made the situation perilous and only by taking a firm hold on the guard-rails and anchor chains was it possible to keep from falling overboard. *Gurkha* was alone in the rough sea with darkness not far off. The situation did not look promising but *Gurkha's* luck had not deserted her completely. Blanks fired at intervals attracted the attention of the cruiser *Aurora* just as night was closing. *Gurkha's* list had by then increased even further. She heeled over onto her starboard side, allowing those who did not fall from the fo'c'sle to climb through the guard rails and sit on the hull. At 1900 *Gurkha* rolled over completely and sank. *Aurora* landed the survivors at Thurso. A notable feature of the sinking was that *Gurkha* was the first Royal Navy destroyer ever to be sunk by aircraft.

* * *

Within hours of *Gurkha's* loss there occurred what became known as the First Battle of Narvick. The port of Narvik is situated in Beisfjord, a small fjord towards the head of the main Ofotfjord. Early on the morning of 9 April ten German Destroyers, under the command of Kommodorre Friedrich Bonte, loaded with two thousand troops, made their way through the 15 miles long Ofotfjord towards Narvik. Three destroyers crossed to Herjangsfjord on the north shore, where the troops were landed to seize an army depot. Kommodore Bonte then entered Narvik and took the port with ease.

By late afternoon Captain Bernard Warburton-Lee of the 2nd Destroyer Flotilla (*Hardy, Havock, Hostile, Hotspur, Hunter*) learned from the Norwegian pilot station of Tranoy, at the end of VestfJord, that a force of German destroyers had proceeded up Ofotfjord towards Narvik. In the early hours of the following morning the 2nd DF entered Ofotfjord in line ahead with *Hardy* leading. Heavy snow-squalls at times rendered the snow-covered shore invisible and at one point *Hardy* almost ran aground. Undetected the small force edged closer to the sleeping port of Narvik. Then quite suddenly they were there. The tranquillity of the early morning came to an abrupt end when, at 0430, a torpedo from *Hardy* exploded in the after magazine of Kommodore Bronte's Flagship, the destroyer *Wilhelm Heidkamp*. Another destroyer was hit by two torpedoes from *Hardy*. She broke into two sections and sank. Further torpedoes scored hits on merchant ships. *Hardy* then retired to leave the way clear for Lieutenant-Commanders Lindsay de Villiers in *Hunter* and Rafe Courage in *Havock*. Both fired torpedoes and used their guns to good effect before withdrawing. *Hotspur*, Commander Herbert Layman, and *Hostile*, Commander John Wright, had remained outside the harbour to guard the entrance. Wright then entered harbour and fired his guns at the destroyer *Diether von Roeder*.

Already suffering damage, the destroyer was soon blazing fiercely. As a parting gift Commander Layman sent four torpedoes into a mass of shipping. Before withdrawing completely, Captain Warburton-Lee led the flotilla past the harbour entrance to allow each destroyer a final burst of fire. The flotilla then raced 3 miles down fjord to take stock of the situation. After a brief report from each ship, Warburton-Lee decided to make another attack.

HMS *Hardy*

Smoke and mist in Narvik harbour made sighting difficult. Gun flashes of the German ships were taken as points of aim. *Hostile* fired four torpedoes, trusting to hit something. Having caused a great deal of damage and confusion the British made smoke and withdrew down fjord. They had steamed a short distance when three German destroyers were encountered. These ships were large enough for one of them to be mistaken for a cruiser. Increasing speed to 30 knots the five H class ships raced seaward. The German ships gave pursuit, but as they were low on fuel the situation for the British looked favourable. Then ahead of the fleeing ships there suddenly appeared two more German destroyers.

The new arrivals, the *Georg Thiele* and *Bernd von Arnim*, had been in Ballangenfjord when ordered to engage enemy destroyers. In the hope that the two ships were British Warburton-Lee made the challenge. Accurate gunfire was the response. *Hardy* was at once seriously damaged but from her yardarm broke the signal *Keep on Engaging the Enemy*. Almost immediately a 5-inch shell smashed *Hardy*'s bridge. The effect was devastating: no one on the bridge escaped death or injury. Warburton-Lee was thrown to the deck mortally wounded.

On the bridge with *Hardy*'s captain was Paymaster-Lieutenant Geoffrey Stanning. Regaining his senses amid a scene of almost total destruction, Stanning realized that *Hardy* was racing along apparently out of control. He called the wheelhouse but there was no reply. Though his left foot had been smashed he made his way to the wheelhouse and took over the wheel from the dead helmsman. He remained at the wheel, steering by looking through a shell-hole, until an able seaman arrived and took over. He then made his way back to the bridge. Damage to steam-pipes was causing *Hardy* to lose way. Not wishing her to come to a stop in mid-fjord, where she could be sunk with greater loss of life, Stanning gave the order to run *Hardy* aground.

HMS *Hunter*

Seeing *Hardy* heading towards the shore, German gunfire was concentrated on *Hunter*, the next in line. *Hunter* was soon well ablaze. Astern of *Hunter* came Commander Layman in *Hotspur*. When Layman saw the burning and disabled *Hunter* swerve across his track, he ordered avoiding action. Unfortunately at that instant a shell struck *Hotspur* beneath her bridge and severed the controls between the wheel and the steering gear and also jammed the engine-room telegraph connection. Layman could do nothing but watch his ship's bow slice into the *Hunter*. He hurried aft to where he could pass verbal orders to the engine-room and the auxiliary steering position. Under punishing gunfire Layman was able to free *Hotspur* from the sinking *Hunter*. Calling for maximum speed Layman continued to head seaward. It was 0640.

*   *   *

Meanwhile the *Havock* and *Hostile* had been engaging the enemy at every opportunity. With their support the battered *Hotspur* was able to clear the fjord. The Germans made no attempt to pursue, and so when *Hostile* encountered the ammunition ship *Rauenfels* on a heading for Narvik, he was able to sink her.

The action at Narvik had cost the Germans two destroyers and nine supply ships. Other vessels had been damaged. The 2nd Flotilla had lost *Hardy* and *Hunter* and *Hotspur* had been badly damaged. The sinking of *Hunter* in mid-fjord resulted in only forty-six survivors out of a ship's complement of 145. Her South African captain, Lindsay de Villiers, did not survive. Captain Warburton-Lee was being floated ashore on a stretcher when he died of his wounds. For his courage and leadership at Narvik, he was awarded the Victoria Cross.

By the end of April the situation for the Allies in central Norway had become tenuous. Operation Klaxon, the evacuation of Allied troops from Namsos, was put into effect. Three French troop transports were made available for the evacuation, which began on the evening of 2 May. Loaded with troops, the last transport sailed from Namsos at 0230 on 3 May. Shortly before 0300 the *Afridi*, commanded by Captain (later Admiral of the Fleet Sir) Philip Vian, embarked the rearguard. Afridi joined the flag of the Vice-Admiral Commanding 1st Cruiser Squadron at 0540 and, with other destroyers, formed a screen on the cruisers *Devonshire*, *Carlise*, and a transport.

HMS *Bison*

At 0850 fifty JU87s (Stukas) and JU88 bombers began a continuous attack on the Allied force, which by then was well out to sea. The French cruiser *Montcalm*, the French destroyer *Bison*, and HMS *Griffin* were escorting one transport. At about 1010 the *Bison* was hit by a bomb which exploded the fore magazine. The whole of her fore part was blown away, including the bridge. *Grenade* went alongside to take off survivors while the *Montcalm* and the transport raced on. Vian hurriedly closed *Grenade* to provide AA protection. To speed up the rescue of *Bison's* crew, the *Afridi* also went alongside. Rescue operations were hampered by two air attacks but by 1130 most of the *Bison* was sunk by *Afridi*. With sixty-nine survivors on board, twenty-five of whom were seriously burned, *Afridi* proceed to join the convoy.

HMS *Afridi*
Captain Vian reports:

> *At 1400 on 3 May, on rejoining the Vice-Admiral Commanding the 1st Cruiser Squadron, when about to pass* Carlise, *who was the rear ship of the force escorted by* Devonshire, Afridi *was hit by two bombs dropped from 1,000 feet from either wing of a Junkers 87 diving from the sun. The ship was proceeding at 25 knots at the time and was under port rudder. Another bomb had missed astern about a minute before. Junkers flights are now learning to synchronise attacks. One bomb passed through the galley and forward boiler room and blew a hole through the port side, which admitted water into No.2 boiler room. It is believed that it was this explosion which set fire to the wireless room. The second bomb blew in sections of the port side abreast Nos 1 and 2 guns, flooded the compartments, and started a fire in the after end of the mess deck. The density of the fumes emitted by the fire prevented any accurate estimation of the extent of the damage forward.* Griffin *proceeded alongside the starboard side of* Afridi *and the port side of* Imperial; *both ships were very well handled and the survivors of the troops and* Bison's *crew transferred without difficulty.* Imperial *passed her towing pendant, which was secured to the towing slip of* Afridi *ready for towing her by the stern, the bows by this time being almost awash, but, as she was about to cast off and swing round, it became apparent that* Afridi *herself was about to founder, so part of her crew which had not by that time transferred to* Griffin *were transferred to* Imperial *at 1400. The survivors, including six ratings who were blown out of the ship by the explosion, were picked up by* Imperial's *whaler.* Afridi *foundered by the bow at 1446, having first turned turtle.*

Fifty of *Afridi's* crew did not survive. Thirty of the rescued *Bison* survivors were lost.

* * *

Towards the end of May it was clear that the Allies had lost the battle for Norway. The evacuation of troops from Norway began on 29 May when four thousand troops sailed from Bodo. On the nights of 4, 5, and 6 June fifteen thousand troops embarked on ships for a rendezvous 189 miles out to sea in preparation for their journey home. Under a destroyer escort this convoy was to proceed south. At 0100 on 8 June it would be joined by the battleship *Valiant* and destroyers from Scapa Flow. *Valiant* was then to escort the convoy safely past the Faeroes before returning to assist in the protection of a convoy of seven ships with ten thousand troops. Ships of this convoy sailed to their rendezvous on 7 and 8 June escorted by the cruiser *Southampton*, five destroyers, and the carrier *Ark Royal* with her own escorting destroyers. The carrier *Glorious* with

Acasta and *Ardent* were to have proceeded with this convoy but permission was given for her to part company with *Ark Royal* and head homeward with *Acasta* and *Ardent*.

Unknown to the Allies the German battle-cruisers *Gneisenau* and *Scharnhorst* had sailed from Kiel on 4 June in company with *Hipper* and four destroyers. This powerful force had put to sea for Operation Juno, an attack on shipping in Andifjord and Vaagsfjord. Of the Allied evacuation nothing was known.

At 1545 on 7 June the *Scharnhorst* sighted smoke 25 miles to the starboard. Half an hour later the *Glorious*, *Acasta* and *Ardent* were made out. A short while later the *Ardent* was seen approaching at speed. *Gneisenau's* 11-inch guns opened fire at 27,800 yards, her target being the *Ardent*. Minutes later *Gneisenau's* guns again roared, this time with the carrier as target. *Glorious* turned away at best speed, but to no avail. The German ships soon began hitting the target. A shell exploded in the forward hanger and fire quickly spread through the hanger, making it impossible to prepare aircraft for an attack. Another shell struck the bridge causing massive damage and killing the captain. Eventually *Glorious* rolled over and sank.

HMS *Ardent*

Ardent, under Lieutenant-Commander John Barker, fought a gallant action against massive odds. The call to action stations had sounded around 1630. Barker then made his way towards the enemy, challenging as he did so. The German reply was a barrage of accurate fire. A hit in one of *Ardent's* boiler rooms reduced her speed. She laid smoke and began zigzagging. But the shells continued to strike. *Ardent*, her 4.7s completely out-ranged, returned fire more as an act of defiance than in hopes of causing damage. She fired a salvo of four torpedoes but without success. Enemy gunfire transformed the destroyer into a tangle of twisted metal and escaping steam and she took on a heavy list to port. Casualties were high. At about 1728 she capsized and sank. Lieutenant-Commander Barker had fought and lost, and it is unlikely that on the bridge no other outcome could have been envisaged. It was now up to *Acasta* and Commander Charles Glasfurd.

HMS *Acasta*

Acasta had found protection in her own smoke-screen. On emerging from it, course was altered to starboard. She then fired four torpedoes from the port tubes. A cheer went up when the *Scharnhorst* was seen to have been hit. *Acasta's* guns opened fire and at the same time she again sought refuge in the smoke-screen but when she cleared the smoke for another attack when she was hit by shellfire and came to a standstill. *Acasta* opened fire, and continued to do so until the end. The final German barrage was at 1810.

Carley floats were dropped into the sea on the order to abandon ship. Commander Glasfurd, a much respected and popular officer, was seen leaning over the bridge. With the use of a loud-hailer he bid his men farewell: *Goodbye, good luck, and thank you. God go with you.* He then waved to the men on the rafts and to those in the water. Almost the entire complements of *Glorious, Ardent,* and *Acasta* were to die within hours of abandoning ship, more than 1,500 men. From the two destroyers Able Seaman Roger Hooke had survived from *Ardent*, and Leading Seaman Nick Carter from *Acasta*. That was all!

*   *   *

The Germans had incurred damage to *Scharnhorst* and had lost forty-eight men. Though the British had suffered heavy losses, the evacuation convoys could easily have met with terrible disaster had not the Germans been engaged. The torpedo from *Acasta* had hit *Scharnhorst* aft and had flooded two engine rooms and put her after turret out of action. Concerned for *Scharnhorst's* safety Admiral Marschall, in command of the German force, at once made for Trondheim. The troop convoys which had sailed from Norway arrived at their destination safely, which might not have been the case had not *Acasta's* torpedo, fired by Leading Seaman Carter, damaged the *Scharnhorst.*

Norway was by no means alone in her forlorn attempt to repel Nazi aggression; elsewhere on the Continent the crushing advance of the German military painted a depressing canvas. Germany had unleashed its war machine against Holland and Belgium on 10 May. It was appreciated that Holland would quickly fall to the German onslaught, and on the evening of 14 May the Dutch lay down their arms. Having attained victory in Holland, the German 18th Army turned south on 15 May to support the 6th Army's drive into Belgium. Two days prior to this move south, General Heinz Guderian's panzers crossed the Muese near Sedan. The German Army was in France.

HMS *Valentine*
Royal Navy destroyer activity throughout the German blitzkrieg had been incessant. The turning point in Belgium's fortune had been the day the German 18th Army had swung south from defeated Holland. The destroyer *Valentine*, Commander Herbert Buchanan, RAN, had spent much of that day providing AA cover for vessels transporting French troops in Flushing roads when she received orders to cover troop transportation between Derneuzen and Beveland. Once clear of the roads *Valentine* increased speed from 15 to 20 knots. Astern of her was the *Whitley*, another of the old V and W class destroyers. The sky was cloudless but conditions which should have made for good visibility were spoiled by a heat haze. Commander Buchanan had his ship in first degree of AA readiness.

Petty officer Frederick Thornton was on *Valentine's* bridge when at 1430 a JU87 attacked from astern. In common with the rest of the bridge party Thornton did not hear the Stuka, but when it was 400 yards off he happened to glance sternward. He saw that the plane was near to completing its dive and had just released four bombs. There was no time for *Valentine* to take avoiding action. Of the four bombs two exploded harmlessly ahead of the ship and another appears to have passed through the after funnel, destroying the after boiler room, whilst the fourth exploded close to starboard and abreast the foremost magazine, tearing a large hole in the ship's side and possibly setting fire to the magazine. No gunfire from *Valentine* met this attack, but *Whitley* reported having shot down the aircraft.

Damaged steam-pipes brought *Valentine's* main engines to a halt and she immediately began to lose way. Commander Buchanan's first impression was that the ship was so badly damaged forward that she would have to be beached. He ordered starboard wheel, his intention being to make towards the nearest bank of the river. Even with a light wind astern *Valentine* hardly had sufficient way on to cover the 500 yards to the bank. It was with relief that she was felt to ground gently forward. An anchor was released in case she slid sternward and back into deeper water.

There was no hope of repairing the damage and re-floating the ship. *Valentine* had a port list of 20 degrees. Her engine room was flooding and several of her compartments were already flooded. All boilers were disabled. A 12 to 15 feet hole in her ship's side forward extended from below the water-line to the upper deck. Internal structural damage was considerable. The oil fuel tanks had been opened. Following a brief inspection Buchanan ordered preparations made for abandoning ship. Dutch ambulances arrived to take the wounded to hospital. Twenty-three of the crew had been killed and eight of the wounded died later.

HMS *Whitley*

After the loss of *Valentine* Commander Buchanan became CO of *Vanity*. He retired from the navy in 1957 as a rear-admiral. The *Whitley*, under Lieutenant-Commander Guy Rolfe, survived *Valentine* by five days. Leading Telegraphist Anthony Story was serving in *Whitley* and in the account which follows tells of her loss:

At about 0620 on 19 May 1940 we were off the Belgian coast between Nieuport and Ostende when we found the Walcheren Lightship adrift, badly damaged, and with the two occupants dead. As it constituted a serious hazard to shipping we laid off and sank it by gunfire. It was another lovely day. I was on duty in the W/T office with an ordinary telegraphist. Barely had the sound of our guns died away when I heard the familiar whine of a Stuka diving on us. This one was different. The bombs sizzled down and all hell let loose. The ship heaved. The lights went out. All power was lost. Equipment flew about. As I tried to obtain power for the transmitter, I realized we had been struck by a mortal blow as our ship lay dead in the water. I sent the ordinary telegraphist onto the upper deck fast, and informed the bridge we were out of action. The familiar voice of my 'oppo' of Penelope *days, Tom Webster, the signalman, called down:* 'It's okay, Tony. We are in contact. Help is on the way. Get up here out of it.' *I reported to the bridge, taking the codes with me.*

The captain was perfectly calm and matter of fact. I looked to port and saw the Belgian coast about four miles distant. Our ship was in a sorry state. The bombs had apparently destroyed the forward boiler room, the men on watch there being killed instantly. We were indeed fortunate casualty wise. Some crewmen were off watch sleeping down below. The captain informed us that help was near. He advised us to stand by to abandon ship and to keep together in the water, and clear of the leaking oil. I then saw Vimiera *and* Keith *approaching from seaward at high speed. I became engrossed with my task of lighting a bonfire of the codes and ciphers on the bridge. Fortunately we were only carrying 'dangerous waters' extracts, relatively easy to ignite.* Vimiera *was preparing to come alongside the starboard side and was lowering life-lines and scrambling nets. The captain ordered abandon ship. The ship was now deserted and looked in a sorry state.* Vimiera *had stood off, and* Keith *was standing by. The captain ordered us into the motor-boat, which was coming alongside. It was obvious he intended to stay with the ship. I remember plucking up courage and insisting he joined us. Eventually he did.*

On board Vimiera *I suddenly felt bereft of all responsibility. Having had no sleep for days, I fell fast asleep on the upper deck. I remember putting into Dunkirk and the ship topping up with assorted passengers, soldiers, and the like, and heading for Portsmouth.*

Three bombs had fallen close to *Whitley*, breaking her back. She had been abandoned at 0720. *Keith* administrated the *coup de grace*.

* * *

Once their line had been breached at Sedan, the Allies found it impossible to contain the Whermacht with its blitzkrieg concept of warfare. Apparently invincible the Germans crushed all opposition in their drive across France. At eight o'clock on the evening of 20 May a forward battalion of Guderian's 2nd Panzer Division reached the Channel at Novelles. Two days later the panzers turned north to seal off the ports of Boulogne, Calais, and Dunkirk. After hard fighting Boulogne surrendered on 25 May. The 10th Panzer Division went into action against the Calais defences. A clash with British armour drove the panzers back. This resulted in the panzers merely sealing off Calais on 24 May. On this day the *Wessex*, under Lieutenant-Commander William Cartwright, was sunk in action off Calais.

HMS *Wessex*

Wessex sailed from harbour at 0700 on the 24th to provide support to the Calais defences. Three hours later *Wessex* was followed by *Wolfhound* and *Vimiera*. The main objective of the trio was the bombardment of road approaches and, if located, any German batteries or units.

Following the bombardment of targets earlier in the day, *Wessex* was closing the coast in company with *Vimiera* and the Polish destroyer *Burza* when at approximately 1640 the three ships attracted the attention of twenty-one Stukas. The German planes divided into three formations. Cartwright called for 28 knots and began zigzagging. His evasive action sent the bombs of the first attack into the sea. A second attack also failed. *Wessex*, the whole of her armament working flat out, was not so lucky with the third attack and three bombs struck her.

The bombs hit *Wessex* in the vicinity of her funnels, penetrating to, and severely damaging, the two boiler rooms. Extensive damage occurred to her bottom and sides and a perforated bulkhead caused flooding in the engine room. *Wessex* began to settle by the head. Even though the ship was sinking, most of her main armament continued to fire until the last moment.

The *Vimiera* and *Burza* did not escape damage. A near miss reduced *Vimiera's* speed. Nevertheless she closed *Wessex* and took off survivors. Meanwhile the *Burza* had been badly damaged forward by two bombs. At 3 knots she struggled to Dover, her bows noticeably lower in the water that when she had left.

* * *

A German assault against Calais the following day failed to take the town. Further attacks on the 26th were successful and by early evening the town was in German hands. That evening the Admiralty signalled Dover: *Operation Dynamo Is To Commence.*

HMS *Wakeful*

Entering the harbour of Dunkirk very soon became hazardous, and at times impossible. It was clear that troops would have to be embarked not only from the harbour, but from the sandy beaches on either side of it. In her three days of operating in the Dunkirk area, HM destroyer *Wakeful*, Commander Ralph Fisher, performed valiantly. Commander Fisher was thirty-six when war broke out. Just before Christmas 1939 he was appointed to command *Wakeful*. On his first trip from the beaches during Dynamo, Fisher landed at Dover 639 soldiers. The commander's permission to reproduce the following extract from his book *Salt Horse* is appreciated.

We anchored off Braye Sanatorium, unable to get nearer than about a quarter of a mile from the beach on which long queues of soldiers were waiting. It was comforting to be in company with plenty of friendly vessels including, next door to us, the new destroyer Jaguar *with much better anti-aircraft armament than* Wakeful. *However, there was a low cloud and rain that afternoon and bombing attacks were few and ineffective but getting the troops on board was painfully slow. Our boat would row in to the beach only to be swamped by eager troops and immovably grounded. There were other boats about but they tended to be abandoned by soldiers who had finished with them and let them drift away. During some eight hours we got about 640 troops on board and sailed after dark. Wisely – or perhaps unwisely as it turned out – I had insisted that all troops should be stowed as low as possible so as to preserve stability in case we should have to manoeuvre at high speed to avoid bombs. At fifteen men to the ton 600 men constituted a serious top-weight consideration in a ship the size of* Wakeful. *Accordingly they were stuffed into engine room, boiler rooms and store rooms. The route this time was by Zuydcootte Pass, where I felt our propellers hitting the sand and then up to the Kwinte Buoy where one would turn west for Dover. So as not to reveal ourselves to aircraft by a bright wake we went at only 12 knots until we neared the Kwinte Buoy where any enemy might be lurking and then increased to 20 knots with a wide zigzag. Phosphorescence was very bright.*

The buoy was brightly flashing once a second and when it was about a quarter of a mile on our starboard bow I saw two tracks like white swords coming towards us from that direction. We avoided one but the other torpedo hit us on the forward boiler room with, I remember, a brilliant white flash. It transpired after the war that these torpedoes were fired by Lieutenant Zimmerman from 'E-boat' S30 hiding behind the brightly flashing buoy. A well planned attack and a good shot. Wakeful *was cut in two and the halves sank immediately until their broken ends grounded on the bottom. The fore part rolled over to starboard and it cannot have been more that 15 seconds before I found myself swimming off the bridge.*

There were perhaps fifty of my men, probably gun crews, in a group in the water with me. All my engine room people had been killed and all except ten of the soldiers trapped inside the ship and tragically drowned. The tide was quickly sweeping our group away from the grounded wreck and we must have been a mile or two down-tide when two Scottish wooden fishing boats on their way to Dunkirk came amongst us. The Nautilus *picked up six, including my first lieutenant, and the* Comfort *sixteen, including myself. We tried for about half an hour to pick up others we could hear shouting in the dark but it was terribly slow work hauling out sodden, half-drowned men. Eventually the shouting stopped. The* Nautilus *went on to Dunkirk and I directed the skipper of the* Comfort *to go up-tide to the wreck, where I had last seen men sitting on the stern portion some 40 feet above the water. When we got there we found the destroyer* Grafton *lying stopped with her boat over at the wreck. The* Grafton's *deck was solid with soldiers and I went alongside her starboard quarter to tell her captain to get out of it as there were enemy about. At that moment some sort of grenade exploded on her bridge and he was killed. Nobody seems to know what this was. At the same time there was a large explosion as a torpedo hit the* Grafton *on the opposite side from where* Comfort *was lying.*

Wakeful *had survived twenty-seven bombing attacks before twenty-six years old Oberleutenant zur See Wilhelm Zimmermann's S30 had caught her with a torpedo. Casualties had been heavy: a hundred of the crew were lost and 640 soldiers. Only forty-seven crewmen and ten soldiers were rescued. Zimmerman survived the war.*

HMS *Grafton*

As stated in Commander Fisher's account the *Grafton*, Commander Charles Robinson, had become the target of a torpedo attack. At about 0250 a torpedo fired by Kapitan-leutenant Hans-Bernhard Michalowski of U62 struck in the vicinity of *Grafton's* wardroom, killing thirty-five army officers rescued from the beach at Braye Dunes. A second hit by a torpedo caused further loss of life and extinguished the ship's lightning. *Grafton*, with eight hundred troops on board, began to sink. There was no hope of saving her and she was eventually sent to the bottom by gunfire from the destroyer *Ivanhoe*.

HMS *Grenade*

The third British destroyer to be sunk on 29 May was the *Grenade*, Commander Richard Boyle. *Grenade* was alongside the mole in Dunkirk harbour. She was at the end of the mole and alongside her to starboard, and also loading troops, was the *Jaguar*. With several hundred troops packing her decks *Jaguar* headed seaward. She was soon found by Stukas. Suffering bomb damage *Jaguar* was obliged to transfer her troops and be taken under tow for Dover. From *Grenade*, still in the harbour, a Stuka was seen to pass to seaward; it then turned and came in for an attack on *Grenade*. A bomb exploded on the mole so close to *Grenade* that crewmen and soldiers were wounded by flying shrapnel. Very soon after this, at 1600, another Stuka attacked. *Grenade* was hit aft by a bomb. A second bomb hit the bridge and exploded in an oil tank below. At once a fierce fire broke out. To lessen the danger of *Grenade* going down at her berth her lines were cast off. Packed with troops the blazing ship drifted out of control towards the harbour entrance, so now even greater danger of her sinking and blocking the harbour entrance arose. Thankfully, this did not happen; a brave trawler skipper, despite the raging fire and further bombing, took *Grenade* in tow and manoeuvred her clear of the entrance. When the fire reached the destroyer's magazines she blew up with a mighty roar. There were few survivors.

* * *

Operation Dynamo had been in progress for almost a week when on 1 June the *Keith, Basilisk,* and *Havant* were sunk off Dunkirk. The flotilla leader *Keith* was active throughout the evacuation, first under the command of Captain David Simson, who was killed in action, and then under Captain Edward Berthon, who was in command on the morning of 1 June when *Keith* was at anchor Braye beach, 6 miles west of Dunkirk. Close by was *Basilisk.* At about 0740 a mass of German aircraft appeared over the Braye anchorage. *Keith* was among several ships attacked by dive-bombers. She was turning hard to port when a bomb went down her after funnel. Severally damaged internally, she came to a halt with a 20 degree list.

HMS *Basilisk*
At about 0815 the *Basilisk* drew the attention of a group of nine Stukas. Commander (later Vice-Admiral Sir) Maxwell Richmond, her CO, ordered port helm when he saw the first bombs released. Richmond says:

As far as I could judge, each aircraft released a pattern of five bombs, one being a large B type, and four smaller bombs with slight delay action. One of the latter exploded at the after end of No.1 boiler room on the port side and blew away the bulkhead, piercing both main and auxiliary steam-lines and main fuel oil supply. All engine room and boiler room personnel were killed. About six of the B type bombs then exploded underneath the ship, flooding the after magazine and shell room and probably the gland compartment and store room just forward of this position. The upper deck and sides of the ship cracked right across in the vicinity of the mainmast. In order to preserve stability the torpedoes and depth charges were jettisoned, and the ship floated comfortably with little increase in draught. I inspected the engine room and No.1 boiler room and found that a small amount of water was making its way through shrapnel holes. These were plugged and collision mats placed over the worst leaks. It was found impossible to get steam to the engines and thereafter the ship remained immobile.

Keith's situation was even worse than *Basilisk's.* The tug *St Abbs* was ordered alongside to embark some of the crew. At 0820 further damage was caused in another air attack. *Keith* was then abandoned completely. Unaware that *Basilisk* was immobile, Captain Berthon ordered her to sink *Keith.* Meanwhile a Belgian tug was persuaded to take *Basilisk* in tow. A line had just been secured when at 0945 a second bombing attack was made on *Basilisk but* no hits were scored. The tug, which had slipped the tow, returned and again attempted to tow *Basilisk* clear of the shore. The tow was in progress when around noon *Basilisk* was again attacked from the air. Commander Richmond says that, *the ship was completely smothered by hits and near misses.* She began to settle immediately and he gave the order to abandon ship. Between them, the Belgian tug and

HM destroyer *Whitehall* took on board 131 of the crew. *Basilisk* sank in about 4 fathoms with her upper deck awash. Her destruction was completed by *Whitehall's* guns and torpedoes. Elsewhere in the anchorage the crew of *Keith* was being picked up from the water. The abandoned *Keith* was subjected to her fifth air attack and at 0915 she was hit and sunk.

HMS *Havant*

The third and final destroyer loss of 1 June was *Havant*, Lieutenant-Commander Anthony Burnell-Nugent. Beginning on 29 May, *Havant* made four runs across the Channel. On her first she left Dover at 1815. By 0900 she was off Braye beach. She returned to Dover at 0400 next morning and put ashore five hundred French troops. She put to sea in the early hours of the 3rd with orders to embark troops from a beach to the east of Dunkirk. By 1700 that evening she arrived at Dover with a thousand troops. She then sailed for Dunkirk and by 2145 was alongside taking on more troops. It took only 30 minutes to hurry on board a thousand soldiers. At 0230, 1 June, they were going ashore at Dover. *Havant* then cleared harbour for a return to Dunkirk, arriving at 0730 at the same berth as before.

At 0800 an intense aerial bombardment began at Dunkirk. Troops were arriving at the jetty at such a slow rate that it took half an hour to embark fifty. During this phase the *Ivanhoe*, just outside the harbour and loaded with troops, was hit amidships. *Havant* cast off and went to her aid. She put alongside *Ivanhoe* at 0840 and began transferring troops and wounded. As Philip Hadow, *Ivanhoe's* captain, hoped to get underway very shortly, he refused a tow. *Havant* at full speed set off for Dover.

While proceeding down channel and parallel to the beach west of Dunkirk, *Havant* came under shore gunfire, high and low-level bombing, and intense dive-bombing. *Havant* was zigzagging as much as the width of the channel would permit when at 0906 she was hit in the engine room by two bombs which tore two holes (one with a diameter of 6 feet and the other of 3 feet) on the starboard side of the engine room just above the water-line. Almost immediately afterwards a large bomb dropped about 50 yards ahead. This bomb had a delay action and exploded directly beneath *Havant* as she passed over it, momentarily giving the impression of lifting the whole ship. By this time the engineer officer and all the ERAs had been either killed or wounded. The after ready-use ammunition lockers had blown up, causing many casualties among the soldiers on the upper deck.

Out of control *Havant* steamed ahead. She had taken on a gradual turn to starboard and this sent her towards sand-banks opposite Dunkirk. It was impossible to enter the engine room to stop this ship. As the cut-off valve on the upper deck was bent and broken the only method of stopping was to let the steam out of the boilers. The chief stoker was able to do this, despite there being a fire in one of the boiler rooms. *Havant* was eventually brought up in four fathoms by the starboard anchor. Signals for assistance were made to the minesweeper *Saltash* and a large yacht. Both vessels came alongside, one on each quarter, and the transfer of troops was undertaken. Bombing throughout the proceedings was almost continuous. A tow was passed between *Saltash* and *Havant*. Towing was taken up at slow speed.

Havant's list to port increased sufficiently for her captain to call alongside another vessel, the *Aegair*, so as to transfer the crew, with the exception of his officers and twenty ratings. About this time *Havant* was attacked by heavy bombers. A group of bombs entered the sea very close to *Havant's* port quarter, causing further damage. With the port side of the upper deck almost awash, the seaworthiness of *Havant* was getting worst by the minute. Following a brief conference with some of his officers, Burnell-Nugent decided to abandon ship. The tow was slipped and *Aegair* went alongside. Those of the ship's company remaining were transferred. As at this time *Havant* was in an area of deep water, her magazines were flooded to ensure her sinking before she could drift on to a sandbank. *Saltash* fired several rounds into *Havant* to hasten the end. At 1015 *Havant* sank from view. Under the circumstances casualties were light: one officer and seven ratings killed and about twenty-five men wounded. At least twenty-five soldiers were killed or wounded. Operation Dynamo was not the only evacuation of Allied troops from France in June 1940. Operations Cycle and Aerial were evacuations, the latter mainly from the Biscay ports. The Royal Canadian Navy destroyer *Fraser*, Commander Wallace Creery, RCN, was part of Aerial when she was involved in a collision with the British cruiser *Calcutta*.

* * *

The great strain during the hectic days of evacuation, together with fatigue from lack of sleep, certainly had an effect on ships officers, particularly those in command. Under such circumstances judgement was always liable to be impaired and an error of judgment may well have contributed to *Fraser's* loss, which occurred on the last day of Aerial, 25 June.

HMS *Fraser*
The evacuation was taking place from the harbour of St Jean de Luz when some guns, thought to be German, were seen to arrive on a hill overlooking the harbour. Previously, around sixteen thousand Polish troops and thousands of refugees had been evacuated. After detailing destroyers to escort merchant ships to England, Rear-Admiral Alban Curteis, flying his flag in *Calcutta*, ordered *Fraser* and HMCS *Restigouche* to escort *Calcutta* towards Bordeaux, where enemy activity at sea had been reported. Nothing became of this and towards dusk on the 25th the small force turned westward for home. In a

manoeuvre carried out as darkness was falling, the *Calcutta*, Captain Dennis Lees, was in collision off the Gironde with *Fraser*. The commanding officers of *Calcutta* and *Fraser* relate events. First Captain Lees.

When the signal to form single line ahead in sequence of fleet numbers was made at 2212, Calcutta was steaming on a steady course of 253 degrees at 14 knots, with Fraser steaming a similar course, bearing about Green 30, distance, apparently about a mile. Visibility was about 10 miles. As soon as the executive signal was made Fraser was observed to alter course to port and appeared to be shaping course to cross Calcutta's bows and come down her port side. I estimate that Fraser crossed my line of advance about 2 cables ahead of me and that at this time her inclination was 160 degrees to the left. I considered that if I held my course Fraser would have passed dangerously close down my port side and I ordered the officer of the watch to put on starboard helm and sound one blast on the siren. About three seconds after Calcutta had sounded one blast Fraser was distinctly heard to sound the same signal. Instead of altering to starboard, however, she altered course to port and commenced re-crossing my bows from starboard. It was then evident that no reversal of helm could save collision so full speed ahead was ordered in order to lessen the impact. Calcutta's stem struck Fraser abreast B gun at which time Calcutta's course was about 265 degrees and Fraser's inclination about 140 degrees to the right.

Commander Creery:

At 2130 manoeuvres were carried out and at 2212, as a result of these manoeuvres the ships were steering at 252 degrees at 13 knots with Fraser in a position 1.5 miles on the starboard bow of Calcutta. It was the end of the evening twilight. At 2216 the admiral made the signal to form Order One. The officer of the watch asked me if he should carry out this manoeuvre. I instructed him to do so. The sequence of the subsequent events was as follows:

2217.   *OOW [Officer of the Watch] gave the order 'Port 10'.*
2217 1/2. *Commanding officer ordered OOW to increase to 20 knots and get manoeuvre over.*
2217 1/2. *Commanding officer realized that the OOW had insufficient wheel on and took the ship over, at the same time ordering 'Port 20' and the 'Hard aport'.*
2219.   *Commanding officer appreciated that the ship would not turn short of Calcutta and decided to try and cross the bows. He gave the order 'Hard astarboard' and 'Sound one short blast'.*
2219.   *It was obvious that the swing could not be checked in time and the commanding officer, in order to avoid a head-on collision, gave the orders 'Hard aport' and 'Full speed astern motors'.*

Shortly after this Calcutta *struck* Fraser *on the starboard side, the angle between the courses of the ships being about 20 degrees.* Calcutta's *stem penetrated to about the centre line of* Fraser, *which broke in two at about the break of the forecastle.* Calcutta's *bow jutted into* Fraser's *wheelhouse and the forepart of the forebridge remained impinged there.*

Fraser's forepart floated away into darkness. Later the after section of *Fraser* was sunk by a scuttling party.

The accident was deemed to have been caused by the use of insufficient helm by *Fraser* when ordered to form single line ahead from a position on the starboard side of *Calcutta*. A misunderstanding of a bridge order is also a possibility. The degree of sea swell may also have contributed. Commander Creery, commenting on the swell, states, *I think it accelerated the swing to port at the very moment I went hard astarboard. I was amazed. The ship had been swinging to port, though not very rapidly, when I went hard astarboard; instead of checking, the ship swung faster to port than before, and it was then obvious that I would not be able to cross* Calcutta's *bow.*

Commander Creery, who had not had a proper night's rest for nine days and nights prior to the collision, had in World War One served in cruisers.

* * *

After the loss of *Fraser* the Royal Canadian Navy purchased HMS *Diana* as a replacement, commissioning her into the RCN on 6 September 1940 as the *Margaree*, the name of a river on Cape Breton Island. Her captain was Commander Joseph Roy, RCN. She was manned with *Fraser's* survivors, plus a draft from Canada, including Commander Roy, which arrived as a replacement for those lost in *Fraser*. As it was the intention to give *Margaree* a refit in Halifax, Nova Scotia, she joined convoy OL8 of four merchantmen as an escort for part of the westward crossing. When *Margaree* joined the convoy it was in charge of a coastal escort. This escort left on 21 October, leaving *Margaree* as OL8's only escort ship.

HMS *Port Fairy*

At 0100 on the 22nd, the convoy was now about 400 miles west of Ireland and 500 miles south of Iceland, the chief engineer of *Port Fairy*, one of the merchantmen, noted that rain storms of short duration were blowing up. These storms had the effect of cutting visibility sharply, but as the duration was brief the chief saw no reason to call the captain. Visibility at this time was such that the other ships could not be seen. At 0125, on the lifting of a blinding rain squall, the fourth officer of *Port Fairy* called the chief officer's attention to a vessel bearing three points on the starboard bow and not more than 400 yards away. As near as could be observed, this vessel was heading on a course about a point to the southward of *Port Fairy's* course. It was soon recognized that it was the *Margaree* and that their courses were converging. At about 0129 *Port Fairy's* chief officer observed *Margaree* bearing Green 35 at 4,000 yards. He then saw her suddenly heel over under port helm heading directly across *Port Fairy's* track. He ordered the helm hard to port and, to indicate that his engines were at full speed astern, sounded three short blasts on the fog-horn.

In *Margaree* the *Port Fairy* may have been sighted at this time; in any event, speed was increased. On hearing the three blasts from *Port Fairy*, the *Margaree* stopped her engines and then went full astern, turning to starboard in the process. (Later indications suggested that after the engines were stopped the port engine was put to full astern.) But there was no time for these moves to take full effect. *Margaree* continued to come to port about and about 15 seconds later, while she was crossing *Port Fairy's* bows at right angles, she was struck on her port side of the after end of the bridge. The freighter's bow smashed through the bridge superstructure, laying open a boiler room and cutting the ship in two. The forward section drifted clear and in one minute had turned over and sunk. Those in the forward section of *Margaree* and on the bridge were beyond help. Under very difficult conditions *Port Fairy* rescued six officers and twenty-eight ratings out of a ship's complement of ten officers and 166 ratings, most of whom had been survivors of *Fraser* four months previous.

The ships of OL8 arrived at their destinations. *Port Fairy* put in at Bermuda on 29 October with the survivors. A board of Inquiry held in Bermuda found that the collision had been caused by a turn to port by *Margaree* when, owing to the variable visibility, she had found herself dangerously close to the convoy. It was believed improbable that Commander Roy was on the bridge at the time of the collision. No blame was attached to *Port Fairy*, it being the responsibility of the escort to keep clear of the convoy.

HMS *Imogen*

Another destroyer to be lost in 1940 through collision was the *Imogen*, Commander Charles Firth. *Imogen* was part of Force C, which comprised five cruisers of the 18th Cruiser Squadron and eight destroyers. At 2010 on 16 July Force C was returning to Scapa Flow from the south east after an operation in the North Sea. Between 2040 and 2343 the ships encountered banks of fog on three occasions. During a manoeuvre in fog, one division of destroyers at a speed of 15 knots cut through the line of cruisers, also proceeding at 15 knots but on an almost opposite course. The final moments prior to the collision, which took place eight miles east of Duncansby Head, is described by Captain Harold Hickling, in command of the cruiser *Glasgow*.

At 2353 a destroyer was observed broad on the port bow of Glasgow *steering on an opposite course. This was HMS* Inglefield. *One long blast of the siren was given and engines put to slow ahead. About 15 to 20 seconds later a second destroyer appeared out of the fog right ahead. The wheel was put hard astarboard and the engines to full astern. HMS* Glasgow *struck HMS* Imogen *just before the bridge at an angle of about 20 degrees to her fore and aft line. The two ships remained locked together.* Glasgow's *engines were stopped.*

The cruiser's stem came to rest deeply imbedded in *Imogen*. Within seconds of the impact a sheet of flame shot up abreast the port side of the bridge, and even blew across *Glasgow's* bridge. A raging fire quickly took hold. The blaze rapidly spread to the fuel in the foremost tanks, and then to the oil fuel in Nos 1 and 2 boiler rooms. Steam was lost at once. With her Downton pump out of action *Imogen* had no means of fighting the fire with her own resources. Though *Glasgow* speedily brought hoses into action from her fo'c'sle and lower deck scuttles, in a short time the whole of *Imogen's* forepart under the bridge was well ablaze. The force of the collision had heeled *Imogen* over to starboard so that her upper deck was just awash. Commander Firth had been thrown from the bridge onto B gun deck and for a time was rendered unconscious. With the fire in the vicinity of her forward magazine there was a danger that *Imogen*, and possibly *Glasgow*, would blow up. The order was given to flood the cruiser's petrol compartment and forward magazine. Carley floats were put into the sea in the event of *Imogen* sinking, and the opinion was that she would do so. Meanwhile her ship's company was transferred to *Glasgow's* bows by means of the lower boom and emergency escape ladders. Others of the crew were transferred across a floating bridge of Carley floats.

At twenty-five minutes past midnight Captain Hickling was informed that *Imogen* had been evacuated; the task having taken 30 minutes. *Glasgow* was then manoeuvred astern to break clear of *Imogen's* side. After breaking free, *Glasgow* circled slowly round the sinking destroyer. *Imogen* was last seen at 0045 heavily on fire in a sea of burning fuel oil. Ammunition was exploding. Seventeen of her crew had probably been killed in the actual collision.

* * *

In July 1940 a torpedo from Kapitanleutnant Wilhelm Rollmann of U34 began destroyer sinkings in the North Atlantic. When war broke out thirty-three years old Rollmann had been in the navy for nearly 13 years, 12 months of that in command of U34. Within days of war breaking out he had sunk the British steamer *Pukkastan*, only the sixth ship of the war to be sunk by a U-boat.

HMS *Whirlwind*

U34 was some 200 miles to the west of the Isle of Scilly when on an evening in July she sighted HM destroyer *Whirlwind*. Recently arrived in the area, U34 had yet to make her first attack of the patrol. The *Whirlwind*, Lieutenant-Commander John Rodgers, was part of convoy OB178 (Liverpool–North America) when around noon on 5 July she was ordered to investigate a submarine sighting. Course was set at 290 degrees, speed 21 knots. An hour had passed when *Whirlwind's* OOW, Lieutenant Vincent Chacksfield, sighted an object on the horizon. With the glasses he identified the sighting as a submarine. He then saw it dive. Course was altered onto the bearing and then as the A/S cabinet directed. After running for 7 miles the course was altered to intercept any attempt by the U-boat to attack the convoy, some 20 to 30 miles away. An A/S search was then undertaken at 15 knots, zigzagging 10 degrees either side of mean course every 10 minutes. Lieutenant Christopher Bax was the OOW when Rodgers informed him that he was going below for a few minutes. Shortly after this Rollmann made his attack.

The torpedo struck *Whirlwind* forward. Lieutenant Bax later had no recollection of being blown off the bridge, right over the funnels, and onto the pom-pom gun platform. Another man was blasted 600 feet into the sea. For Lieutenant (E) Douglas Cook, in his cabin when the torpedo hit, the explosion had such little effect that his first impression was that a ship elsewhere had been torpedoed. On reaching the upper deck he was surprised to see the bows of his own ship drifting down the port side. *Whirlwind's* forepart had been blown away just forward of the bridge, which itself was a mass of twisted metal and the mast was down. The ship's back had been broken aft. The whaler and motor-boat had been wrecked, and the skiff so damaged that it sank when lowered. Only the Carley floats were intact. Hands were ordered to muster on deck. Lieutenant-Commander Rodgers had taken a blow to his head.

By good fortune a Sunderland flying boat appeared overhead. It flew away but returned at 1900 and signalled that help was near. The Sunderland had informed Lieutenant-Commander William Seagrave of the destroyer *Westicott* that *Whirlwind* was in need of help. At 2055 Seagrave went alongside *Whirlwind* and in 20 minutes had transferred *Whirlwind's* crew.

After consultation the decision was made to sink the ship, mainly because her back was broke and she appeared to be settling. It was thought that she would sink in about 4 hours. After 5 minutes of shelling, Seagrave fired a torpedo at the derelict. The torpedo surfaced, ran badly, and just missed the stern so gunfire was resumed. Fires broke out, but no vital hits were made. Throughout this time *Whirlwind* slowly settling. At 2245 another torpedo was fired. This hit below the after funnel and minutes later *Whirlwind* sank.

Following the sinking of *Whirlwind* Rollmann, during the next six days, sank five more ships. Then on his homeward run he sank HM submarine *Spearfish*. He did not survive the war, being sunk in November 1943 by American aircraft.

As part of the build up for Operation Sealion[Hitler's proposed invasion of Great Britain] German aircraft were raiding ports and harbours from Ramsgate to Southampton. Convoys in the English Channel had the full attention of the Luftwaffe and air attacks on convoys in the Straits of Dover were fierce. Only essential coastal traffic risked a Straits passage during July. One such convoy was the Southend-Portsmouth CW7.

HMS *Brazen*

Convoy CW7 consisted of more than twenty ships and it left Southend at 0700 on 20 July with four destroyers as escort. Patrolling between the lightships South Goodwin and Lydd was *Brazen*. Aware that CW7 was due in his patrol area around 1600, *Brazen's* captain, Commander Sir Michael Culme-Seymour, decided to remain in the vicinity of CW7 to give additional cover during its passage through the area.

By 1800 CW7 was south of Dover. *Brazen* had taken station on the convoy's southern flank. Around 1815 a large number of aircraft were sighted to the eastward. They were making towards the rear of the convoy at a height of about 8,000 feet. *Brazen's* bridge party counted twenty-two Stukas in formation at the head, followed by a number of planes in line ahead, thought to be He111s, accompanied by fighters. When the aircraft broke formation to attack, they concentrated on the centre of the convoy and on *Brazen*, whose guns opened fire at the first opportunity. Commander Culme-Seymour tells us what happened to *Brazen* over the next two hours.

Speed was at once increased to 24 knots, and to full speed approximately two minutes after sighting. It is thought that a maximum speed of 28 knots was reached. Course was maintained with the wind on the starboard bow to keep all guns bearing and the ship fairly steady during the aircrafts' approach. The main attack was up wind from the port side and consisted of about eight to ten JU87s and five to eight Heinkel 111s. These carried out dive-bombing and shallow dive-bombing attacks respectively on HMS Brazen. Most aircraft came very low, and machine-gunned the ship as well. All attacks were pressed well home. The wheel was put hard aport as the bombs from the first wave were released. When these were seen to be falling clear to port, the wheel was reversed to avoid the second wave, whose bombs pitched clear to the starboard. A third series fell ahead of the ship, which was steadied in order to gather speed and avoid a high-level attack from the starboard quarter which had not previously been seen. This manoeuvre was successful but a salvo of two heavy and four smaller bombs were dropped from close on the port beam immediately after and could not be avoided because of insufficient time. These did not hit the ship but burst underneath due to their forward velocity carrying them on, and to a delay-action fuse. There was a most violent concussion. The steering gear and all lighting were put out of action but the engines were continued ahead and the ship remained on a steady course. Further attacks, including machine-gunning, were continued but without success. All guns were able to continue firing so long as targets were available.

It was thought possible that one bomb only had exploded underneath the ship and another on the surface close alongside to starboard. Whatever the case, the damage was serious. Commander Culme-Seymour again:

The keel was split at the engine room/boiler room bulkhead and both compartments flooded immediately. The forward boiler room also flooded due to its after bulkhead being pierced. There were a large number of shrapnel holes in the starboard side of the engine and boiler rooms. The upper deck was distorted, being raised about 8 inches above the engine room and boiler room bulkhead and in waves on either side of it. The ship's side plating was also bulged out-board by about 6 inches on each side of the ship. As a result of the explosion high-pressure steam was blowing in the starboard forward end of the engine room and it was impossible to reach the machinery there. Secondary lighting and torches only were available. The steam pressure was falling rapidly, and steam was shut off the main engine in the hope of conserving steam from the forward boiler room to run the main circulators; this, however, proved useless and the boiler rooms and engine rooms had to be evacuated. In the after boiler room there was a considerable fire due to the explosion. The casing plates were thrown off the boiler and oil fuel caught fire. The oil fuel pumps and sprayer valves were immediately shut off and this kept the fire under control. The engine rooms and boiler rooms having been evacuated, the after engine room bulkhead was shored up and all the after lower deck hatches battened down and shored. Watertight doors throughout the ship were secured down.

In their attack the German aircraft had not escaped damage or worse. Pom-pom fire from *Brazen* hit one aircraft before it could release its bomb and it crashed into the sea. Another plane was hit but not actually seen to fall. A third attacker was hit and seen to fly off with its port wing in flames.

Once the aircraft had been driven away, more attention could be directed towards saving the ship. *Brazen's* captain concludes his story:

It became apparent that the after part might break away, the upper deck being awash amidships. The order was therefore given to abandon the after part, and all men mustered on the forecastle. It still seemed possible, however, that the ship could at least be beached, and HMS Boreas, *proceeded to take her in tow. This was done using HMS* Boreas' *wire and cables in both ships. The tow parted although little apparent strain was put on the wire, which may have become foul on the bottom. HMS* Boreas *then came alongside and took on board the wounded and the majority of the ship's company who were of no use in* Brazen. *The conditions for this operation were exceedingly difficult but it was performed entirely successfully with little damage to either ship. A volunteer party of five officers and sixteen ratings were kept on board* Brazen *to man the forward guns and work the cables. All boats were lowered, the forward motor-boat alone proving seaworthy.* Boreas *then shoved off taking* Brazen *in tow, but* Brazen's *towing-wire was crippled at the end so that no cable could be secured to it. It was then decided to await the tug which was by then approaching. The ship was settling in the water amidships but it was found possible to take her in tow by the tug and* HMS Boreas *together. Considerable progress was made towards Dover for about three-quarters of an hour before the ship finally broke amidships and sank. The bow continued to float with the deck nearly vertical and the bridge under water. I then gave orders finally to abandon ship. The party on board was taken off by motor-boat at approximately 2030. The forepart was sunk by gunfire from* HMS Boreas, *though it continued to float for a long period with considerable stubbornness.*

Ships of the convoy had also been under attack. Over the next three days the merchantmen *Pulborough* and *Terlings* were sunk and three others damaged. On the morning of 22 July convoy CW7 entered harbour.

✻   ✻   ✻

The harbour at Dover was very much in the forefront of German air attacks. A week after the sinking of *Brazen* the flotilla leader *Codrington*, Captain George Stevens-Guille, was bombed in the harbour.

HMS *Codrington*

The depot ship *Sandhurst* was berthed at the north wall of the submarine basin in Dover harbour with *Codrington*, in the process of boiler cleaning, moored alongside her. At 1430 on 27 July fighter-bombers raced over the harbour. In this attack the destroyer *Walpole* suffered slight damage when two bombs exploded close by her. That evening, at 1745, the harbour was again attacked by fighter-bombers. A bomb exploded under the *Codrington*, breaking her back. *Sandhurst* was also seriously damaged, but luckily had no casualties.

The Luftwaffe had blown *Codrington* out of the war. She was aground from No. 3 gun to the stern, and the whole of the ship forward of this position was lying at an angle of 15 degrees to the after part and slightly out of the fore and aft alignment with it. The fore-end contained a considerable portion of its buoyancy for about 6 days. *Codrington*, the seventh destroyer leader to be sunk, had three of her crew slightly injured.

HMS *Wren*

Saturday 27 July was also the day on which the *Wren* met her end. On the morning of the 27th six minesweeping trawlers and the minesweeping sloop *Halcyon* left Harwich to sweep what was termed Gap E in the mine barrage near Aldeburgh. The *Wren* and *Montrose* accompanied the sweepers as AA ships.

At 1655 fifteen German aircraft put in an appearance. To allow themselves sea-room for the coming battle, *Wren* and *Montrose* moved clear of the sweepers. At 1700 the aircraft dived to attack. Air activity became intense, the aircraft attacking in flights of three. *Montrose* was attacked by three flights: one from ahead, one from astern, and the other from almost directly overhead. Bombs falling close to her caused damage, her steering gear being put out of action so that she was steaming in a large circle.

The noise of the alarm on *Wren* had sent Lieutenant Guy Horsey hurrying to the bridge; aircraft were approaching. HMS *Wren*, captained by Lieutenant-Commander Frederick Harker, put up a strong barrage. Horsey explains:

> *B gun, the 12-pounder gun and the pom-poms were firing at the aircraft but this did not prevent the leading flight from making a most determined dive-bombing attack. One or two bombs slid down the starboard side and burst below the water-line abreast the wardroom and the cabin flat. I ordered the hands who were not closed up to turn out the boats and Carley floats and went aft. I saw nobody on the quarter-deck or down below. All the after compartments were already badly flooded. I then went forward on the port side. I had just got to the after steering position when I heard a rending noise and saw that the ship had split across the upper deck. A few seconds after this another bomb exploded in the water, and as a result of the blast I had no further recollections of the sinking of the ship.*

At least twenty bombs fell in the vicinity of *Wren*, and she received direct hits from two or more bombs. After one of the attacks on *Wren*, Commander Cecil Parry of *Montrose* saw her list heavily to port with her upper deck awash as far as the after torpedo tubes. She sank in about 2 minutes, except for her bow which remained vertically afloat for 15 to 20 minutes. Her survivors, four officers and ninety-nine ratings, were rescued by Commander Eric Hinton of *Halcyon* and by the trawlers. *Montrose* was towed to Harwich by *Worcester* and *Halcyon*. Lieutenant-Commander Harker, who had served in submarines between 1922 and 1926, did not survive the loss of *Wren*.

HMS *Delight*

Forty-eight hours after the attack on *Wren*, bombing accounted for the loss of *Delight*. On the afternoon of 29 July the *Delight*, Commander Mark Fogg-Elliott, sailed from Portland with the Clyde as her destination. She was 20 miles SSW of Portland Bill when at 1830 she sighted fifteen enemy aircraft. Approximately

5 minutes later the planes launched an attack. The first bombs fell close to the ship with no appreciable effect, but from the second load of bombs one hit the destroyer a glancing blow on the port side at the break of the forecastle. The explosion caused structural damage to her side. A fire in the low-power room became serious when fed by oil fuel from a damaged forward fuel tank. The main steam-pipe was fractured and all lighting failed. Her ship's company fought a gallant action but the strength of the attack was overwhelming. Both boiler rooms were put out of action. The forward magazine group became flooded. And she was blazing fiercely.

Delight's W/T apparatus was knocked out early in the engagement, but fortunately a report by the station at Portland Bill alerted the naval base at Portland and a number of vessels were dispatched to help her. On approaching the scene of the attack, *Delight* was seen to be ablaze fore and aft. Fighter protection arrived in the area.

Sixty of the one hundred and forty-seven survivors were either wounded or injured. Including those who later died of burns and wounds, eighteen of the crew did not survive. The end for *Delight* came soon after 2130, at which time a heavy explosion occurred forward in the blazing ship.

* * *

By August the bombing raids on south-east England had grown in intensity. On 13 August the Luftwaffe launched its great air offensive against Britain, designated Operation Eagle by the Germans. While the young heroes of Fighter Command were immersed in their aerial battles, two divisions of Royal Navy destroyers put to sea for mine-laying operations in the North Sea.

It was 1430 on 31 August when the minelaying destroyers *Esk, Icarus,* and *Ivanhoe* sailed from Immingham on Operation CBX5, a minelay off Texel. At 1640 the minelayers joined *Express* and *Intrepid* off the Humber Lightship. *Express, Ivanhoe,* and *Esk* formed the 39th Division, and *Icarus* and *Intrepid* the 40th Division. The force proceeded in divisions and in single lines ahead with the 40th Division 800 yards astern of the 39th. Course was shaped to pass through a gap in the minefield.

HMS *Esk*

At 2047, having passed through 53.37'N/02.24'E, course was altered to 099 degrees. At 2215 course was again altered, to 109 degrees. Speed was 22 knots to make 20 knots with paravanes streaming. Although the night was dark the sea was very phosphorescent so when at 2305 *Ivanhoe's* port paravane was carried away Lieutenant Allan Phipps, on the 0.5-inch gun platform, noticed it at once and was able to report the incident to the bridge. Almost simultaneously with Lieutenant Phipps' report an explosion took place on

Ivanhoe's port quarter. The lost paravane had set off a mine. A minute later *Express* struck a mine which blew off her forepart almost as far as the bridge. *Ivanhoe's* captain, Commander Philip Hadow, turned and closed *Express* to assist, having passed her port side after the mining. While proceeding alongside *Express*, *Ivanhoe* met *Esk* bow to bow, *Esk* presumably having stopped to avoid collision and perhaps rescue men in the sea. An attempt by Commander Hadow to communicate with *Esk* failed, frustrating Hadow's intention to send her to join the 40th Division. At about 2310 Commander Hadow proceeded alongside *Express'* starboard side, bow to bow. During this period around twenty hands were taken off *Express* before the ships drifted apart.

About five minutes after *Express* had been mined the *Esk* set off two mines in a space of 10 minutes, the second of the tow being a particularly heavy explosion in the vicinity of the foremost funnel. Commander Hadow lowered the whalers to rescue survivors. After the second explosion *Esk* sank very rapidly, probably in less than 2 minutes.

HMS *Ivanhoe*

The sinking of *Esk* did not end the night of disaster. At 2325, while manoeuvring to get alongside *Express* for a second time, *Ivanhoe* struck a mine forward. All three ships of the 39th Division had now been mined. Hadow at once ordered the forward magazine flooded. Watertight doors were secured and hands ordered to their abandon ship stations. Fire had broken out forward. Shortly after the explosion Lieutenant (E) Andrew Mahoney, *Ivanhoe's* engineer officer, reported that the engine could be moved. Hadow went briefly sternwards to clear *Express* and to avoid crushing men in boats afloat. Then water in the oil feed suction line caused the loss of steam-pressure.

During the period in which *Ivanhoe* was stopped and drifting *Express* signalled that she could proceed astern and that her first lieutenant was in command and requested orders. He was instructed to proceed westward and, if able, to send assistance.

By 0145 *Ivanhoe* had raised steam. She proceeded stern-first to westward at about 7 knots. It soon became apparent that the propeller shafts had been damaged, and were in fact out of line. At 0400 the main engines had to be stopped because of the damaged propeller shafts. At first light, around 0445, Commander Hadow and Andrew Mahoney inspected the ship's damage.

When news of the minings was received ashore, several MTBs[Motor Torpedo Boats] were dispatched in search of survivors, and they rescued a number from ships' boats, as did the Germans. MTBs joined *Ivanhoe* at about 0800. Retaining MTB15 Commander Hadow sent the others on their way with wounded and nearly forty of the crew.

It was imperative that steam be maintained for the working of pumps and electrical generators. At 1030 Mahoney reported that water in the oil fuel made it unlikely that steam could be held. Just over 3 hours later the steam-pressure failed. The engine room had been slowly flooding, and so the loss of steam meant that the inflow of water could not be contained.

The decision was made that the extent and nature of *Ivanhoe's* damage was against her being towed the 150 miles to harbour. A further consideration was that a Dornier flying boat had arrived in the area and so at 1430 the remaining hands boarded MTB15. When Hadow left *Ivanhoe* she was listing 15 degrees to port. Her upper deck abreast the engine room was level with the deck of the MTB. It was estimated that she would sink in 30 minutes.

Commander John Allison of *Kelvin* sighted the *Ivanhoe* shortly after 1620. She seemed to be down about 8 feet by the stern with her port scuttles awash. Damaged was observed between the funnels, probably from enemy bombing. It appeared that her keel was broken. The extent of the damage was emphasized by the manner in which the funnels leaned towards each other, leading Allison to believe that *Ivanhoe* was snagging amidships. He sank the derelict with two torpedoes.

The mining of *Esk*, *Express*, and *Ivanhoe* had taken place 40 miles north-west of Texel when the 39th Division encountered the northern flank of the German mine corridor laid to defend the invasion fleet of Sealion. *Esk* suffered heavy casualties, one hundred and thirty-five hands being lost and twenty-five taken prisoner. The mine struck by *Ivanhoe's* port paravane caused serious underwater damage aft which, though not at first apparent, was ultimately the governing factor in the decision to abandon ship. *Ivanhoe's* keel plate was probably fractured by the explosion, her after structure thereafter resting partly on the propeller shafts. Following her move sternwards to clear *Express*, both shafts fractured. The damage and flooding caused forward by striking the mine was such that attention was focused on this part of the ship. Eight of her crew had been lost and twenty-three taken prisoner.

The captain of *Esk*, Lieutenant-Commander John Couch, did not survive the mining. He had been in command of *Esk* since February 1938. Forty-three years old Jack Bickford of *Express* had been mortally wounded and died in a Grimsby hospital. Fifty-nine of the crew had been killed and twenty wounded. A new forepart was built for *Express* and joined to the rest of the ship. She later fought in the Battle of the Java Sea.

HMS *Venetia*

A mine also accounted for the loss of *Venetia*, an old destroyer completed in the Great War. Her captain, Lieutenant-Commander Lisburn Craig, had, in 1937, been appointed CO of the gunboat *Seamew* in China. Returning home in 1940, he was appointed to command *Venetia*.

During the night of 18/19 October, 1940, Craig was patrolling off Dover. At 0530 he left the patrol area and set a course for Sheerness in company with

Walpole and the new Hunt class destroyer *Garth*. At 0850, the ships were by then in the swept channel, a muffled explosion occurred on *Venetia's* starboard side in the vicinity of her engine room. It was quickly followed by a second explosion further aft. For a few moments a column of water completely enveloped the ship. Thirty seconds later she broke in half. The after end remained afloat for 15 minutes. The forepart soon turned over to the starboard, about 12 feet of it remaining above water for an hour.

Walpole rescued forty survivors and the *Garth* forty-seven. Another five were picked up by the paddle-steamer *Balmoral*. Lieutenant-Commander Craig, below deck when the mining took place, was lost with five of his officers. He had at one time served in the Royal Yacht *Victoria and Albert*.

HMS *Sturdy*

Lieutenant-Commander George Cooper had qualified for destroyer command in April 1936. He had served in *Sturdy*, his first command, prior to his becoming her captain on 31 July 1939. Cooper was thirty-one at the time *Sturdy* was wrecked on the Isle of Tiree, off the Scottish coast. On 26 October *Sturdy* and *Shikari* had joined an outward bound Atlantic convoy until dusk the following evening, their orders then being to join convoy SC8, on its way from America, in position 55.40'N/16.20'W around 0800 on the 28th.

By 0800 Cooper reckoned his position as 55.38'N/14.33'W, and he estimated the convoy bore 272 degrees and 50 miles. The sky was cloudy and only one star-sight had been obtained under poor conditions. By midday there was still no sight of the convoy. The weather was deteriorating, visibility was less than 4 miles. From the convoy situation report of the night before, it was likely that the convoy was late. Around 2200, *Sturdy* lost sight of *Shikari*.

At 0800 on the 29th neither the convoy nor *Shikari* were in sight. Cooper decided to proceed to Londonderry. By noon *Sturdy* found herself in very rough weather, but by 1800 the weather had eased slightly, though conditions were still bad. Lieutenant-Commander Cooper explains:

My appreciation of the situation at 2000, 29 October, was as follows: I had had no sight since 1440, 28 October. During this period I had encountered the full fury of a North Atlantic gale from SSE. Seas had at times been 30 feet high, wind up to 50 knots or more. The ship was short of fuel and therefore light. I had made considerable allowance for surface drift. I was expecting to come under the full influence of the tides in the North West Approaches during the night. I considered my position might be in error owing to the difficulty of making an accurate estimation of the course and speed made good in a 900 tons destroyer in a North Atlantic gale. I therefore decided to set a safe course for Inishtrahal. At 0430, approximately, I sighted a white light of foam fine on my port bow which I thought was the backwash of a large wave. A second or two later I realized it had the appearance of breakers, and at that moment the ship hit rocks, a slight bump forward (probably the dome) followed by a heavy crash under the bridge. I immediately stopped engines. The ship had come up all standing, badly damaged. I went on the wing of the bridge to view the situation. I felt certain that the screws drawing almost 15 feet had hit, and this was confirmed by breakers round the stern. I decided first to try slow astern both, to see if the propellers would revolve as I did not wish to knock them off by going full speed astern and then be adrift on a lee shore and risk the ship sinking in deep water. It was at once obvious that any chance of getting her off in a manageable state with the surf raging was impossible and I decided to remain where I was in the hope of saving life. The ship was driving slowly up the rocks, crashing and grinding and listing from 10 degrees to starboard to upright and back. Great waves were breaking over the ship. All watertight doors were closed immediately after grounding without orders, and hands were ordered to get out rafts. Rocks could be seen 30 yards ahead but no land could be picked out. Distress signals were made and the 24-inch searchlight and 10-inch SPs burnt to pick out the shore. Low-lying land could be seen about 100 yards inside the rocks. A raging surf was beating over the rocks close ahead of the ship. It was decided to send a raft with two men in it to try and get a line ashore. The raft capsized but the two men got ashore and immediately went for help. It appeared likely that the ship would break up, as she was pounding heavily and waves were breaking right over her. It seemed wise then to try and get men ashore in floats and attempt to get a line from the bows to the shore. Unfortunately the float kept being sucked back in the backwash and could not be kept under control. It was therefore decided to try the whaler. Thirteen men were sent in the boat. At this moment all the lights failed as the boiler rooms could no longer keep steam owing to the water in the fuel tanks. The whaler capsized on the rocks close ahead of the ship, and the occupants of both the whaler and the float were lost to view in the blackness of the night. Shortly afterwards, at about 0510, the ship broke in half, the stern portion being swept round to the port by successive waves until it lay at right angles to the forepart.

When the tide appeared to be going down, and the bows to be getting nearer to some rocks just awash but being swept by a 12-foot surf, an Able Seaman Smith bravely went ashore with a line. As daylight broke, the surf had receded from the bows and it was possible to disembark everyone down the line taken ashore by Smith. Five men had lost their life. The atrocious weather and an insufficient allowance for drift had been contributing factors in the grounding.

HMS *Cameron*

The last of thirteen destroyers to be lost in 1940 from bombing was the *Cameron*, in dry-dock at the time of the attack. At approximately 2050 on 5 December during a raid on Portsmouth the *Cameron* was hit by a bomb which fell to port abreast the foremost funnel, exploding in the dock in which she was resting. *Cameron* listed to port almost instantaneously when many of the shores holding the ship upright were blasted away. Within a few seconds a large fire broke out on the upper deck abaft the midship superstructure, probably in some oil drums containing waste oil fuel. The fire was a considerable distance abaft the place where the bomb hit and may have been caused by a small incendiary bomb, though this is thought improbable, oil fuel in the wing tanks caught fire and ran blazing across the bottom of the dock, setting alight the dock blocks and shores. With fires inside and outside, *Cameron's* interior was soon blazing fiercely.

Steps were immediately taken to flood the dock, and flooding began some 15 minutes after the explosion. As the water-level rose, burning oil fuel floated up the dock and helped spread the fire. At about 2115 a small explosion occurred in *Cameron* which threw debris a considerable distance. It was not until the early hours of next morning that the fire in *Cameron* was brought under control. Early morning workers saw *Cameron* on her side at an angle of 45 degrees with water lapping through the upper hatches and with her masts and B gun broken from their moorings. A layer of oil on the surface of the water gave the impression that the dock was full of oil. The funnels were distorted and broken and the brass structure of the bridge had melted.

HMS *Acheron*

Although her sea-going days were over, the *Acheron* was lost off the Isle of Wight with considerable loss of life. She had been in dry-dock as a result of bomb damage caused the previous August. By December *Acheron*, under Lieutenant John Wilson, was ready to run trials following her extensive repairs. At 0400 on the 17th *Acheron* set off for her trials in the vicinity of the Isle of Wight. Donald Sleeman opens the account of *Acheron's* loss with his experience of the day's events.

Early one cold morning in December 1940 HMS Acheron *left her anchorage on the Spithead and steamed eastwards towards the English Channel. As she passed the Nab Tower the morning watch was called, and with sleep still in my eyes I took my place alongside the depth charge levers on the after bridge, pondering on the position I now found myself in. This was my first ship and my first voyage to sea in a man-of-war, and she was about to undergo steam trials in the Channel, south of the Isle of Wight.*

The persistent ringing of a nearby telephone bell called me to my job at hand. Lifting the receiver I learned that I was being called from the quarter by the leading seaman of my watch of torpedo men. He was not very pleased to know that a new member of the crew, without any experience, had been put on the depth charge levers. Completely unimpressed with my statement that the TI had given me a demonstration and full instructions beforehand, the leading seaman told me he was going to relieve me with another more experienced man who was on the quarter-deck telephone. I was to remain until he arrived. A few minutes later he appeared. After a casual exchange of words I made my way aft to the quarter-deck, and a biting north-east wind which made me seek what shelter there was behind Y gun mounting. After a short while my eyes became accustomed to the darkness and I was able to pick out landmarks from the black mass of coastline that had become discernable on our starboard beam. It was a new experience for me to follow the coast in such an unfamiliar setting. With this new interest my discomfort was forgotten. Further off in the distance the weaving pencils of light from searchlight beams began probing the sky for enemy raiders over Portsmouth. How relieved I felt not to be on shore. The rhythmic hum of our engines, the vibrations of the deck from the screws, the steady roll of the ship, all produced a sense of confidence and assurance the like of which I had never experienced ashore.

We were due south of St. Catherine's Point when I noticed a change in the tempo in the rhythm of our screws. The deck beneath me began to vibrate faster, causing the shell of the Y gun to rattle. The noise increased and the ship commenced a swaying motion as she thrust her way ahead at the peak of her steam trial. Suddenly the deck sloped away to port beneath my feet and I clutched at the bulkhead behind me to steady myself whilst the ship slewed. The turn to port was made when above the thunder of our screws I heard a muffled roar and a sudden unfamiliar hiss. The blackness of the night was transformed by a brilliant light. Peering around the after structure, I was horrified to see the ship on fire. Great flames were leaping skyward just forward of the funnel, completely enveloping the bridge. Our speed rapidly reduced. For a brief moment I stood transfixed to the spot, too dazed and bewildered to move. I was soon brought to normal thinking by the presence of the chief bosun's mate who ordered me to make sure that the depth charges were all were set at safe. I checked the port throwers and all was well. The deck was now tilting alarmingly to forward and it was with great difficulty that I crossed over to the starboard throwers. A quick examination assured me that these depth charges were also set at safe. The ship was now completely submerged forward of the 3-inch gun monitoring, so it was easy to slide down the sloping deck into the dark waters. 'This is the end', I thought as I swam away from the ship in the direction of land that was so far off and hopelessly beyond my capacity to reach. My immediate thoughts were to get as far from the stricken vessel as possible. The woollen Balaclava, saturated with water, began to stifle me. I snatched it off and became aware of the presence of oil fuel which stank with nauseating aroma and burnt with every mouthful of water that the choppy sea washed into me. Looking over my shoulder I was surprised to see how far I had swum. Some 200 yards behind me the stern of HMS Acheron *was poised vertically above the sea – then, accompanied with a tremendous gurgle, she slid into the dark waters. It took all my effort to keep afloat whilst the sea eddied and swirled around me. I sank, swallowing a horrible mixture of salt-water and oil fuel. Spluttering and choking I broke surface for a further effort. Again I sank, once more coming to the surface with my strength almost spent. I spied a light bobbing on the water ahead of me and, with desperate endeavour and all the remaining strength in my possession, I struck out towards it. Would I ever make it? Had the light, my only hope, appeared to tantalize me? It drew painfully nearer. In my dazed state I saw that it was a calcium flare on a Carley raft. With flagging strength I floundered forward and, with a grasping outstretched hand, I just grabbed the rope handhold on the raft. I clung there unable to move, exhausted and panting for breath. In a moment I felt someone grab me under the arms and haul me upwards and heard a voice saying, 'You're okay now, chum'. I flopped over the side of the raft and found my feet on the wooden base of the raft up to the waist in water. I rested, leaning on the side of the raft until fully recovering my normal breathing. By now other men had joined us and I helped them aboard the raft. Soon it was full to capacity, and several men clung on the hand-lines around the raft. So commenced the most harrowing vigil in all my experience.*

Acheron had struck a mine. Her first run on the trials course had been without incident. Lieutenant (E) Stewart, her engineer officer, says, *We had just turned round when there was a sudden sharp explosion and the lights almost immediately went out and the ship took an immediate list to port of about 10 degrees. The port list quickly increased to 45 degrees.* Stewart climbed up the deck to the starboard side. He climbed over the side and took to the water. *I looked back and the ship had sank except for the stern which was sticking out of the water about 30 feet, practically vertically,* continues Stewart. *I assumed that from the time of the explosion to when I jumped over the side was about three to four minutes. Acheron* is believed to have sunk at about 0700.

Reg Willis was one of the few to survive the sinking. He states:

I was logging down all readings from the bridge with the engineer, Lieutenant M. Stewart, when a loud bang went off. I tried to open both forward hatches but could not do so. I went to the stern one. On getting out I saw the mast on fire and disappearing. The stern end was rising up. I called down to abandon ship. All got out of the engine room. I jumped with a mate of mine from my home town but did not see him again. There was another explosion. I lost my clothes. I became covered in oil, which I think helped save me. The only Carley float which got away was filled up by the time I got there, and so I hung on a rope. The sea was bitterly cold and the spray was like being jabbed with needles.

Those of the crew who made it safely to the Carley float were the only survivors. Donald Sleeman concludes his narrative:

Slowly the time passed. The silence of the deep was broken at intervals with the plaintive cries for help from our unfortunate comrades out in the inky blackness beyond us, and by the wash of the heaving swell around us. I realized for the first time that morning how rough the sea was; there were times when, as I stood, the water was just below my waist, and then suddenly it would rise up to my neck. This occurred with every motion of the raft on the heaving crest of the swell. The cold was intense and the biting wind rapidly penetrated my sodden clothing. An awful sense of weariness began to assail me, and every effort of will was needed to prevent nodding off to sleep. Time seemed interminable. Would the daylight never come? And with daylight, what then? The only hope lay with the coastguard lookout high upon the cliffs above the Needles; surely the fire from the ill-fated ship must have been seen by them.

The miserable moments slowly passed and the grey light began to break eastwards. But all of our party were not destined to see that dawn for one by one our unfortunate comrades clinging to the raft lost their handgrip and, despite efforts of those near them, broke away, throwing their arms frantically above their heads as they disappeared beneath the cold sea. Only one remained, and he was floating on a fender which one of our company had tied to the Carley float.

At last day was fully with us. In its early light, far away head I could see the faint outline of the white cliffs of the Isle of Wight. Around us drifted the flotsam and jetsam of wreckage, all that remained of HMS Acheron. *Away to port in cold mockery to our lost shipmates drifted an empty Carley raft, too far for us to reach. We tried to sing to keep up our spirits but our voices came harsh and tuneless as the croaking of frogs and we gave it up and lapsed into silence.*

At long last a ship appeared. We made her out to be an escort vessel. Frantically we waved and shouted. What were their lookouts up to? Would they never see us? At last she altered course and bore down on us. She hove to, and we drifted alongside. One by one, wearily and with painful effort, we climbed up the scrambling nets and fell into the arms of our rescuers. Stripped of our wet clothing and swathed in warm blankets, and filled with hot cocoa and rum, we sank into the blissful oblivion of sleep and safety.

Loss of life was heavy: around six officers and 145 ratings perished, plus dockyard personnel. Survivors totalled about fifteen. Lieutenant Wilson was lost with the ship. The exact position of the sunken *Acheron* remained unknown for many years. All attempts to find her came to nothing until April 1984 when diver Martin Woodward of the Bembridge Maritime Museum on the Isle of Wight located her about 5 miles south of St. Catherine's Point.

HMS *Khartoum*

The Italians came into the war on 10 June 1940. But it was not in the Mediterranean that the first destroyer loss of the war with Italy took place. On the morning of 23 June 1940 the Italian submarine *Torricelli* fought an engagement with five Royal Navy ships. The Italian fired her torpedoes and gun. Knowing that defeat was inevitable her captain scuttled his command. The action had taken place to the north of the small island of Perim, which lies in the strait known as Bab el Mandab at the southern end of the Red Sea. At the end of the fighting the British made towards Aden, except for the *Khartoum* which continued to patrol the area. She had on board three Italians from *Torricelli*. All three were in a bad way, two dying of wounds despite every effort to save them. Arthur Johns was serving in *Khartoum* at the time and remembers clearly the events of 23 June.

We had got back to our allotted position on Perim patrol and had just had our dinner when there was a terrific explosion aft. I thought that we had been bombed, but soon found out what it was. Our engineer officer had had his lunch and was sitting aft of the officers' gallery in the after superstructure with all the doors open to get the effect from the breeze which the movement of the ship might give him. Suddenly he found a torpedo war-head passing over his body. He was terribly burned, as the galley was oil-fired and the war-head had broken through all the pipes and had caught fire instantly. The war-head, having passed over the engineer officer, carried on aft and passed through the hydraulic pipe system of X gun turret; so we had a situation where approximately 90 gallons of hydraulic oil, all burning fiercely, mixed with the galley fuel oil, was catching everything alight inside the superstructure and pouring down the hatchways to the wardroom and the after cabin flats. Meanwhile the war-head had passed through the bulkhead aft of the superstructure and had come to rest on the stern white-hot. I've never seen steel catch fire and heat up so quickly. It burned right through the deck and down into X turret magazine and the depth charge magazine. But the speed of the fire amazed me.

The explosion had occurred at 1150, about six hours after the fight with *Torricelli*. The starboard wing torpedo tube of the after torpedo mounting was the source of the explosion, which it is thought was the result of shell splinter damage received in the action with *Torricelli*. The explosion, caused by damage to a torpedo's air vessel, was so violent that the after body of the torpedo jammed into the rear of the tube and the war-head was discharged aft at high speed. The war-head passed through the after gallery, severing the feed-pipe from the 80 gallons gravity oil feed-tank for the galley, and instantly started a fire. The war-head then passed through an after gun support, and then on through the after gun power unit compartment. It continued onwards through the after bulkhead of the superstructure before striking a starboard winch. The war-head's safety pistol proved effective and the head, though it split, did not explode.

Damage to fire-mains and hoses accentuated the problems of fire fighting. The fires created dense smoke as they spread. *Khartoum* was manoeuvred stern to wind to reduce the draught. After almost 15 minutes without any noticeable effect on the fire, Commander Donald Dowler, *Khartoum's* captain, set course for Perim harbour 7 miles away.

Steaming on one boiler *Khartoum* made towards the harbour entrance. Commander Dowler intended to beach ship on a shoal known as Prince's shoal, just inside the harbour. If possible he would venture even farther in. On approaching the harbour entrance the order was given to clear the boiler room of additional hands. Unfortunately this order was incorrectly received as an order to clear the boiler room of all hands. Before evacuating the boiler room the main fuel supply to the fires' sprayers was turned off, which at once resulted in the ship losing way. The loss of steam caused the dynamo to come off the board, with a consequent loss of electrical power. A steaming watch was hurriedly sent to flash up the boiler. The 50 lb of steam-pressure sufficient for manoeuvring main engines at slow speed was raised, but there was insufficient time to raise the pressure required by the steam dynamos to restore electrical power needed to operate the steering gear. The loss of speed and the failure of the steering power shortly after passing the harbour entrance nullified the attempt to beach on Prince's Shoal and *Khartoum* came to anchor in about five fathoms.

After anchoring, the order was given to flood the gear room, the intent being that it would act as a buffer if, as expected, the after magazine blew up. On the order of Lieutenant-Commander (E) Allan Reed Nos 1 and 2 magazines and shell rooms were flooded as the extent of the explosion could not be known. Many of the crew were ordered to take to the water and swim ashore. Small boats from ashore greatly assisted in the recovery of the crew. At 1245 there was a heavy explosion in *Khartoum's* after end, presumably in No 3 magazine. The explosion caused *Khartoum* to settle aft and she was felt to touch bottom. It was thought that the flooding would probably extinguish the fire, and that further danger had passed. Then at 1259 a second and much heavier explosion took place when a large number of depth charges in the warhead magazine detonated. Personnel on the fo'c'sle were lifted several feet off the deck. The explosion blew off a considerable length of *Khartoum's* stern and she settled much deeper aft and heeled 25 to 30 degrees to port. Subsequently, as air was expelled from compartments forward, the bows settled and *Khartoum* came to rest on an even keel. Commander Dowler was pleased to note that, *Throughout, the conduct and bearing of the officers and ship's company was exemplary.*

HMS *Escort*

HMS *Escort* became the first Royal Navy destroyer to be sunk in the Mediterranean when Capitano di Corvetta Giulio Chialamberto of the submarine *Guglielmo Marconi* attacked her 100 miles east of Gibraltar. The circumstance which led to her loss indirectly involved the passage of two convoys from Malta to Alexandria. As the Italians could be expected to attack the convoys, it was decided that their passage should take place under cover of a fleet operation. As a diversion Force H (*Hood, Valiant, Resolution, Ark Royal*, with cruisers and destroyers) was to cruise in the Western Mediterranean and carry out an air attack on Cagliari. Force H sailed from Gibraltar at 0700 on 8 July. When south of Minorca the ships met with continual heavy air attack, pressed home with such determination that Vice-Admiral Sir James Somerville considered that the risk to *Ark Royal* outweighed the advantage to be gained from a minor operation. He therefore turned about and headed for Gibraltar. It was during this return to Gibraltar that *Escort*, under Lieutenant-Commander John Bostock, was attacked by *Marconi*.

At 0300 on 11 July *Marconi* sighted two dark shadows sternwards. These were the *Escort* and *Forester*. At 0320 Chialamberto fired a torpedo at *Escort* before diving hurriedly to prevent being rammed by *Forester*. The torpedo struck *Escort* at the bulkhead between Nos 1 and 2 boiler rooms, causing instant flooding. The bulkhead between Nos 2 & 3 boiler rooms was split and No.3 started to flood more slowly. A huge hole was torn in the upper deck over the forward boiler room, the bulkhead between No.1 boiler room and the mess and low power room burst, flooding the compartments. With a steadily increasing list to port, all but three hands abandoned *Escort* at 0630 when she was listing about 30 degrees. Two hours later No.3 boiler room was three-quarters flooded, but the bulkheads were holding, though the list was still increasing. Shortly before 1100 water passed through the watertight door on the port side of the galley flat and *Escort* gradually went over onto her beam ends, displaying the 20 feet hole made by the torpedo, clean cut from about 4 feet below the upper deck to beyond the keel. The hull now began to bend, and the bow and stern came up until they were standing vertically together out of the water. The stern then broke off and sank. Nearly 30 minutes later the bows also went down. *Forester* returned to Gibraltar with survivors.

HMS *Hostile*

The second destroyer loss of the Mediterranean war was the *Hostile*, captained by Lieutenant-Commander Anthony Burnell-Nugent who had commanded *Havant* during Operation Dynamo. In the early hours of 23 August the *Nubian*, *Mohawk*, *Hero*, and *Hostile*, in that order, were in line ahead *en route* from Malta to Gibraltar as a temporary loan to Force H when at 0110 *Nubian* signalled *Mohawk* – four cables astern – that owing to an engine defect she was unable to continue and that the others should proceed without her. With *Mohawk* leading, the three raced onwards at 30 knots.

At 0318 Yeoman of Signals Frances Cherry in *Hero* reported that *Hostile*, four cables astern, had hauled out to port and that he had observed a column of smoke and water astern of her. Aware that an Italian dive-bomber squadron was based 20 miles away at Pantelleria, Commander Hilary Biggs, *Hero's* captain, thought it probable that *Hostile* had been dive-bombed, as the bright moonlight was ideal for such attacks. He signalled Commander John Eaton of *Mohawk* that *Hostile* had been bombed. Both ships closed *Hostile*, then stationary about 2 miles astern; her position was 125 degrees Cape Bon Light 17 degrees. *Hostile* had been mined just abaft the engine room. The after torpedo tubes had been blown into the sea, along with two able seamen who did not survive. Electrical power having failed at the same time of the explosion, Burnell-Nugent with a hand-torch signalled *Mohawk* that *Hostile* had been mined and that Commander Eaton was to close on the starboard side. A bridge-to-bridge discussion took place as to how the situation should be met. *Hostile's* after part was flooded and her back appeared to be broken at the after torpedo tubes. Her buoyancy was such that pre-war she could have been towed to harbour. All things considered it was decided that she would have to be sunk. By 0355 the transfer of her ship's personnel to *Mohawk* had been completed.

Hostile's stern was under water as far forward as the searchlight platform and she appeared to be settling further when from 300 yards *Hero* fired a torpedo which struck *Hostile* in her forward boiler room. There was a violent explosion followed by a rain of debris over a wide area. Within 40 seconds there was nothing above water except 40 feet of *Hostile's* bows, floating with the upper deck vertical. While sinking her stern was completely destroyed by exploding depth charges. After circling for 5 minutes, *Hero* proceeded to join *Mohawk*.

Commander Eaton decided to make for Malta in preference to continuing for Gibraltar as *Mohawk* had 166 extra personnel on board. The passage to Malta was completed without incident.

HMS *Hyperion*

The last destroyer loss of the year took place off Pantellaria. The battleship *Malaya* was escorting the empty *Clan Forbes* and *Clan Fraser* from Malta to Gibraltar. Ahead of the small convoy the *Hyperion*, Commander Hugh Nicolson, had the task of sweeping a few miles ahead to deal with any troublesome U-boats or E-boats. At about 0127 on 22 December *Hyperion* obtained an echo, considered to be that of a U-boat. Nicholson made two attacks and was turning in readiness to make a third attack when *Hyperion* set off a mine in the vicinity of Y gun. Her position was about 24 miles east of Cape Bon. Both main engines were put out of action: the port engine being jammed and the starboard engine was bumping, due probably to hull distortion. A number of compartments were flooded. The destroyer *Ilex* arrived in the vicinity at about 0245 and the wounded and most of *Hyperion's* crew were transferred to her. At 0345 *Ilex* took *Hyperion* in tow but 25 minutes later the tow parted. While it was being recovered and re-passed Captain D14 in *Jervis* arrived with *Janus* and *Juno*. By 0445 *Hyperion* was again in tow, but not for long. Captain D decided that with daylight not far off and the close proximity of Pantellaria, *Hyperion* would have to be sunk. At 0454 he signalled Nicolson to prepare ship and that he would go alongside to transfer the remainder of the crew. By 0510 the transfer had been completed. *Janus* was then signalled to sink *Hyperion*. An observer in *Jervis* noted that:

> *Nobody spoke a word as we stood on the bridge, together with some of Hyperion's officers, waiting for the end. There followed a flash from the torpedo tubes, a few seconds pause, and then a deep, muffled explosion. The shock of the explosion broke off the after funnel, a column of water and smoke shot skywards from amidships, and the Hyperion slowly rolled over. There were no flames or subsequent explosions. Very gently she sank and one of her officers remarked, 'How gracefully she goes down. She was a graceful ship.' It was a moment of great sadness. As the ship heeled over, her gaping wound could be seen. Then only the keel was visible as she gradually disappeared from view. When we thought she had gone for good her bows suddenly broke surface again and she remained thus perpendicular for some minutes, presumably owing to air pockets, before the waters finally closed over her.*

HMS *Exmoor*

Twenty-eight of the 1941 launchings were Hunt class destroyers. *Exmoor*, one of the Hunt class, was the only destroyer to be sunk off the British coast in 1941. Her loss, on 25 February, came less than 4 months after her completion by Vickers-Armstrong on 1 November 1940. At the time of her loss *Exmoor*, Lieutenant-Commander Robert Lampard, was part of the escort for a Southend to Methil convoy. *Exmoor* and *Shearwater* were to remain with the convoy until passing Sheringham Buoy, off Norfolk, and then proceed to meet a Methil–Southend convoy. On the night of 25/26 February there was considerable E-boat activity on the east coast between the Humber and Lowestoft and it was a torpedo from an E-boat that struck *Exmoor* aft. The explosion split the ship's hull and caused severe internal damage. Oil fuel sprayed over the after end by the explosion was ignited almost immediately and the after end was enveloped in flames, the fire spreading rapidly forward. *Exmoor* heeled over 20 degrees to port. Taking an increasingly pronounced list, she finally capsized. *Exmoor* then stood on end. About ten minutes after the torpedoing she went down. It was 2115.

First news of the sinking came in a signal from *Shearwater: Am picking up survivors from Exmoor at 5 buoy. Approximate position 52.27N/01.56E. Proceeding to Yarmouth.* Loss to the ship's company was heavy: Lieutenant-Commander Lampard, three officers, and a hundred ratings went down with the ship. The attack had taken place off Lowestoft and had been carried out by the S30, the E-boat which had accounted for *Wakeful* during Operation Dynamo. Command of S30 had passed from Zimmermann to twenty-nine years old Oberleutenant zur See Klaus Feldt, who survived the war.

HMS *Mohawk*

On 17 May 1940 *Mohawk* left England for the Mediterranean, where she met her end. At dusk on 15 April the *Jervis*, Captain Philip Mack, *Janus*, Commander John Tothill, *Nubian*, Commander Richard Ravenhill, and *Mohawk* left Malta to intercept on Axis convoy of five merchantman escorted by three destroyers. The convoy was reportedly off Cape Bon and on a heading for Tripoli. Captain Mack's intention was to intercept the convoy in the area of the Kerkenna Banks. The flotilla was proceeding at 25 knots when the convoy, after some searching, was encountered at 0158 about 6 miles away. At 0220 Captain Mack opened fire with 4.7s and pom-pom, scoring hits and so battle commenced.

Commander John Eaton, last in line with *Mohawk*, engaged the rear merchantman and reported:

This ship was hit at the second salvo and burnt fiercely. Fire was checked after firing about eight salvos. Fire was opened spasmodically for the next few minutes, as the merchant ships were being repeatedly hit by the destroyers ahead of Mohawk *and I did not wish to waste ammunition. At 0223 an enemy destroyer of the Navigatori class was sighted on the starboard bow steering an opposite and parallel course at high speed. She was immediately engaged by* Nubian *and* Mohawk, *hit and set on fire, and was last seen stopped and on fire about a mile astern. At 0230* Nubian *led round to port across the bow of the leading merchantman, which immediately altered course to starboard and tried to ram* Mohawk. *The ship appeared to be quite undamaged and, on avoiding her and crossing over to the port side, I turned to starboard with the object of engaging and sinking her. As the ship was still under helm and turning to starboard a torpedo struck on the starboard side about Y gun. The ship was at once stopped and I ordered the engineer officer to report to me as to the extent of the damage. The foremost group of guns then opened fire on the merchant ship in direct firing and hits were at once obtained, the ship catching fire and stopping. No ship could be seen in the vicinity which could have fired the torpedo, apart from the enemy destroyer who was stopped and on fire over a mile astern of* Mohawk, *and I came to the conclusion that it must have been a stray torpedo fired by this vessel, possibly with the object of getting rid of top weight. The engineer officer then reported to me that although most of the stern had been blown away the propeller shafts and propellers were still in place and that he would try to move them and get way on the ship. About 5 minutes after the first torpedo had struck, a second torpedo struck* Mohawk *on the port side approximately on the bulkhead separating Nos 2 and*

3 boiler rooms. The ship commenced to settle rapidly on an even keel and I ordered all hands on deck. Less than a minute after this order had been given, the ship took up a very heavy list to port and settled on her beam ends with the after part submerged as far as the after end of the torpedo tubes. The order was then given to abandon ship as I considered it only a matter of minutes before the ship sank. Six Carley floats were got out and manned, the remainder of the hands jumping into the sea. It was not possible to lower the boats owing to the rapid listing of the ship, but the hands abandoned ship in an orderly manner and I consider that under the circumstances it was not possible to get out the remainder of the Carley floats.

Petty Officer Harry Whitehorn had joined the navy in 1921. As the director layer in *Mohawk*, Whitehorn was at his station on the bridge. If need be, he could fire all eight of the ship's 4.7-inch guns at the squeeze of a trigger. Whitehorn recalls:

Our captain ordered the director to engage a destroyer approaching fine on the starboard bow and making smoke. She appeared to be burning inside the bridge. Immediately after, there was a big bump. Although I did not know it at the time, our stern had been blown off together with the after twin 4.7s. We then engaged a merchant ship hurrying away from the conflict and had managed about four salvos when there was another big bump. We had been torpedoed again, this time on the port side. On the captain giving the order to abandon ship I climbed out of the director and down to the signal bridge and then to the upper deck. Putting my hands in front of me I slid down the ship's side just like going down the chute at a swimming-baths. I was fully dressed and wearing wellingtons and sea-boot stockings, which came off in the water as I swam away. My last sight of Mohawk *was of her on her beam ends with bow out of the water. It was now a question of survival. I had great faith in our other destroyers and I knew that they would look for us when the action was over. And this was so. I was picked up by* Jervis *and eventually landed at Malta.*

Leading Seaman Ray Bromley had joined *Mohawk* at Alexandria in November 1938. He well remembers the action of 16 April:

My position in Mohawk *was as operator of the secondary control. This was situated in the after flat of the destroyer and its function was to take over from the TS (Transmitting Station) should there be a breakdown. It could also be used to control X and Y guns independently of the TS control. Our twin 4.7s were firing and the battle was in full swing when we suddenly heeled over to a very sharp turn as if trying to avoid something. The sharpness of the manoeuvre suggested that it was an emergency turn. We had just started to straighten when there was an almighty explosion between the after lobby and Y gun which took away Y gun and the quarter-deck completely. The lights went out but darkness prevailed only a few moments as the emergency lighting came on at once. Under the direction of a petty officer the after flat was filled with men operating the ammunition lifts to the twin 4.7s above. On hearing shouts that the after gun and quarter-deck had gone, I looked through the after door. There was no sign of anything, no men or debris in the water. Then came the order to batten down the lower hatchways. This we did, although we could hear the men calling for help in the magazine below. An order is an order and it had to be carried out regardless. The petty officer in charge ordered me to the bridge to report the after situation to the captain. I was reporting to the skipper when the engineer officer arrived on the bridge to report that one screw was okay and could probably get us back. The skipper then replied,* 'Please do that, Chief'. *The EO then left. It was at this point that I really became of what was taking place. All hell seemed to have broken loose. It was a classic example of destroyers in action: the for'ad guns, the .5-inch and pom-pom and Oerlikon, all were engaging targets. I was waiting for further instructions when a second torpedo hit us, this time in the boiler room. The old* Mohawk *began to heel over and the order to abandon ship was given. I blew up my lifebelt and jumped from the bridge with other crewmen. There was no panic. At first I tried to swim away from the ship, then decided to swim along her side. On seeing my mate Tom Mayel, who with others was trying to get a Carley raft into the water, I shouted for him to join me. Owing to the din he did not hear my call. Alone, I passed the stern and swam clear to escape any likelihood of suction taking me down. I had been swimming for about an hour, covered in oil fuel for much of the time, when I began to feel sick through having swallowed oil fuel. By this time I was quite tired and I was reflecting on the notion that one's past life flashes before one towards the end when I heard singing. I thought,* 'Bloody hell, when I have been in a choir?' *I then recognized the tune as* Roll Out the Barrel. *In making my way towards the singing I spotted a Carley raft with several of my shipmates on it. Sighting the raft gave me renewed strength and it was not long before I was being hauled aboard. Then, for the first time in my naval service, I was violently sick.*

Shortly after, the raft was closed by *Nubian* and the survivors taken on board to be landed at Malta.

The Flotilla had struck hard at the convoy. In line ahead and with all guns bearing it had raced along the convoy's starboard flank. The sudden appearance of the British from astern had taken the Italian escort by surprise. The destroyer *Baleno* as soon hit and she drifted in a sinking condition into shallow waters. The *Lampo* was hit and badly damaged and she was taken by the current on to the Kerkenna Banks. The *Luca Toriga* was quickly ablaze: between 0247 and 0259 Commander Tothill engaged her on various courses, and at speeds varying between 16 and 30 knots. Tothill says that an explosion occurred amidships and a very fierce fire broke out. Although the ship was finished her crew bravely fired three torpedoes, two of which hit *Mohawk*.

By 0320 *Mowhawk* lay on her side with about 50 feet of her fo'c'sle above water. *Janus* was ordered to completely sink the wreck. She opened fire with a gun, obtaining four hits. Air inside the hull was released and the wreck sank. The position was logged as 34.56.5N/42.4E. Two officers and thirty-nine ratings had been lost with the ship. At 0430 Captain Mack departed the battle area. The action had cost the Axis almost 19,000 tons of shipping. The Afrika Korps had been denied reinforcements of troops, three hundred vehicles, and 3,500 tons of stores. *Mohawk's* captain survived the war and went on to become Vice-Admiral Sir John Eaton. Philip Mack became a rear-admiral. He was killed in a plane crash in April 1943.

HMS *Jersey*

On 28 September 1940 HMS *Jersey* joined the 5th Destroyer Flotilla, which at that time had Captain Lord Louis Mountbatten in *Kelly* as Captain D. The flotilla left Plymouth for the Mediterranean on 21 April 1941, arriving at Malta a week later. In company with the cruiser *Gloucester* the flotilla carried out raids on shipping. Unfortunately the *Jersey* had only four days at Malta before she sunk. The *Kelly, Jersey, Kashmir,* and *Kipling* were returning to Malta from patrol. *Kelly* safely entered harbour but the *Jersey,* next in line astern, hit a mine in the swept channel close to the harbour entrance. Reginald Beck, who was then thirty-one, recalls the incident as follows:

The ship's company had been at action stations during the night's patrol. I was employed in a junior capacity as a coder of the watch in the W/T office. For my part the watch had been quiet with little decoding for me to deal with. For want of something to do, I blew extra air into my Mae West. It was nearing the end of the morning watch and soon we would be closing down the W/T watches and going down below to our messes for breakfast. But this was not to be, for suddenly there was an almighty bang. Petty Officer Telegraphist Guinevan did not forbid me when (survival instinct at work!) I said I would go outside and find out what had happened. The auxiliary lighting must have been switched on, as I found the W/T office door-handle without difficulty. Out on deck I could see that there was already quite a list to starboard and a white cloud of steam aft. I decided to report it to the office, but just then all the fellows were coming out from forward and so I couldn't get to the door. On returning to the port side I saw the ship's 'postman', a staid hand. No orders of any sort were being given. 'Posty', looking after number one, went down the port side into the harbour. I then followed him and I swam quickly so as not to get taken down. I was picked up by a Maltese dghaiso. The men picked up were put to bed after a tot of rum and the skipper came round to see that we were comfortable. Later we were taken to Gibraltar.

Jersey sank in less than 5 minutes. Her captain, Anthony Burnell-Nugent, had also been in command of *Havant* and *Hostile* when they had been sunk.

So ended 1940. The year's thirty destroyer losses were in part offset by the forty-one destroyers which in the same period ran down the slipways.

Chapter Three

1941

On 6 April 1941 Hitler invaded Greece and Yugoslavia. It took only 11 days to subdue Yugoslavia. A week later the Greeks surrendered. On that day, 24 April, the Allies put into effect plans to evacuate the Imperial Expeditionary Force. The first of more than fifty thousand troops that were eventually rescued from Greece was lifted on the night of 24/25 April. On the third night of the evacuation (26/27) in excess of twenty-five thousand troops embarked at several locations for passage to Crete. Of the embarkation points on that third night, one was at Nauplia and another at Tolon, both in the Gulf of Argolis. Under the command of Captain Dennis Lees in the AA cruiser *Calcutta*, the destroyers *Diamond*, *Griffin*, *Havock*, *Hotspur*, and *Isis* were all escort to the large transports *Slamat* and *Khedive Ismail*.

It was essential that the troops be embarked with all speed so as to enable the convoy to get beyond the range of enemy dive-bombers during darkness. Failure to leave the pick-up points by 0300 would almost certainly lead to air attacks later. At Nauplia, the embarkation point for the *Slamat* and *Khedive Ismail*, the loading of troops began at once. When the time came to weigh anchor the *Slamat*, loathed to depart when many troops were still on shore, remained where she was. She left almost an hour late, and so it was not until after 0400 that she joined the convoy for the return to Crete.

Daylight on Sunday 27th revealed that the *Khedive Ismail*, *Slamat*, *Calcutta*, *Diamond*, *Hotspur*, and *Isis* were still in the Gulf, and so within range of dive-bombers. At 0700 enemy aircraft were sighted and 15 minutes later two bombs hit *Slamat*, killing all on the bridge and in the wheelhouse. The *Diamond*, Lieutenant-Commander Philip Cartwright, was detailed to rescue survivors of *Slamat*. Under heavy air attack the ships raced on. Though they continued to attract the majority of aircraft, the *Slamat* and *Diamond* were also attacked, and so it was some time before Cartwright was able to concentrate fully on rescuing survivors.

The *Western*, *Wryneck*, and *Vendetta* sailed from Suda Bay with orders to join Captain Lees, and so enable *Hotspur* and *Isis*, both packed with troops, to proceed at high speed to Crete. The trio met Lees at 0910. As *Diamond* had signalled for help in her new rescue work, the *Wryneck* was directed to join her. Commander Lane, *Wryneck's* captain, closed *Diamond* at about 1000. Lane was soon involved in rescuing survivor's from rafts and boats, taking on board about fifty. Cartwright, with five hundred survivors of *Slamat*, was keen to be on his way and so torpedoed the burning *Slamat* at the first opportunity. He then formed astern of *Wryneck* and at 28 knots proceeded towards Crete.

HMS *Diamond*

It was shortly after midday when *Diamond* and *Wryneck* came under sudden and devastating attacks from aircraft. Unseen and unheard, dive-bombers swooped low out of the sun with engines switched off. There was scarcely time to sound the alarm rattler before *Diamond's* decks were being riddled with machine-gun fire. A near miss forward by a bomb tore a large hole in her side. Another bomb exploded in the engine room, bringing down the mast and the after funnel. There was steam blow off in all directions. The boats were smashed so men jumped into the sea. *Diamond's* bows suddenly rose perpendicularly and then she disappeared stern first.

HMS *Wryneck*

The *Wryneck* fared no better. A bomb struck the forecastle near A gun and killed or wounded everyone at the gun, on the bridge, and in the sick-bay. The same bomb shattered the stokers mess deck. Another bomb passed through the engine room hatch, destroying steam-pipes and a third bomb struck aft, setting an ammunition locker on fire. *Wryneck* was proceeding at about 18 knots with a heavy and increasing list to port. The whaler, slightly damaged, was lowered.

The only officer to survive from the two destroyers was the engineer officer of *Wryneck*. After having put an army officer survivor to bed in his bunk, he was changing in his cabin when the ship was hit. Although wounded by splinters, he went on deck to ensure that the boilers were made safe and to assist fore and repair parties. Seeing the hopelessness of the situation he returned to his cabin where he found the army officer lying in oil fuel and with injuries to both legs. Assisting him to the upper deck, he adjusted his lifebelt and left him by a raft while he went forward to examine the ship. By now the deck on the port side was awash. The list, oil fuel, which made the deck slippery, and weakened by his wounds, he lost his grip and slid into the sea. Floating clear of the propellers as the ship continued to move ahead, he saw the list grow steeper, until *Wryneck* finally rolled over to port and disappeared.

Commander Lane was seen on a Carley raft. He was wounded, as were others on the raft, and covered in oil. In the rising sea he was unable to hold on and was lost. Philip Cartwright was observed on a crowded raft but when a further two men gained a hold of the raft's life-line, he dived off the raft to make room for someone else. He swam away, and was not seen again. And so neither commanding officer survived.

The number of those who survived the sinking of *Slamat, Diamond,* and *Wryneck* totalled only fifty: one officer, forty-one ratings and just eight out of the many hundreds of soldiers.

HMS *Juno*

The evacuated troops had for most part been transported to Crete, 60 miles south of Greece. On 15 May, two weeks after the withdrawal from Greece, the Luftwaffe began its bombing of the island. As a seaborne invasion could take place at any time, Royal Navy ships were formed into groups and deployed as required. One such group was Force C, a mixture of cruisers and destroyers. Throughout 19 May, Force C ships left Alexandria at various times and much of the following day was spent patrolling south of the Kaso Strait. In the evening course was shaped to pass through the Strait but at 0950 on Wednesday 21st, the force was attacked by aircraft and these attacks continued for some time. During this period the destroyer *Juno*, Commander St John Tyrwhitt, was attacked and was hit in her after magazine and a boiler room. In less than two minutes she had sunk. The ship's medical officer states:

Suddenly there was a blinding flash, the lights went out and I could just sense redness. I have no recollection of any noise or great concussion. I and my small first aid party climbed up ladders and quickly followed others who were jumping over-board.

A rating who still has a vivid recollection of this day is John Tilley. *Juno*, was his first ship and he was a breech loader of a 4.7. He recalls:

We were hit by three 1,000 lb bombs dropped from a high-level Italian plane, whose height made it look like the thickness of a pencil. At the time, I was in the gun turret with the rest of the gun crew. We all heard the bombs coming down. One of my shipmates was bending down with me; as I struggled to get up he fell dead to one side with a piece of shrapnel through his brain. My leg was through the deck and was swollen, bleeding, and felt dead. I am afraid we did not wait for orders to abandon ship, as per sailors manual. Those that were able to do so, dived or dropped into the sea. Juno *listed to one side but I managed to get over the guard-rails on the opposite side to the list. Many of the crew were killed on board ship. In the water I heard a lot of men praying to be saved. Some were non-swimmers and others, including myself, could not swim owing to injuries. We were all covered in oil and must have drunk pints of it through ducking under the water to avoid the tracer bullets from the enemy planes trying to catch the oil alight. I was close to exhaustion when I heard a voice say, 'Come on, Jack'. Looking up I saw a ship about 20 yards away. A sailor, who had jumped overboard from* Nubian *to help those in the water was swimming towards me pushing a ship's spar. 'Hang on to this,' he said. I managed to do as he said and he pulled me to his ship's side. After that I do not remember any more until I woke up on board the* Nubian. *That sailor saved my life, although, I heard later that he was cautioned as he had 'abandoned' ship. In the* Nubian *survivors were everywhere: on stretchers, below decks and in the sick-bay. After a couple of days we returned to Alexandria, and then went off to hospital.*

Two of the three bombs which hit *Juno* opened the after boiler room and the engine room to the sea. The third bomb exploded the after magazine. Six officers and ninety ratings were rescued, but 119 hands were lost. Completed in August 1939, the *Juno* had in two years of hard fighting gained seven Battle Honours.

HMS *Greyhound*

When the *Greyhound* was sunk the following afternoon, almost half her crew went with her. *Greyhound*, part of a battleship's screen, was detached at 1325 to sink a caique. At 1345 she was proceeding to rejoin when attacked by dive-bombers. The right Stukas scored three hits, and the *Greyhound* sank in less than 15 minutes. Machine-gunning by aircraft on men in the water took a great many lives. Five officers and seventy-four ratings were lost.

The loss of *Juno* on the 21st and *Greyhound* on the 22nd was followed on the 23rd by the loss of *Kashmir* and *Kelly*. At about 0800 on the 23rd a formation of twenty-four Stukas found *Kashmir* and *Kelly* to the south of Crete. Captain Mountbatten of *Kelly* signalled Commander Henry King of *Kashmir* to act independently, and then went full ahead.

HMS *Kashmir* and HMS *Kelly*

The dive-bombers attacked in waves of three and *Kashmir* was the first to be sunk. She was proceeding at top speed when hit by a 1,000 lb bomb. Two minutes later she was gone. *Kelly* was hit by a bomb while doing 30 knots under full starboard rudder. Captain Mountbatten recalls:

The bomb hit by No.3 gun deck the starboard side. I immediately gave the order 'Midships.' The navigator, I think it was, repeated the order to the coxswain. The coxswain replied, 'She won't answer her wheel, sir.' I said, 'Slow both'. The reply came back, 'Telegraphs won't work, sir'. I leant over the side and said, 'Keep all the guns firing as another wave is coming in'. A useless order as all the guns were firing. As she went over I could see some of the guns' crews being washed away from their guns while they were still firing. I realized she was going over.

Kelly turned over to port and after 30 minutes of floating upside down, she sank. Survivors of both ships were fired on by aircraft.

Commander Aubrey St Clair-Ford in *Kipling* witnessed the attack from about 8 miles away. Closing the area he moved from raft to raft picking up *Kelly* and *Kashmir* survivors. Air attacks on *Kipling* were frequent and she often had to go racing away at full speed, zigzagging and with guns blazing. With the greatest difficult *Kipling* rescued 279 officers and men. She left the area at 1100. Air attacks only began to ease as she drew farther from the aircrafts' base of operations. Near misses had damaged her and she had taken on a list. Speed had been reduced to about 17 knots. She was still on a heading for Alexandria when she ran out of fuel. A minesweeper was able to assist with fuel, and so *Kipling* was able to steam into Alexandria to a rousing welcome.

* * *

The situation in Crete was grave. German airborne troops had landed in Crete on 20 May. At noon on the 27th they entered the Cretan capital of Canea. At 1500 the decision was taken to evacuate Crete. The cruisers *Orian* (wearing the flag of Rear-Admiral Henry Rawlings), *Ajax*, *Dido*, and the destroyers *Decoy*, *Hereward*, *Hotspur*, *Imperial*, *Jackal*, and *Kimberley*, sailed from Alexandria at 0600 on 28 May to embark troops from the Heraklion area. The passage to Crete was quiet until 1700 when the Luftwaffe found the squadron 90 miles south of Scarpanto. At about 1720 the *Imperial* was attacked by Stukas. Lieutenant-Commander Charles Kitkat, her captain, states, *in spite, or because, of maximum speed and rudder, five bombs narrowly missed the after part of the ship.* Although we thought we had escaped damage, *later we were to find otherwise.* Later that night the *Ajax's* hull was damaged by a near miss. She was ordered to Alexander.

HMS *Imperial*

Arriving at Heraklion at 2300, the embarkation of four thousand troops began at once. In silence and with a minimum of fuss the troops boarded the destroyers. By 0325 the squadron had re-formed and was speeding east at 29 knots towards the Kasos Strait. Things seemed to be going well for a successful dash from the danger area when at 0345 *Imperial's* steering broke down. A collision between *Imperial* and *Kimberley*, and then *Imperial* and the cruisers, was narrowly avoided. Lieutenant-Commander Kitkat again:

The ship slewed violently to port and starboard and showed no inclination to answer the wheel. Nor could she be steered by main engines, the yaw being so violent that she could only be checked with the use of steam on the appropriate engine. Tiller-flat steering was tried but proved equally fruitless. An investigation in the tiller-flat disclosed an extensive leak of oil in the ram cylinders allowing the ram to traverse at will, and consequently the rudder to swing freely from side to side. The system was refilled. The rapidity with which it again emptied disclosed the serious nature of the leakage.

It was not possible to trace the position of the leak, but it was considered probable that it was the result of a fracture of one of the ram cylinders. The fracture was almost certainly caused by the bombing of the previous day.

Hotspur, Lieutenant-Commander Cecil Brown, was detached to inquire of the situation in *Imperial* and to stand by her. Kitkat signalled *Hotspur* that *Imperial* was completely unmanageable. *Hotspur* made an alongside and *Imperial's* crew, together with about 320 soldiers, was transferred. At 0445 two torpedoes from *Hotspur* sank *Imperial*. Brown then made full speed to rejoin the squadron, which had reduced to 15 knots. *Hotspur*, with nine hundred troops on board, rejoined and speed was increased to 29 knots.

HMS *Hereward*

Admiral Rawlings was speeding southward when, at 0600, aircraft attacked the squadron. Twenty-nine years old Lieutenant James Munn was in command of *Hereward and recalls:*

Being the junior boy of the party, just a lieutenant, I was the port-wing ship of the screen and the nearest to Scarpanto. Three Stukas attacked me: one each side of the boy, which I saw and managed to avoid their bombs, and another Stuka, which I didn't see in time, came up my stern, and his bomb actually went down my foremost funnel and burst on top of the boiler room. It felt like being in a tube train pulling up at a station – one's body sagged forward as from 28 knots we came to a grinding halt.

Lieutenant (E) Desmond Callaghan says of the attack on *Hereward:*

I remember being knocked off my perch in the engine room by a big explosion and watching the steam-pressure gauges falling rapidly back to zero and the engines dying away to silence. I remember clambering up the ladder and making my way along to the boiler room, finding two out of the three completely demolished and mutilated bodies lying all over the place. While I was still surveying the scene, another bomb fell into the engine room which I had just left. I realized we were powerless to move and would soon disappear beneath the waves.

Lieutenant Munn continues his narrative:

It would have been murder for any of the squadron to have taken off our ship's company and we were left to our own devices, which were nil. We were on fire forward and every boat had been damaged so I decided to abandon ship to save as much life as possible. In addition to our ship's company we had about two hundred soldiers on board. I was horrified at the carnage in the galley flat area and as every officer had been issued with morphine we gave the desperate ones an overdose to put them out of their misery. I just kept my sub-lieutenant, Page, and engineer officer, Callaghan, to prepare to sink the ship and get rid of the confidential books. One or two soldiers who could not swim also stayed. After dealing with the Cbs my chief passed up the wardroom chairs, of which we made a raft. Unfortunately he said there was a bottle of port and one of brandy on the side-board; this may well have been responsible for the ghastly cramp we got after being in the water for an hour or so. We were just preparing to trundle a depth charge down into the engine room when the Stukas, who had left us alone when they saw we were stopped, came back and cut the ship in half with a stick of bombs. By this time the majority of the ship's company was a half-mile or so up wind of us, due to the ship drifting. Our raft vanished but I found an empty petrol drum and I tied a line from this round my neck to keep my head up if I passed out as it was surprising how cold the sea was, and not made any more pleasant by the Stukas machine-gunning us in the water. When I complained about this later at Scarpanto, they said that we had carried on firing after we had been hit. The Italians sent out some of their MTBs, which was a very friendly gesture.

Lieutenant Munn and Callaghan both survived PoW camps in Italy and Germany to become admirals.

By 2000 the squadron had arrived at Alexandria, very battered and with crews utterly exhausted. Almost eight hundred men had been killed or taken prisoner. The last troops to leave Crete were lifted from Sfakia on the morning of 31 June, and a curtain descended on what was perhaps the most intense period of combat between ships and aircraft to be fought in the European war. The Battle of Crete had cost the Royal Navy 1,828 killed and 183 wounded. Three cruisers and six destroyers had been sunk, and many ships damaged.

HMS *Mashona*

On 18 May the battleship *Bismarck* and the heavy cruiser *Prinz Eugen* sailed from Gdynia on Operation Rheinbung: Admiral Reader's attempt to concentrate a naval force against Atlantic convoys. In the hunt for the *Bismarck* the Tribal destroyers *Tartar* and *Mashona*, both low on fuel, were proceeding at 15 knots towards harbour when daylight of 28 May revealed *Mashona*, under Commander William Selby, in station a mile on *Tartar's* starboard beam. From Selby's report of aircraft attacks on his ship, it is apparent that the fighting, which had taken place about 70 miles off south-east Ireland was at time very hectic. The engagement was over a period of two hours, beginning at 0840. Selby reported:

Aircraft were reported by the OOW. On my way to the bridge I ordered AA defence stations to be piped. On arriving on the bridge I sighted three aircraft on the starboard bow, and I identified them as hostile. 'Repel Aircraft' stations were rung on the alarm rattlers and a V/S signal report was made to Tartar. Mashona *was in first degree of AA readiness by 0850. The first attack developed at about 0855, and avoiding action to starboard was taken at about 25 knots. These bombs fell clear between* Tartar *and* Mashona. *The third boiler was connected at 0905. Three attacks were made on* Mashona *between 0850 and 0910, the first two by one aircraft and the third by three aircraft approaching from the starboard bow, the beam, and quarter. Luckily only one of these dropped bombs, which missed, as avoiding action would have been difficult. The fourth attack was commenced just before 0912 and was made by a Heinkel 111 which came in on the port quarter in a shallow drive from about 8,000 feet, bombs being released at 5,000 feet. Speed was increased to 25 knots as the run in commenced, and course altered slightly to port to bring all guns to bear. Fire was opened when the range was about 6,000 yards. Just before bomb was released, full speed ahead and port 30 degrees was ordered. The aircraft, however, seemed to anticipate this move and altered slightly to port at the moment of bomb release. A stick of six bombs was observed, the fourth of which was seen to be falling some way to port of the remainder. Wheel was put amidships, and then the swing checked by starboard wheel in an endeavour to avoid, but by this time it was obvious that the fourth bomb would hit. The ship was still listing slightly to starboard. The order 'Take cover' was passed. The first three bombs fell on the port beam and short, the nearest being about 50 yards clear. The fourth bomb struck just above the water-line at No.74 bulkhead. The fifth bomb fell about 10 yards clear abreast the torpedo tubes, starboard side, and the sixth bomb well clear to starboard. All bombs exploded on impact. The hitting bomb damaged compartments on the port side from No.30 to 98 bulkheads, extensive damage being done to No.4 oil fuel tank, stoker petty officers' mess and Nos 1 and 2 boiler rooms. The largest hole, which was 14 feet 5 inches wide, was in No.1 boiler room. Splinters caused extensive damage to No.1 boiler and to the steam and feed lines in that boiler room. The size of the bomb appeared to be about 250 lb. The splinters from the fifth bomb penetrated the gear room and office flat and caused some casualties aft.*

Immediately the hit occurred all lights went out and all power, except batteries, failed in the W/T office, but the turbo-dynamos remained running. All emergency lighting functioned correctly and steam-pressure appeared normal. Steps were immediately taken to isolate No.1 boiler. The telegraphs were put to 'Stop' immediately after the bomb hit. Orders were passed to the W/T office to make the signal Have 'Been Hit By Bomb', but as all aerials had been carried away a jury-aerial had to be rigged. The signal was passed on 210 kcs[kilocycles] and 107 kcs 7 minutes later. The ship very soon took on a list to port.

It was discovered that a splinter had started a fire in B magazine, which was partially flooded by the repair ERA as the fire-main was out of action. The flooding was stopped when the fire was put out and the watertight doors replaced. It has since been discovered that the correct damage control drill was being carried out at the time, and investigation of all the damage was being proceeded with. At this time the fifth attack was made from the port beam. The bombs dropped clear on the port bow. As all power had failed and primary control was out of action, the order 'Sector firing' had been passed, and the aircraft was engaged by X gun and pom-pom. Shortly after this, about 10 minutes from the time of the hit, the main engines were reported ready to me on the bridge with Nos 2 and 3 boilers in action. At this time the ship's head had come up to and passed the wind, which was now blowing from the port bow, and at this time the sixth attack was commencing from the starboard quarter, 'Half speed ahead – 10 knots', was put on the telegraphs. This aircraft was engaged by B, X, and Y guns and the pom-poms.

As soon as the ship had gathered way it was decided that the rudder was jammed hard to starboard. The coxswain immediately went down and passed the order to steer from the tiller flat. The ERA noticed that though the steering motor switches were made there was no reading on the ammeters, so the ship was put to hand-steering and the rudder brought amidships. At the same time the port engine was put half astern and revolutions increased gradually to 190 in order to turn the ship to port and take avoiding action for the sixth attack. The bombs from this attack fell on the starboard quarter, the nearest bomb falling about 50 yards on the starboard quarter. The bomb exploded on striking the water, and the splinters penetrated the wardroom and the cabin flats and caused further casualties aft. By this time the ship had been turned sufficiently to get the wind on the starboard bow and revolutions were reduced. Steam was failing owing to lack of feed-water. With the list on the ship the starboard propeller was nearly out of the water. Revolutions had been reduced to 90 but both engines had to be stopped through lack of steam as at this time No.2 boiler had water in the furnace and had to be abandoned.

The orders to jettison torpedoes, depth charges, and ready use ammunition on the port side were being carried out, and endeavours were being made to unreel the 4 inch wire in case towage was possible. This was impossible as the reel was under water. In spite of great difficulty due to the heavy list, the torpedoes, depth charges, and the ready use ammunition on the port side were jettisoned. The time was then about 1015. Meanwhile X gun was engaging an aircraft on the port side which dropped bombs well clear. At this time the engineer officer reported that the ship was flooded from Nos 30 to 98 bulkhead and that 98 bulkhead was starting to leak, so I gave the order 'Everyone on the upper deck'. The whaler was lowered and the wounded placed in this and one Carley float. Unfortunately the whaler could not get clear of the ship and was stove in by the starboard bilge keel as the ship rolled. It became obvious that there was no hope of saving the ship and at 1030 I gave the order to abandon ship. As the ERA left the engine room he noticed that the list was then 60 degrees but engine room bulkheads were quite intact. After the ship was abandoned she slowly capsized and floated bottom up, being sunk later by gunfire from HMCS St Clair.

Before abandoning ship there had been twenty casualties including one killed. Later the casualties were calculated as forty-six hands killed, including an officer and ten ratings who died from exposure after having been picked up.

HMS *Dainty*

HMS *Dainty*, Commander Mervyn Thomas, was sunk while supplying the garrison at Tobruk. During her brief say at Tobruk she was then ordered to carry out a night patrol. Accordingly at 1845 on 24 February she proceeded out of harbour in company with *Hasty*, Lieutenant-Commander Lionel Tyrwhitt. The destroyers were just clear of the outer boom when aircraft attacked the harbour. *Hasty*, three cables astern of *Dainty*, had a bomb explode in her wake. Both ships opened fire. The boom was 2 miles astern when course was altered and almost immediately the sound of a falling bomb was perceived. Within 2 seconds a heavy bomb exploded in the captain's after cabin, at once igniting the oil fuel tanks beneath the cabin. Observing that *Dainty* had been hit Tyrwhitt reduced speed and ordered *Hasty's* whaler to be made ready for lowering. The after part of *Dainty* was seen to be heavily on fire. The whaler was lowered with orders to track *Dainty's* wake to pick up anyone blown overboard. Both ships had opened fire on the aircraft, but only as it flew off. Commander Thomas considered that the plane had attacked with its engine off. After releasing its bomb the plane had revved up its engine, and it was this sudden noise that had attracted the attention of those on the bridge.

Less than two minutes after the bomb exploded, the ready use ammunition on X gun deck started to explode. The warheads from the after torpedo tubes opened with the excessive heat and burned fiercely. Within five minutes of *Dainty* being hit Commander Thomas realized that the fire aft was beyond any means available for controlling it. It was impossible to communicate orders aft to flood the after magazine, which it was later realized may have been flooded by the initial explosion. To avoid shrapnel from exploding shells, all available hands were ordered onto the fo'c'sle. The order was given to prepare to abandon ship and *Hasty* was signalled to make an alongside on *Dainty's* starboard bow. By 1914 *Hasty's* stern had been positioned as ordered. A line was passed between the ships to assist the transfer from *Dainty's* fo'c'sle owing to *Dainty's* bow having risen. '*First to go across was our monkey*', recalls 'Bungy' Edwards. '*I remember watching her and thinking to myself how I would like to go across the rope like she did*'. While *Hasty* was securing alongside, the air vessels of *Dainty's* after torpedoes exploded. This shook *Dainty* considerably and threw up a mass of torn metal, causing injuries. The foremost torpedo tubes then exploded, and *Dainty's* stern began to sink rapidly. At this point the order was given to clear the ship. Those remaining in *Dainty* jumped over the side or onto *Hasty's* quarter. Three Carley floats were dropped into the sea from *Hasty*.

Having to abandon *Dainty* was a particularly sad moment for Leading Seaman Samuel Stocker as he had been in the ship since joining her at Hong Kong in April 1938; he recalls:

I jumped into the water. 'Knocker' White, who was standing on the anchor, followed me into the water. It was a bit chilly. As I swam to the Hasty *someone said 'She's going', so I stopped and looked around. In the glow from the fire at the stern, the bows slid beneath the water followed by the stern section. I felt rather sad as the ship had been my home for three years and by that time I had been on board longer than anyone. I swam to the* Hasty. *When alongside I caught a line thrown to me. As I was being hauled up by the ship's side my knuckles were scrapped over the splinter shield and I fell back into the water and began to drift astern. I was not a strong swimmer and thought I'd had it as oil fuel was in my eyes and mouth. I felt awful, and could not see very clearly. In desperation I swam for the* Hasty, *which fortunately was drifting towards me. This time I took the line around my chest. I was hauled on board like a drowned rat.*

Twenty-three minutes had passed since *Dainty* had been hit when Commander Thomas entered the sea, the last to leave the ship. Commander Thomas: *I estimate that the bows were about 60 feet on the air by this time. As I emerged from the oil and water, the bows were vertical. They soon turned over further, until the fo'c'sle deck inclined at 70degrees with the surface of the water.*

From Torbruk some trawlers and motor-boats arrived to help rescue survivors. Next morning at Alexandria the survivors were stepping ashore from *Hasty*. Some of them were lost in other ships.

* * *

The besieged garrison of Tobruk was, for a time in 1941, second only to Malta as a difficult supply problem. The 242 days siege of Tobruk lasted from 12 April to 8 December 1941. During this period supplying the garrison became a hazardous ordeal. Luftwaffe attention soon prevented the slow and underarmed merchantman ships from supplying Tobruk. The task then fell to warships, mainly destroyers and particularly the Australian *Stuart*, *Vendetta*, and *Waterhen*, the three working a regular night service from Alexandria to Tobruk. The siege had been in force almost two months when *Waterhen* was sunk.

HMS *Waterhen*
At 1945 on Sunday 29 June the *Waterhen* in company with *Defender* was on a heading for *Tobruk*. The ships were in position 32.20'N/25.13'E on a course of

306 degrees and proceeding at 23 knots with *Defender* a mile on the port side beam of *Waterhen* when about fifteen Stukas were sighted to the south-west. The Stukas made for a position astern of the ships and at 2000 they attacked. The opening attacks were against *Defender*. With guns blazing she increased to full speed, using the helm to spoil the aim of the aircraft. The first three Stukas were closely followed by three more, the attacks coming from both quarters and form astern. Another wave of about nine Stukas attacked, five or more on *Defender* and four on *Waterhen*. All bombs aimed at *Defender* fell within a radius of 100 yards, the nearest being about 5 yards from her stern. After the attack two Stukas were seen to be trailing smoke as they left. A stick of bombs aimed at *Waterhen* fell about 30 feet clear of the port bow, shaking her considerably and starting a leak in No.1 oil fuel tank. The W/T aerials were also carried away. Another load of bombs fell 50 feet astern. But the bombs which caused serious damage to *Waterhen* and led to her loss were the bombs of the third attack which fell close alongside. In a fourth attack the bombs fell wide to port.

After the third attack *Waterhen's* wheel jammed and she took on a list. The boiler fires went out, bringing her to a standstill. An 8 feet wide hole was discovered just below the water-line at the bulkhead dividing the engine room from No.3 oil fuel tank. The engine room had immediately filled with water and fuel. There was water in the compartment above No.3 tank. The section abaft of this, the main cabin flat with No.4 oil fuel tank, also quickly filled, via a hole below the water-line. The tiller flat was leaking and the bulkhead between the engine room and the after boiler room was buckled and leaking. *Waterhen* was badly down at the stern and listing to port. To lighten ship the deck cargo for Tobruk was jettisoned. Depth charges were released and torpedoes fired. *Waterhen* rightened and then took on a list to starboard. Following a report by the engineer officer, and after he himself had made an inspection, Lieutenant-Commander James Swain, *Waterhen's* captain, decided to abandon ship. At 2015 *Defender* made an alongside and all on board were transferred. Shortly after making the transfer *Waterhen's* starboard list increased considerably. Swain judged that she would sink within 30 minutes. It was decided to keep her in sight until she sank.

At 2142 a U-boat was sighted and *Defender* made an attack. It was not until around 2330 that her captain, Lieutenant-Commander Farnfield, was able to close *Waterhen*, still afloat more than 2.5 hours after it was thought she would have sunk. Swain, his first lieutenant, his engineer officer, and ten ratings were put on board. *Waterhen* had by then a list of more than 30 degrees. After inspecting the ship Swain did not feel justified in ordering a steaming party below. He decided to see how *Waterhen* fared under tow.

At 2350 the tow was secured. *Waterhen's* starboard list made it possible only to tow by going half ahead on the starboard engine with the port engine stopped or going astern, and by carrying 15 to 25 degrees of port wheel. At 0015,

30 June, *Defender* was signalled that *Waterhen* was in danger of sinking and requested that the towing party be taken off. Keeping her engines at slow speed, *Defender* lowered a whaler. At 0150 *Waterhen* capsized. Five minutes later Farnfield was proceeding at 25 knots towards Alexandria, arriving at 1030.

HMS *Defender*

Eleven days after the loss of *Waterhen* the *Defender* was also bombed out of the war while supplying Tobruk. *Defender* and the Australian destroyer *Vendetta* made a night run to Tobruk. After unloading, the two ships passed through the boom at 0112 on 11 July. They headed east for Mersa Matruh. It was a clear moonlight night with a calm sea. At 0200 course was altered to 095 degrees and *Vendetta* took station 1 mile on *Defender's* starboard side. No damage or casualties resulted. For the next 2 hours the zigzagging ships continued towards Mersa Matruh. Then at 0518 came disaster.

The destroyers had arrived in position 31.49'N/25.50'E when the sound of a large bomb was heard approaching *Defender*. A 1,000 kilos delayed-action bomb entered the sea in the vicinity of the starboard anchor and exploded beneath the ship just abaft the engine room forward bulkhead. A column of water deluged the bridge, and the ship appeared to lift bodily several feet. The immediate consequence was that water entered the engine room and after boiler room to the level of the water-line, stopping the steering motors. The W/T was put of action and all power failed. A large buckle about a foot deep appeared on each side of the iron deck, just abaft the engine room forward bulkhead, with a fore and aft rent of two feet wide on each side of the deck. *Defender* took on a 5 degrees starboard list. All upper deck gear on the starboard was moved to port to help offset the list. Torpedoes were fired and depth charges released. Boats and Carley floats were lowered and towed astern. It was considered that the ship's back was broken and that she was being held together by her sides and upper deck. There was reason for believing that *Defender* had been holed the starboard side but, as the midship section was awash, no close check could be made to confirm this. The after bulkhead of the engine room was shored up. The remaining bulkheads appeared to be holding. It was considered that the flooding boundary was between the forward bulkhead in No.2 boiler room and the after bulkhead in the captain's cabin flat. Steam-pressure had been lost almost instantaneously. As there were no connections remaining between No.1 boiler room and the after end of the ship, no attempt was made to maintain steam.

Lieutenant-Commander Rodney Rhoades, RAN, in command of *Vendetta*, was signalled to make an alongside to take off army personnel. He closed *Defender* and embarked 275 soldiers, only moving away after 15 minutes when, at 0607, an Italian aircraft was seen approaching. Under fire from both ships the aircraft made off. Whilst lying off *Defender's* fo'c'sle preparatory to taking her in tow Rhoades took the opportunity to transfer ratings to *Vendetta*.

At 0645 towing got underway at 6 knots. Fifteen minutes later fighter cover arrived. Speed was increased gradually until *Defender* seemed to be towing satisfactorily at 9 knots. The situation appeared to be in hand when at 0752 a yaw, causing a sudden strain on the tow and produced a tearing of *Defender's* hull. *Vendetta* was ordered to slip the tow and close *Defender* to embark all hands not required for towing. As the midship section was under water it was not possible to get to the after end. The steering party and others in the after part were ordered to *Vendetta* by whaler. Even at this late stage Farnfield hoped that, providing the upper deck held, he would get *Defender* to harbour, or at least beach her.

At 0812 towing was resumed but within minutes the tow parted. By 0900 towing was again underway. Over the next 90 minutes the situation deteriorated appreciably: the forward torpedo tubes became awash and further rending noises were heard with increasing frequency. It was apparent that she could not withstand the strain of towing and that she was sinking. With great reluctance Gilbert Farnfield ordered abandon ship, *Vendetta's* whaler taking off the remaining hands. It was considered advisable to clear the area as quickly as possible as *Vendetta* had 720 men on board, and she was well within bombing range of German occupied North Africa. At 1058 Rhoades fired a torpedo at *Defender* to expedite her sinking. This was followed at 1105 by two salvos of 4-inch shells, fired into vertical bows. Ten minutes later *Defender* sank in 58-eight fathoms.

HMS *Fearless*

Operation Substance was an attempt to sail a convoy through to Malta. The convoy sailed from the Clyde on 11 July and reached Gibraltar on the 19th. But on 23 July the convoy, then south of Sardinia, came under heavy air attack. Though aircraft from *Ark Royal* engaged the enemy, the cruiser *Manchester* was damaged and had to return to Gibraltar. In the attacks the destroyer *Fearless* as hit by a torpedo. The *Fearless*, Commander Anthony Pugsley, was part of the destroyer screen. She was proceeding at 13 knots when at 0941 six Italian torpedo-bombers were sighted directly ahead and steering slightly across starboard to port. Gunfire was opened from *Fearless* and adjacent destroyers, *Fearless* and *Faulknor*. When in range the aircraft divided: three to port and three to starboard. *Fearless* concentrated her fire on the starboard group, and in particular on an aircraft to the extreme left of the group which approached her fine on the port bow. At 1500 yards the aircraft dropped a torpedo. Pugsley altered course to port until it was seen that the torpedo was crossing ahead at a distance of 80 to 100 yards. Then the nearest aircraft of the port group approached with the clear intention of attacking *Fearless*. This aircraft was at once engaged with all available weapons. The wheel was put hard to port and the engines to full ahead. Through this strong gunfire the pilot bravely held his course. The aircraft was hit by the port 0.5-inch AA guns but this in no way deterred the pilot who released a torpedo at 800 yards. The torpedo ran shallow and broke surface abreast the destroyer's stem, on the port side, at a distance of 30 feet and when on approximately an opposite course to *Fearless*. As full port wheel was on, it was felt with confidence that the torpedo would miss. Unfortunately for *Fearless* the torpedo altered course to port and a second or so later, at 0945, struck *Fearless* at an angle of about 15 degrees. *Fearless*, which had worked up speed to 22 knots, was stopped immediately as the rudder was hard aport and could not be put amidships owing to the loss of electrical power. Fire broke out instantly and when the smoke cleared it was seen that the ship was ablaze from the searchlight platform to Y gun. It was considered that the blaze was the result of large quantities of burning oil fuel thrown up through all the cabin flats by the explosion. A survivor from aft reported that the wardroom deckhead was burning fiercely within seconds of the ship being hit. The engineer officer's inspection was not encouraging: all the after oil fuel tanks and the after part of the ship was ablaze and the port shaft was out of action; all lighting and electrical power in the ship was off owing to the switchboard being wrecked, which in turn resulted in both steering motors failing; the after engine room bulkhead was split and oil fuel was entering the engine room; the starboard engine could not be worked.

The situation confronting Commander Pugsley was (1) *Fearless* was unable to steam (2) the rudder was hard over and could not be straightened for some time to come (3) although there was hope of preventing the fire from spreading it could not be extinguished and would have to be left to burn itself out, which might take about 5 hours. Whether or not the ship could have survived under tow in the prevailing conditions was not put to the test as *Forester* later closed and at 1057 sank *Fearless* with torpedoes. An officer and fifteen ratings had been killed in action and a further nine ratings died of their burns while in *Forester*. Without further loss to escort or convoy the operation was completed on 24 July when the freighters arrived at Malta.

HMS *Bath*

The destroyers *Bath*, *Broadwater*, *Cossack*, and *Stanley* were all engaged in convoy duty when between August and December they fell victim to U-boat attacks. Convoy OG71 (UK–Gibraltar) began assembling at Milford Haven in early August. On 15 August vessels from Scottish ports joined the convoy off Rathlin Island. The twenty-three ships formed into seven columns. Its escort was the sloop *Leith*, six Flower class corvettes, and *Bath*, a Town class destroyer which since her commissioning from the United States Navy had been manned by the Royal Norwegian Navy. OG71 was heading south when at 1000 on Tuesday 17th a Kondor was sighted low on the horizon. From the Kondor's report, seven U-boats were positioned for an attack. During the early hours of the 19th *Bath*, Commander Christian Melsome, RNN, was 2 miles astern of the convoy zigzagging at 12 knots. She was altering to the port leg of the zigzag when at 0107 an object was sighted on her starboard beam. Commander Melsome ordered hard astarboard, presumably intent on ramming a U-boat. Almost at the same instant the wake of a torpedo was seen to starboard and *Bath* fired star-shell. The torpedo then hit *Bath and* the explosion, in the vicinity of the engine room, heeled *Bath* to port. She then righted before later breaking in two and sinking. The corvette *Hydranger* closed the vicinity of the sinking to rescue survivors. She took on board nine, most of whom were injured. After this sinking the convoy was savaged by the U-boats. The convoy fared so badly that it had to seek refuge in neutral Portugal. Ten ships had been sunk with a loss of more than four hundred lives. German losses were zero. *Bath* had been sunk by twenty-three-year-old Kapitan-Leutnant Walter Kell of U204. Two months later U204 was lost with all hands.

Another convoy savaged by U-boats was SC48. Ten merchantmen were sunk, along with two warships. SC48 left Canada for the UK on 5 October. Heavy weather was all the sixty-nine ships of the convoy had to contend with until the night of 14/15 October when U553 sighted the convoy some 400 miles south of Iceland. U553 was first to strike when at 0600 she sank the British *Silverceder*, laden with steel. As more and more ships were sunk, four United States Navy destroyers were detached from another convoy to reinforce SC48. Additional support was provided by HMS *Broadwater* and the French corvette *Alysse* which joined from Reykjavik. But despite these reinforcements the night of 16th/17th brought the U-boats much success, seven ships being sunk and one damaged. But the worse was over.

HMS *Broadwater*

On the 18th only the escort *Broadwater* was sunk. Her captain Lieutenant-Commander William Astwood and her attacker Kapitanleutnant Ernst Mengersen of the U101. There being no moon the night of 17/18 October was very dark; too dark for zigzagging considered Astwood. Towards midnight he retired to his chartroom to rest a while. Sailing at 6 knots SC48 continued its journey into Saturday 18th. It was nearing 0200 when the 12-inch gun crew saw a torpedo pass the stern of *Broadwater*. Another torpedo was not so obliging, it struck the ship port side forward, blowing away the forepart and most of the upper bridge and stopping *Broadwater* dead in her tracks. The deck abaft the fourth funnel was seriously buckled and the working of the ship at both sides at this point indicated that her back was broken. The front of the wheelhouse was blown away completely, though for some reason the wheel was left standing. The bridge party suffered heavily: Lieutenant John Parker, RNVR, and Sub-Lieutenant Richard Sampson, RNVR, were blasted 50 feet aft. Lieutenant Parker, an American from Boston, is believed to have been the first American serving in the Royal Navy to lose his life in the war. Sub-Lieutenant Sampson died on board a trawler soon after rescue. Two signalmen on the bridge were killed. Lieutenant-Commander Astwood was asleep in the charthouse when the torpedo struck. Badly injured about the head, he first became aware of what had happened when he came to about 20 minutes later to find the coxswain waiting to report the damage. Though suffering the effect of his injuries, Astwood took charge and it was he who ordered the ship abandoned when it was realized that she was beyond help. The trawlers *Cape Warwick* and *Angle* closed to assist. An attempt by a trawler to go alongside and transfer *Broadwater's* crew was unsuccessful. The destroyer was broadside to the wind and making much leeway. The trawler had gone alongside but owing to the swell she was unable to remain without incurring damage, and so she had withdrawn without taking anyone off. When Astwood became too weak to supervise the ferrying of the crew to the trawler, the duty fell to Lieutenant Francis Brooke-Smith, who as a bomb disposal officer had been awarded a George Cross for coolly working on a bomb which began ticking. By using *Broadwater's* whaler and the *trawler's* boats Brooke-Smith was by 0945 able to complete the transfer of personnel. By noon *Broadwater* was some 3 feet lower in the water and slowly settling by the bows. At 1240 she took on a starboard list and both propellers became visible. Five minutes later a trawler opened fire with her 4-inch gun to hasten the sinking. At 1341 *Broadwater* sank. Four officers and forty-one ratings had been lost, as well as eleven survivors rescued by Astwood from sunken ships. U101 and her captain survived the war.

HMS *Cossack*
For a time HM destroyer *Cossack* was the most famous ship in the navy. Her rescue of prisoners from the *Altmark* will long be remembered. Just over a week after the sinking of *Broadwater* the *Cossack* was hit by a torpedo from U563. The incident took place on 23 October while *Cossack* was escorting convoy HG75 from Gibraltar to the United Kingdom. Kapitanleutnant Klaus Bargsten made the attack, his first as commander of a U-boat. The corvette *Carnation*, Lieutenant-Commander George Houchen, RNR, had reported sighting a submarine at about 2225. In *Cossack* the alert was passed to hands at their stations. When nothing came of the sighting, the hands were ordered to rest at their stations. Lieutenant Brain Moth was on duty as gunnery control officer. At the order to rest, Lieutenant Moth did not remain in the director but lay down at the back of *Cossack's* bridge. Twenty minutes later Moth was startled by a torpedo exploding forward. Lieutenant Moth:

At about 2310 there was a terrific explosion. I found myself lying on the bridge surrounded by flames. The whole bridge superstructure seemed to have collapsed forward, and the deck was sloping forward at a steep angle.

Though the engine room and No.3 boiler room appeared almost free of damage, No.1 boiler room was flooding with oil fuel and was expected to catch fire, and No.2 boiler room had to be evacuated. Also, the lighting had failed. In the forepart of the ship the blaze was fierce, and exploding ammunition meant that nobody could get near it. After discussing the condition of the ship, and as no effective measures could be taken with her own resources, it was decided to abandon ship. It was after taking to the water that Lieutenant Moth saw that: *The forepart of the ship had been opened out like a kipper, and I realized that the fore-magazine must have blown up in the first explosion.*

Several of the escort ships, including *Carnation*, had arrived to assist, but Commander Richard Jessel of *Legion* ordered them to rejoin the convoy. Observing *Cossack*, George Houchen saw that she was burning wildly round the remains of her bridge structure and that all forward of this had been destroyed above water, and seemingly below. At 0145 Houchen laid *Carnation* alongside *Cossack's* stern so as to allow a party with lines to leap on board from the fo'c'sle head. This was done several times until a volunteer party led by *Carnation's* engineer officer, Commander (E) Robert Halliwell, and her first lieutenant had boarded. *Carnation* remained fast to *Cossack's* stern and held her before the wind to prevent the fire spreading. When at 0600 *Cossack* looked as if she might founder, Houchen evacuated all hands and cast off. But fears of the destroyer sinking were unfounded and a party was again put on board, later returning to *Carnation* for the night. In consequence of *Cossack's* plight becoming known at Gibraltar, the corvette *Jonquil* received orders at 0315 on the 24th to raise steam. Her captain, Robert Partington, took the tug *Thames* under his orders at 0615 and made 12 knots to pass through the Strait. At 1300 on the 25th, *Cossack* as sighted and within 2 hours *Thames* had her in tow for Gibraltar with *Jonquil* and *Carnation* constantly involved in A/S sweeps. At 0830 on the 27th Partington closed *Cossack*. At this time she was much further out of the water aft and deeper forward. The sea was sweeping over her and it was considered an unjustifiable risk to attempt to re-board. At 1037 *Thames* reported that *Cossack* as sinking and 6 minutes later *Cossack* sank in position 35.12'N/08.17'W. She went down by the bows until her stern was vertical; then she sank completely. Captain Edward Berthon, *Cossack's* captain, had been in command of *Keith* when sunk off Dunkirk. During the Great War he had served in the battleship *Agamemnon* and other destroyers. He had taken part in the raids on Zeebrugge and Ostend, for which he was awarded a Bar to his DSC. Aged forty-six, he did not survive the loss of *Cossack*.

HMS *Stanley*
The Town class destroyer *Stanley* was the ex-United Sates Navy *McCalla*. She was torpedoed and sunk while escorting the thirty-two ships of Convoy HG76 which assembled at Gibraltar in December for passage to England. Since

the autumn, German attention towards the Gibraltar convoys had increased with each passing week. British Naval Intelligence reported that HG76 would be the object of concentrated U-boat activity. The Admiralty elected to meet strength with strength. The 36th Escort Group formed the nucleus of warships gathered at Gibraltar to escort HG76. Captain of the sloop *Stork* and senior officer of the 36th Escort Group was Commander Fredereick Walker, an officer of exceptional ability. Adding strength to Walker's nine ships were three destroyers, two sloops, and a corvette. Perhaps the most important ship of HG76 was *Audacity*, the navy's first escort carrier. On her deck were stowed six American F4F Grumman Wildcat aircraft, known in the Royal Navy as the Martlet. At about 1800 on 14 December the convoy began its passage to Liverpool.

On the afternoon of the 17th U131, already damaged by an attack from the escort, was sunk. At 0916 next morning U434 was sighted by *Stanley* and *Blankney*, who attacked and sank her. It was the early hours of the following morning that *Stanley* reported by RT to Commander Walker the sighting of another U-boat. In the excitement of the moment *Stanley* failed to indicate her own position or the bearing of the U-boat contact. At that time *Stanley* was some 2 miles astern of the convoy with *Stork* 6 miles to starboard, and also astern of the convoy. Commander Walker ordered *Stanley* to indicate her position with starshell. Just at that moment *Stanley* reported, again by RT, that torpedoes were passing from astern. She was then observed using her Aldis lamp. Moments later she erupted in a sheet of flame hundreds of feet high. The torpedo had hit *Stanley* at about 0405. Just prior to this she might have been a target of another attack as Lieutenant Michael Reade, RNVR, states that:

> *Torpedoes were fired at us and we altered course to execute zigzag No.31 which was in the hands of the quartermaster ... We increased to full speed. We ran for 12 to 14 minutes and then altered to north and came down to 20 knots. We sighted the convoy about three minutes later and exchanged peanuts with* Stork.

After 5 minutes at 20 knots, course was altered to port 20 degrees to keep out of the convoy. *Stanley* had just begun to swing to port when a torpedo struck port side slightly abaft the bridge. *Stanley* heeled over to starboard. Yeoman of Signals Alexander McEwen:

> *I was on the bridge watching the* Stork *when the torpedo hit us and the bridge collapsed and I went into the water. The bridge seemed to break to pieces and I went through and finished up in the water. When I looked up, the bows of the ship were almost above me so I swam away.*

In the darkness McEwen heard voices, but saw no one. It would be 2 hours before he was taken from the sea. *Stanley* broke in two within 5 minutes of being hit.

Oberleutnant zur See Dietrich Gengalbach of U574 had made the attack. At 0845 *Stork* rammed the U-boat just before her conning tower. U574 hung for a few moments on the ship's stem before being rolled over and sent scraping along her keel to the stern, where a pattern of ten depth charges awaited her. Gengalbach was not among the few survivors and neither was *Stanley's* captain, Lieutenant-Commander David Shaw, among the few survivors of his ship.

At noon on the 23rd the convoy arrived at the Western Approaches 'safe area'. With air support now available the U-boats were called off. At least nine of them had attacked HG76. Three merchantmen had been sunk.

* * *

In December 1941 what had been termed Force K was operating in the Mediterranean under the command of Rear-Admiral Henry Rawlings, flying his flag in the cruiser *Neptune*. Two more cruisers, *Aurora* and *Penelope*, and the destroyers *Kandahar*, *Havock*, *Lance*, and *Lively* completed the force. In its 3 months of operations Force K had a fair measure of success, but in December 1941 it had a day of disaster.

Force K sailed from Malta on the afternoon of 18 December. In overall command was Captain Rory O'Conor, the squadron having sailed so hurriedly that it was unable to wait for Admiral Rawlings to board ship. The haste was in response to the discovery of an Axis convoy bound for Tripoli. Force K headed south into a rising sea. In single line ahead in the order *Neptune*, *Aurora*, *Penelope*, *Kandahar*, *Lance*, *Lively*, and *Havock*, Force K was proceeding at 28 knots when at 0106 and in approximate position 39.09'N/13.20'E *Neptune* exploded a mine to port. Two minutes later the *Aurora* also set off a mine. Seeing explosions against the two ships ahead of him, Captain Angus Nicholl of *Penelope* thought that they had been torpedoed. On seeing *Aurora* haul out to starboard, he did the same. Captain Nicholl reports:

> *At 0110 there was an explosion abreast the bridge, port side, and I realized that we were in a minefield. No serious damage seemed to have been sustained, however, and the main engines and steering gear were in working order. I turned northwards to get clear of the minefield and then followed the stern of Aurora, who was proceeding on a course of 30 degrees at a speed of 10 knots. Meanwhile at 0116 Neptune hit two more mines in succession, apparently in the after part of the ship.*

HMS *Kandahar*

Kandahar was closing *Neptune* to go alongside when at 0318 a mine exploded under the destroyer's stern. A quick examination revealed her to be flooded up to the after engine room bulkhead. The bulkhead was shored. Boats and Carley floats were lowered. Confidential books, charts, and documents were thrown overboard. All lighting had failed and the propellers had been blown away. At 1630, more than 12 hours after the mining, the destroyer *Jaguar* left harbour to assist *Kandahar*. At 2200 that night a Wellington aircraft arrived over *Kandahar*. It closed the ship at intervals until *Jaguar* arrived the following day. In the meantime *Kandahar* had to see out the night in an area where the enemy could at any time put in an appearance. In his report of the mining Commander Geoffrey Robson states:

> *The report of six E-boats in the vicinity was received from the Wellington and it was estimated that they were 7 miles to southward of ship about 2300. It was realized that* Jaguar *was somewhere in the vicinity though the idea of her whereabouts was not given by the Wellington, probably rightly, because he wished to reduce VS signalling to a minimum. During the night the weather was deteriorating rapidly, with a rising wind and sea, and at about 0400 the ship took a list of 15 degrees to port; having being listed to starboard this made the engineer officer think that she had lost stability due to the engine room bulkhead having collapsed. Correctly he reported to me immediately and I ordered everyone on the upper deck and made a signal on 465 kcs to* Jaguar: *'Am Sinking'. Further investigation proved that the bulkhead was holding and that the change of list must have been entirely due to wind getting on to the starboard quarter of the ship. I therefore cancelled my at 0615 Am Sinking signal.*

When Lieutenant-Commander Lionel Tyrwhitt arrived with *Jaguar* he saw that the whole of the after part of *Kandahar* was under water from the funnel to the stern. At this time a force 4 wind was blowing from the NNW and the sea was moderate. At 0420 Tyrwhitt proceeded alongside bow to bow and began to embark hands over the forecastle. It soon became evident that the motion of the two ships put *Jaguar* at risk of being damaged. Tyrwhitt moved off and lay to windward while those left in *Kandahar* jumped into the sea. He then rescued the men as he drifted towards them. Once this was completed, Tyrwhitt at 0545 fired a torpedo at *Kandahar*. Five minutes later she sank stern first in position 32.57'N/14.17'E. At 0600 Jaguar set course for Malta. Of the two cruisers mined that day, only the *Aurora* returned to harbour. When *Neptune* sank, more than seven hundred of her crew were lost. There was one survivor.

*   *   *

HMS *Thracian*

In December 1941 the Allies faced a new and brutal enemy – the Japanese. The first Royal Navy destroyer lost in the Far East war was *Thracian*, Commander A. L. Pears. *Thracian* was one of the very few naval vessels at Hong Kong when the Japanese invaded, and consequently her activities were numerous and varied: she laid mines, she attacked junks and sampans attempting to land troops and she evacuated Allied soldiers out of areas deemed untenable. Thomas Quilliam was one of the few survivors of *Thracian*. When taken prisoner at Hong Kong, he had been in the navy for 14 years. The fighting had been in progress for more than a week when *Thracian* was damaged sufficiently for her fate to be sealed. Tom Quilliam takes up the story.

Much heavy work, little sleep, and the constant bombing was by this time having an effect on everybody, but the patrolling was resumed with the two-watch system of Action Cruising Stations. *At about 2330 on the night of 15 December a long signal was received from BHQ. The captain decoded the first part, which said go to Kowloon Bay with all speed.* Thracian *was then about 5 miles SE of Lantau Island. We cracked on at full speed through the pitch blackness of that night. With the captain still busily decoding the long signal about his instructions to destroy the invasion forces embarking in Kowloon, the officer of the watch had no time for precise navigation through the islands and into harbour via the Lamma Channel and Green Island entrance. Speed was all important and, in the absence of all blacked-out navigation lights,* Thracian *'cut the corner' of Lamma Island too closely and tore a hole in the bottom of the starboard fuel tank. The ship listed rapidly but the hole was very soon given a temporary plugging. Still listing to starboard* Thracian *went into Kowloon Bay with guns firing as rapidly as they could be reloaded. Anything in sight that was floating was sunk. The ship then returned to Aberdeen Dockyard, after yet again dodging all the gunfire directed at her by the Japanese on the Kowloon side. At first light the next day, the ship was deammunitioned ready for docking. Before the dock gates could be closed behind her, a dive-bombing attack put the gates and the dock pumps out of action. The ship was badly damaged by flying pieces of concrete and bomb fragments. The engineer officer, Lieutenant Birkett, had a large hole torn in his back. He survived the war though was never able to walk again. Three ratings were killed outright. With only a half-fuel capacity* Thracian *would never now be able to get away to either Manilla or Singapore, and with the docking facilities blown up she could never be repaired in Hong Kong. The Commodore, Captain A. C. Collinson, CBE, RN, decided that the torpedo tubes and guns could be taken off and mounted in a defensive position ashore, and then the ship destroyed to prevent her falling into enemy hands. All through that night the ship's company worked to get all the stores ashore and up to Aberdeen School (a temporary naval base). By dawn she was empty. The captain and skeleton crew then took her and ran her aground on a rock in Repulse/Deepwater Bay area. The next day she was re-boarded and preparations made for the arrival of the floating crane and barge that would lift out her torpedo tubes, guns, etc. Depth charges were placed and primed ready to blow up the ship as soon as the lifting operation was completed. All hands then went ashore for the first sleep in more than 48 hours. Two hours later Aberdeen was shelled, possibly from a cruiser at sea somewhere near the Lamma Islands. During the night the Japanese landed on Hong Kong Island.*

Instead of lifting off the guns and torpedo tubes and then blowing up the ship as planned, *Thracian's* crew was issued with rifles. Several were killed in the fighting. On Christmas Day Governor Sir Mark Young surrendered the Colony to Lieutenant-General Taikaishi Sakai. *Thracian* was salvaged and in November 1942 commissioned into the Imperial Japanese Navy as Patrol Boat 101. When the war ended she was located at Yokosuka in Japan a white Ensign was run up: *Thracian* had rejoined his Britannic Majesty's Navy. In February 1946 she was scrapped at Hong Kong.

Chapter Four

1942

For the Destroyer Service 1942 was by far the worst year of the war. Fifty-three destroyers were lost. Of these losses only the *Vimiera*, *Vortigern*, and *Penylan* were sunk in British waters.

HMS *Vimiera*

Weather conditions in the Thames estuary for the afternoon of 9 January as observed by Lieutenant-Commander Angus MacKenzie, RNR, as: fresh NNW wind, sky clear with occasional light snow-squalls, sea slight and visibility excellent. The tide was at half-flood. *Vimiera*, with MacKenzie in command, was an escort of a convoy proceeding towards harbour at a steady 4 knots. She was holding a course requisite to keep in the swept channel. From *Vimiera* a signal ordering ships to follow in the wake of the next ahead and to keep in the swept channel was being hoisted when a mine exploded beneath her forward boiler room, throwing up a column of water 100 feet high. MacKenzie, on the bridge, was sent sprawling and received a hard blow to the side of his head. Regaining his senses he found that he was lying near the guard-rail on the port side of the fo'c'sle, which was listing about 70 degrees to starboard. The entire forward portion of the ship had broken away just abaft the bridge and was being separated from the after part by the tide and wind. The forepart was rapidly filling with water, and it quickly sank. Says MacKenzie:

> *I had removed my inflatable life-jacket shortly before the explosion occurred. I stripped to shirt and trousers and got into the water to swim to the after part of the ship, which was afloat but some distance away. I found Able Seaman Henderson, the starboard Oerlikon gunner, in the water.*

Henderson had both legs broken. Taking Henderson with him, he eventually managed to reach the after part of the ship, where he gained a hold on a line. When near exhaustion he and Henderson were hauled onto a Carley float.

The explosion attracted the attention of Motor Minesweeper 19, which was a mile away delivering mail to a trawler. MM19 at once proceeded at full speed towards *Vimiera*. At 1400, about 7 minutes after the mining, MM19 made an alongside at the after part, which by then was floating at an angle of 15 degrees. The sweeper tried to take it in tow but it was settling and the submerged part ran aground. Unable to move it, and having four badly wounded men on board, MM19 made towards harbour with twenty-four survivors. That approximately a hundred of *Vimiera's* crew had perished was attributed to the majority being forward at the time of the explosion.

German Schnellbootes, called E-boats by the British, were a constant menace to east coast and Channel convoys. Any calm and moonless night was liable to bring an E-boat attack. Sometimes the attack would be made by a single boat, and other times a group would strike at a convoy. The *Vortigern* and *Penylan* were both sunk by E-boats.

HMS *Vortigern*

Vortigern had caught the tail-end of World War One, she being completed in January 1918. In the Second World War she lasted up until March 1942. Convoy FS49 (Methil-Southend) of eight ships sailed from Methil at 1115 on 13 March. As it made its way south, merchantmen from other ports joined the convoy till FS49 numbered twenty-five ships. From 2246 on the 14th up until 0446 on the 15th the convoy was subjected to E-boat attack.

The night of 14/15 March was calm and very dark, ideal for E-boat activity. FS49 was off Cromer when the *Vortigern*, one of the escort ships, was sunk. The E-boats were engaged by the destroyers *Holderness* and *Wallace*. One raider was sunk by *Holderness*, and *Wallace* damaged another. The *Guillemot*, a 500-ton patrol sloop, heard the commotion and at once closed the scene and began sweeping eastwards in search of the enemy. Within minutes she sighted an E-boat and *Guillemot* opened fire, scoring hits. At that moment another E-boat was sighted in a favourable position to attack *Guillemot*, so she gave chase. But the E-boat's superior speed quickly got her clear of trouble and it disappeared into the darkness. Returning to the sunken *Vortigern* twelve survivors were rescued, two of whom died on the return to harbour. *Vortigern*, Lieutenant-Commander Ronald Howlett, had sunk at about 0155 on the 15th. She had been hit port side by two torpedoes, and had sunk in less than 3 minutes. Out of ten officers and 147 ratings, only those picked up by *Guillemot* survived. Her captain did not survive.

HMS *Penylan*

A few months after *Vortigern's* loss E-boats torpedoed and sunk the *Penylan*. At his home in Cornwall, Edward George well remembers the night he was dragged more dead than alive from the sea. He had been eighteen when called up for naval service at the end of 1941. After training at HMS *Raleigh* he was drafted to HMS *Drake*. He recalls:

While at Drake I was part of a working party in the dockyard, which meant going on ships that were having a refit in the yard. When working on these ships it made me wonder what I had let myself in for. They looked awful, and felt the same: cold and mess everywhere. Not a bit like I thought a navy ship would be. On returning to barracks one evening there was a draft-chit waiting for me. The next morning I mustered with about a hundred others. The ship to which we had been drafted was just a number, as no names were used. There was a buzz that it was a frigate or a corvette. At this time, early 1942, there was a railway station in HMS Drake and drafts left from there. So, one evening off we went to join our ship. We arrived at Barrow-in-Furness around noon the next day. There we met our ship's buffer and the coxswain. We then marched to Vickers-Armstrong's yard. On the way, and when crossing a bridge, we were stopped and shown our new ship in the basin: HMS Penylan a Hunt class destroyer, Type III, Pennant No. L89. Before going on board we went off to the canteen for a meal. That over, we made our way to the ship where we were met by our captain and first lieutenant. When I got on board it was just what I expected of a Royal Navy ship. She was spick and span. Even the paint wasn't dry in places. I was so pleased to have been selected for this new ship. My station was on A gun as fuse-setting operator. We spent a day or two getting ready for sea and the first trip couldn't have been better. It was a lovely day. We carried out speed trials around the Isle of Man and the returned to Barrow. The next day we had gun trials, with a night shoot. Then it was good-bye to Barrow. We were sent north to the Clyde. After a time spent there working up, we moved to Scapa Flow. There we did all sorts of work. Apart from the awful weather, I really enjoyed it. Just after the Dieppe raid we had a new captain, Lieutenant-Commander J. H. Wallace, DSC. He had been captain of HMS Calpe at Dieppe. We found him to be a man of steel. He could handle a destroyer like my folk could handle their small fishing boat in the cove. Again, I was so proud to work under him. He made sure we all knew our jobs. We then left for Portsmouth to join the 1st Destroyer Flotilla.

The night of 1/2 December 1942 was spent with an MTB off the French coast. We were looking for enemy shipping and as we had been at action stations all night, we thought that on arriving at Portsmouth next morning, it would be oil ship, clear away, and then catch up on some sleep. Not so. It was off to sea again to do some gunnery practice to the east of the Needles. When this was over we picked up a convoy going west.

The convoy joined by *Penylan* was PW257 (Portsmouth-Bristol Channel). It consisted of seven ships divided into two columns. The escort, of which Lieutenant-Commander Wallace was senior officer, consisted of five trawlers and three MTBs. *Penylan* took station 7 to 8 cables to seaward on the convoy's port bow.

PW257 had by 0400 passed the area of Sidmouth without incident except that one ship, the *Honsburg*, had struggled. John Wallace says of the incident:

> *HE effect was heard first off Portland and an RDF contact obtained on the same bearing. Investigation proved this to be a ship of the convoy, SS* Honsburg, *who was directed to rejoin the convoy. This she did not immediately do, and the A/S operator was told to disregard the HE effect, being informed what it was. HE effect was subsequently heard on approximately the same bearing during the night and, until the explosion, was disregarded by the operator. A fatal error.*

The convoy was in the area of Start Point when the E-boats attacked. The lieutenant in command of HM trawler *Ensay* reports:

> *While stationed ahead of the convoy, at 0622 HE was reported by the A/S apparatus: bearing Green 30 degrees and moving rapidly across the bow to Red 20 degrees. At 0625 two starshells were fired on that bearing. At the same time* Penylan *was hit and appeared to be breaking amidships. A continuous firing of starshell and shrapnel was maintained at the E-boats, which were moving forward again. At this time another torpedo was seen approaching our port bow. Avoiding action was taken and it passed ahead of the ship. In the loom of starshells two E-boats, out of an apparent total of three, appeared to be endeavouring to come in from ahead again. Course was altered to bring our 12-pounder and port and after Oerlikons to bear. Several HEs were seen to burst quite near and above the E-boats, while a whole magazine from the port Oerlikons appeared to be hitting. This appeared to drive them off, as no more were seen.*

On being hit *Penylan* had listed heavily to starboard. Her midship section had sagged until it was under water. Shortly afterwards she broke in two, her bows and stern rising vertically, with the former sinking last. The new destroyer had sunk just 15 minutes after being hit. The E-boat's torpedoes had been sighted by several of *Penylan's* crew, but not in time to give warning. Edward George continues his narrative:

> *I was on the port side leaning over the breakwater talking to Ordinary Seaman John Worthington, who did not survive, and Charles Landen, when coming towards us I saw two white wakes. There was a tremendous explosion. We had been hit amidships by two torpedoes. They blew poor old* Penylan *in half. Half-dazed I was blown across the deck. First thing I remember when I came to was hearing our captain giving the order to abandon ship. Now this was going to be difficult as the bows were 50 feet out of the water. I climbed up the forecastle and out through the guard-rail. Sitting on the anchor I took off my boots and blew up my life-jacket. Being a non-swimmer death was staring me in the face. By this time things*

were terrifying. Those of the crew who had got away were struggling to swim in the oil. Just as I was going down for the last time, my pals Arthur Perkins and George Roberts pulled me away from the ship and got me onto a piece of wood that was just buoyant enough to keep me afloat. While on this I saw Penylan *go down. Sitting on her bow was a shipmate. Afraid to jump, he went down with her. As time went by, one got colder and colder. It became harder to hold on to my piece of wood. At one time I thought it was all up, as another shipmate tried to climb onto my piece of wood, and I knew it would not support the two of us. He didn't make it. I saw him go down through the water to his grave.*

With the coming of daylight I could make out a boat down tide of us. I thought at first that it might be an E-boat and even if it was, that would do, just so long as I could get out of the water and oil. I drifted down to the boat. As I remember, the crew threw us ropes. I tried to catch a rope in my mouth as by now my arms and legs were dead. I drifted right under the boat, my head banging on its bottom as I did so. With the last bit of life I had left, I gave a shout. The boat was a British Mine Layer. One of its crew jumped overboard and pulled me out. Once on the ML I lay just like a dead thing. I recall what might have been a doctor came along. He said that my shipmate beside me was dead, and so could be left on deck. I then made a noise with my mouth. 'This chap's still living', I heard him say. I was then stripped of my clothing, as it was covered in oil, and washed down with water. Draped in a table cloth I was carried down to the galley where there was some heat. The small galley was filled with my shipmates who had been picked up alive. I then moved to the engine room to thaw out. We were landed at Mill Bay Docks, Plymouth.

There were a number of E-boat groups in the Channel that night. A group of four boats (S81, S82, S115, and S116) had attacked PW257. Oberleutnant zur See Joachim Klocke's S115 had sunk *Penylan*. The situation might have been helped if steps had been taken earlier in the evening to make the straggler *Honsburg* take up her station, as HE effect from that direction would then have had a more positive meaning. *Penylan's* casualties included the loss of two officers and seventy-four ratings.

HMS *Gurkha*

The first of twenty-nine destroyers sunk in the Mediterranean in 1942 came on 17 January. She was sunk by Kapitanleutenant Hermann Hesse. Born in Cologne on 10 March 1909 he was, in January 1942, almost thirty-three, getting on in years for a U-boat officer. His first U-boat command was the U133. With this boat he sank one ship only – the destroyer *Gurkha*. The loss of the Tribal class *Gurkha* in the Norwegian campaign was a great disappointment to the Regiment of Gurkhas. The Gurkhas requested that another ship bear their name, and to add weight to its request the Regiment was quite willing to finance another HMS *Gurkha*. At this time the L class destroyer *Larne* was under construction at Cammell Laird. It was agreed that *Larne* should become the new *Gurkha*. She was completed on 18 February 1941. After trials and working up, *Gurkha* did some Atlantic convoys and also convoys from Greenock to Freetown. Then she entered the Mediterranean and did Malta convoys, first from Gibraltar and then from Alexandria. One of the convoys from Alexandria in which *Gurkha* took part was MW8B. The convoy, consisting of the *Clan Ferguson* and the *City of Calcutta*, sailed on the afternoon of 16 January 1942. *Gurkha* and the destroyers *Legion*, *Maori*, and the Dutch *Issac Sweers* was the convoy escort for the passage west. At 0738 the following morning, *Gurkha* was making 18 knots to the north of Sollum, the A/S operator reported an echo to starboard. Commander Charles Lentaigne, *Gurkha's* captain reports:

> *I immediately moved towards the A/S hut, while the A/S control officer, Sub-Lieutenant G. A. de G. Kitchin, went to take up the spare telephone receiver. Almost directly, the operator classified his echo as 'non-sub', qualifying it as a 'very small extent of target, moving rapidly'. At this moment, a matter of seconds after the first report of the echo, the torpedo hit on the starboard, aft. I am of the opinion that there was a double explosion. Certainly I observed a bright flash extending to a considerable height as I started to regain my feet after being thrown down onto the deck of the bridge by the explosion of the torpedo. The double explosion is borne out by a large number of ratings who were knocked down twice. The ship immediately commenced a violent shudder, so I ordered both telegraphs to 'Stop'. Subsequent inquiry showed that both engines were in fact stopped by the engine room artificer of the watch owing to the failure of the forced lubrication pumps and, in the case of the starboard engine, the snapping of the propeller shaft. The ship carried her way for some distance after the explosion. The situation as it now appeared to me was (a) the ship was seriously damaged aft, flooding having already reduced the freeboard enabling the sea to break over the quarter-deck (b) two large fires were burning, the first an oil fuel fire both inside and outside the hull and spreading outwards to windward of the surface of the water, the second a fire both inside and outside the after superstructure mainly fed by the ready use ammunition on deck.*

The situation was complicated by the firemain having been fractured and the 70-ton portable pump being out of reach in the heart of the fire. A hole of 20 to 30 feet in length was reported to extend a foot above the waterline down to an undetermined depth. Immediate flooding in the vicinity of the explosion spread rapidly to most compartments abaft the engine room, and the engine room flooded slowly.

When *Gurkha* took on a list to port, the immediate removal of all top weight was ordered. This returned *Gurkha* to an even keel, but by 0820 she was showing definite signs of foundering. The fire had increased and was spreading forward. As by this time there appeared little chance of saving the ship, preparations were made to abandon her. Able Seaman Frank Hall served in *Gurkha* from her commissioning to the day she sank. Of his experience during the sinking he states:

> *I was on the morning watch. Facing aft, I was leaning against the bridge on B gundeck savouring a cuppa when about 0740* Gurkha *suddenly trembled and turned to starboard at high speed. Flags running up the mast denoted a submarine attack. We had made little progress when there was a cloud of smoke aft in the region of the wardroom. I heard nothing of the explosion owing to the speed of the ship. I said to my 'oppo', a rating from Elland in Yorkshire, 'Bugger me, there goes our cuppa. How deuced inconsiderate of the cads', or words to that effect! But 'Elland' said, 'don't worry, Scouse. I'm going to brew up', and the crazy sod disappeared below. I didn't get a drink. Anyway, the order was: 'Ditch all ammunition from lockers'. This we did. But it made no difference, as the bows began to rise out of the water. Meanwhile repair parties were manning hoses that had no water. The sea was on fire, the fuel tanks having apparently ripped open. The HOs did themselves proud – no panic. Finally the skipper gave the order to abandon ship. Non-swimmers took to the whalers and everyone else jumped overboard. The bows were rising higher, and yours truly stripped to his underpants and money-belt and jumped from B deck.*

Hall believes he went down quite deep before beginning his struggle towards the surface. This seemed to take an age and he remembers thinking of his mother and how she would grieve the loss of her eldest son. With lungs seemingly near to bursting, he broke surface. Taking a few moments to recover, he swam towards the *Issac Sweers*. He continues:

> *The crew rigged us out the best they could, I myself finishing up in football boots. Not long afterwards the* Gurkha *rose perpendicular and smoothly slid backwards beneath the waves. The new ship I thought unsinkable was gone forever – her radar, asdics, twin 4-inch high-angled guns all to no avail.*

Commander Lentaigne boarded *Isaac Sweers* at 0950, around 2 hours after the torpedo attack. He at once ordered a muster of all ratings. With the exception of five officers and four officers' stewards who were missing from the time of the explosion, the entire ship's company, about 190 hands, had been rescued.

Kapitanleutnant Hesse survived only until June 1943, he being lost when his new boat, the U194, was sunk by the RAF. As he did not sink anything with U194, the *Gurkha* remained his only sinking.

HMS *Matabele*

Matabele, Punjabi, Somali, and *Achates* were all lost in 1942 while escorting convoys to northern Russia. It is unlikely that those who sailed in the Arctic convoys, particularly during winter, will ever forget the experience. Conditions were truly fearsome: mountainous seas whipped into a frenzy by roaring blizzards and freezing spray would have to be hacked from masts and rigging and upper works to prevent some types of vessel capsizing. But above all it was the cold – a cold of such intensity that to the watch keepers it seemed in no time at all to penetrate the very core of the body. Ships surviving the winter passage put in at Murmansk, while those in summer made for Archangel, ice-free in summer only. The famous PQ convoys began in September 1941, three months after the German attack on Russia. The loss of *Matabele* occurred when she was an escort of PQ8's passage to Murmansk.

On 8 January the *Somali* and *Matabele*, Commander Arthur Stanford, were ordered to provide the destroyer escort for PQ8. The Tribals fuelled at Seidisfiord, Iceland, and on the 10th sailed as ordered. PQ8 fared well until 17 January, when nearing the Kola Inlet, the steamer *Harmatris* was torpedoed by U454, Kapitanleutnant Burkhard Hacklander, and had to be towed into harbour. Later that night Hacklander attacked *Matabele*. Lieutenant-Commander John Cooke was on Somali's bridge when his attention was attracted by what he at first thought was a flash at the stern of a tanker. *Shortly after that I saw* Matabele, says Cooke:

> *She appeared to be illuminated. She was, also, signalling. We then got slightly ahead of the oil tanker by increasing speed.* Matabele *appeared to have an Aldis lamp pointed down her starboard side. She also had steam coming from the engine room. About three minutes after that she was quite clear and appeared to be very nearly stopped. Due to her white colour she was easy to see. The whole ship seemed to jump slightly out of the water, but remain whole, and then she just split right open. It appeared that B magazine had gone up. The actual explosion extended aft, I should say to No.2 boiler room, and right forward to the bows. All the upper works fell straight down through the bottom of the ship.*

There was only two survivors from *Matabele*, William Burras who had joined the ship a month previous and was on his first trip in her, and Ernest Higgins. Both were stationed on X gun. It was around 2330 that *Matabele* had been torpedoed to starboard. She had heeled over to starboard and then rightened. Burras left X gun and hurried down a ladder leading to the upper deck with the intention of proceeding forward to shut watertight doors. But flames moving aft prevented this. The ship then listed to starboard. Burras slipped on the icy sloping deck and slid into the sea. The waves swept him away from the ship. When about 200 yards from *Matabele* he saw her blow up amidships. The two halves separated. In the oil–covered sea Burras saw perhaps fifty or more of his shipmates. The situation looked very grim. For more than an hour William Burras clung to his life. Mercifully a ship appeared. Burras swam to the side of the ship, then blackness closed in on him and he remembers nothing of being taken aboard ship, cleaned, and put to bed.

Ordinary Seaman Higgins later recalled:

Ten minutes before the first explosion I went down to the mess to get tea for the gun's crew. Then I came back to X gun. It was my turn to put the phones on. It was so cold we were walking up and down to keep warm. Just before the explosion came I could hear something coming through the water. Then the ship was hit. She shuddered as if someone was shaking her and I was flung against the splinter shield. It seemed as if the ship was hit on the starboard side. She came straight up again. The first lieutenant came up and gave orders to some of the lads on X gun to go down aft and close the magazine doors. Just as he said this somebody shouted out that there was a fire forward, and then the ship seemed to blow out altogether. I was flung up against the guard-rail but nevertheless managed to take off my sheepskin coat and jump over the side. I swam for about 200 yards. It seemed as if one of the depth charges went off. It hit me in the back as I scrambled in the water. I heard some of the lads in the water shouting for help. A lot seemed as if they had lost their nerve. I swam about another 100 yards, and then patterns seemed to go off.

Hacklander was one of fourteen survivors of U4545 when in August 1943 she was sunk by the RAAF.

HMS *Punjabi*

Punjabi (Commander Hon. J.M.G. Waldgrave) was lost on 1 May. Three survivors, D. W. Braybrook, P. W. Phillips and R. C. Morgan relate their experience of the sinking. David Braybrook had been called up for naval service in September 1941. By early December he had passed out as an ordinary seaman trained to operate a 285 gunnery radar.

On 30 April we went out with the covering force of King George V, *USS* Washington, *the American cruisers* Wichita *and* Tuscaloose, *and the aircraft carrier* Victorious, *between the Arctic convoy and Norway. On the fateful 1 May, in mist and just before the change of watch at 1600, somehow a signal was made execute too soon, so that the destroyers in line ahead were turned across the line ahead of the battle waggons.* Punjabi *was the unlucky one to cross the path of the lead ship, the* King George V. *I had just gone to the toilets, prior to cutting up for tea two large apple pies I had cooked, when the* King George V *struck* Punjabi *just near the torpedo tubes, sending us over in a giant roll with a shattering of glass and a tearing of metal. I came out on deck with others. Above us we saw the side of a battleship sliding by like a train through a station.* Tirpitz, *I thought.* She's rammed us. *When we had all gathered on the fo'c'sle, the other large ships sailed by towing their fog-buoys, which I interpreted as spent torpedoes. The first thing I had seen after* King George V *had passed was the stern of a ship, in our colours, disappearing. Only the* Eskimo *had these Arctic camouflage colours so I assumed 'They' had also sunk the* Eskimo *in this old style battle. There were explosions aft as radar-primed charges went off under the* King George V, *but I heard no sound, only saw the spray and smoke from aft, probably the after galley. I had no lifebelt so I was allowed one of the cork ones from the locker. With this over my head, but untied, I sat with others and contemplated whether it was better in the water or holding on in the ship as long as possible. Those in the water were in a bad way, all one heard was the bleating of a flock of sheep. Beyond the mist one hoped there was a ship coming to assist. One fellow was throwing forms and tables out for those in the water. As the deck was steeply sloping I tried vainly to clear some cork matting from under a hawser. I borrowed a knife from one of the new fellows, but the knife had no edge to it and my hand was so shaking I had no strength to cut, so we sat waiting. Each time a pocket of air bubbled out, the ship rocked and one thought of going, but the plight of those in the water made one think again. Finally, when the deck was steeply sloping, Signalman Stocker said, 'Are you going, Bray?'. 'Yeah', I just about said. I took off my boots and put them neatly beside the guard-rail alongside about twenty other pairs left there. After waiting for another man to get well down the rope, I followed. Then came Stocker. As I entered the water a tight band came up my body to my chest. I swam after the supply assistant into the oily water and mist. I was no great swimmer so I just turned on my back and struck out for a destroyer which I could make out some 300 yards away each time I was lifted on the swell. Fortunately it was a calm sea, but the water not much above freezing point. I was conscious only of keeping my limbs gently moving and glancing over my shoulder occasionally. Then I came upon a floating barrel, the type with a rope and eye used for taking a hawser to a buoy for morning. I had the idea I could sit on it and so keep warmer. I got astride. I stayed up for a second or two and then plunged head-first back into the water. The next time I managed 3 seconds. Though I kept trying I could not improve on that. Each time I went over I got colder and swallowed more water and oil. There was no future in that for me so I reluctantly gave up my own 'command' and swam on. I now doubted ever making the destroyer. I felt very alone but somehow not lonely; after all it was about tea time at home and I thought my mum making tea and not particularly thinking I was in the water. I just hoped she wouldn't worry about me not getting home – after all I was in no pain, I just couldn't feel a thing. Then something came behind me and a voice said, 'All right, Sparks, we've got you', and then I was being hauled into a motor-boat.*

Able Seaman Patrick Phillips had joined *Punjabi* before the war. He was in the ship when HM submarine *Thetis* sank in June 1939 and *Punjabi* went to assist. Of *Punjabi's* loss he says:

At 1545 hands fell in to clear up decks. My position was on the port side of the iron deck. We mustered there and were detailed for our chores, the operation being to ensure that the ship was clean inside and out before night fell. The weather was calm at the time with a slight swell. It was foggy with dense patches. We were steaming at about 10 knots in company with a large force covering a Russian-bound convoy.[1] This force consisted in part of HMS King George V *and* Victorious, *the USS* Washington, Wasp, *and* Tuscaloosa, *and a destroyer screen. None of these ships were visible from our iron deck at 1545. Within 2 minutes of falling out I was standing alone, as I recall, looking to port. I then saw an enormous bow and quadruple turret appearing out of the fog, and coming straight for me. It was immediately obvious that collision was inevitable. We were turning heavily to port, but much too late. I remember, quite foolishly in fact, calling a warning down to the engine room. There was no way they could have heard me. Also, there was no time for me to do anything but go forward. I had only reached the davits of the motor-boat at the break of the fo'c'sle when the* King George V *stuck* Punjabi *at about the point where I had been standing. It was like a knife through butter. The davit met my head somewhat forcibly, but not enough to prevent me blowing up my inflatable lifebelt and making my way to the fo'c'sle where paint-stages were being passed over the side with the ends secured to get the guard-rails; this was to allow survivors to enter gently into the water rather than jump from the deck-level when the time came. Standing on that fo'c'sle was an eerie experience.* King George V *had by now disappeared. The rest of the capital ships went by in succession. Meanwhile our stern floated away and sank. I believe in fact that it exploded because I don't recall that there were any survivors from there. The bows however remained afloat in an increasingly rising attitude for some 45, enough time to allow rescue ships to be sent. We were eventually brought back to Scapa Flow. We went from Thurso to Devonport by train. We had our own carriage set apart. Conditions were what one might describe as 'wartime primitive!' But we were alive and many poor devils were not.*

Able Seaman Rees Morgan had joined the navy in February 1939 as a *seven-and-five*, that is 7 years active service followed by 5 years in the Royal Fleet Reserve. He had joined *Punjabi* on her return from the scene of the *Thetis* disaster. On seeing the big Tribal for the first time, he thought she was a cruiser. *Believe me, she was very efficient*, says Morgan. *What one might call a pusser ship. An example: scrubbing and washing down the quarter-deck at dawn, Dress No.3. Nevertheless she was a happy ship.* Of events during the collision he recalls:

It happened during the first dog-watch. I was having tea in the watch keeper's mess, which is below decks. I was actually sitting on my locker when we were struck. Lights went out, but the secondary lighting soon came on. We did not know what had hit us – whether we had come across the Tirpitz, *struck a mine, or had been bombed. My own thought was to get up on deck. As stated, I was sitting on my locker; no way was I going to stay and search my locker for my lifebelt or my many personal effects in it. We scramble to the one and only stairway. What a rush! To avoid being left I went behind the stairway and went up backwards, bruising and cutting my fingers. Nevertheless I got to the top. The one thing in my mind was to get outside and to go to my abandon ship station, where a locker was placed with life-jackets. When I got there, however, all the life-jackets were gone. By the time I got to the canteen flat we had a list of 75 degrees and were in semi-darkness. When I arrived abreast the galley, I stopped dead. I could not go any farther. I looked down. There were bodies hanging on pipes. Steam was hissing. On looking round I saw the stern of the ship about 100 yards away. We had been cut in two. I can see my mates now, waving on their half of the ship. I looked in a few lockers for a life-jacket but they had all gone. By this time we were on a level keel with the sea, so it was just a matter of cutting the falls and getting clear. The fog was pretty bad but the sea was calm, and covered in oil. I just stood where the whaler had been. I could see the boat going into a blanket of fog. I was dressed in overalls and was wearing gumboots. I took my gumboots off and waded into the sea. There was no need to dive, just push off. My aim was to get to the whaler. I had just enough strength enough to reach the whaler. The boys pulled me inboard. I was covered in oil, cold, and was trembling. We still did not know what had hit us. I grabbed a spare oar. We pulled as hard as we could to get away from the ship in case she blew up or sucked us under. I believe it was HMS* Marne *who was standing by to pick us up. When we got alongside, the officer in charge asked for volunteers to stay in the whaler and make a few trips to pick up survivors. As I had no life-jacket I asked my opposite number for his, he not wanting to volunteer. He duly obliged and then scrambled up the net to board* Marne. *We circled the area for a long time, marking four or five trips to the* Marne. *When we got on board the* Marne *we were told that we would be recommended for an award, which I for one never saw.*

The foggy conditions of 1 May had of course contributed greatly to the collision. The screening destroyers were 8 cables off the heavy ships, with *Punjabi* in the starboard column of destroyers. So as to avoid losing contact with the fleet in deteriorating weather, the distance could be reduced at the discretion of the leader. Closing and opening the screening distance was accomplished by following a small fog-buoy trailed at the end of a long grass-line by the next ahead. When just before 1600 the weather closed in, the starboard leader moved towards the heavy ships. In the manoeuvre the *Punjabi* lost sight of the fog-buoy of the leader, which was next ahead, and ran in towards the fleet line of advance at an angle of 80 degrees. At 25 knots the *King George V* struck *Punjabi's* ready-use depth charges which exploded, causing slight damage to *King George V* and injuring survivors in the sea. *Martin* and *Marne*, in line astern of *Punjabi*, went full astern and were fortunate to avoid collision with *Wichita* and *Victorious* respectively. Around fifty of the crew had been lost. Commander Waldegrave, the captain, had been in command for little more than three months. Regrettably he was lost when in February 1944 the *Penelope* was torpedoed off Anzio.

HMS *Somali*

Somali was the third Tribal to be lost in Arctic Waters. Lieutenant-Commander Colin Maud was her captain when in September she was torpedoed by U703 while an escort of the Russia-UK convoy QP14. On Sunday 13 September the fifteen ships of QP14 sailed from Archangel under Commodore John Dowding, RNR, who in the previous July had been commodore of the ill-fated PQ17. For about a week foggy conditions prevented the U-boats finding QP14, but by the 20th this began to clear. On this day the U-boats attacked, the minesweeper *Leda* and the steamer *Silver Sword* being sunk. Another victim was *Somali*. She was attacked at 1857 by Kapitan-leutnant Heinz Bielfeld of U703 to the west of Bear Island. The torpedo hit port side in the vicinity of the engine room, which together with the gearing room and a boiler room at once flooded. *Somali* took a list to starboard. Five ratings had been killed and four wounded. HM trawler *Lord Middleton* made an alongside and transferred all but sixty of *Somali's* crew. *Ashanti* then closed to take *Somali* in tow.

Wednesday 23rd was the fourth day of the tow. Speed was maintained at 6 knots throughout the day. Pumping and the removal of top weight had reduced *Somali's* list from around 20 to ten degrees and she was perceptibly lighter to tow. *Ashanti's* captain, Commander Richard Onslow, was optimistic of reaching harbour provided the weather held. A gentle north-westerly breeze for most of the day freshened on the evening. After midnight the wind freshened further. At 0230 on the 24th the tow parted. Commander Onslow turned about to investigate. Snow was falling quite heavily and it was not until Onslow was close to *Somali* that he saw she had broken in half. Her bow was rising at a steep angle. The ship's company, or what remained of it, was seen at the fo'c'sle head. There came at this time the first strong gusts of what within minutes had developed into a gale. Destroyers were ordered to close *Somali*, keeping to windward of her. *Somali's* bow was rising fast. Several hands were observed dropping from her fo'c'sle into the sea, a drop of 100 feet or more. Lieutenant-Commander Maud was seen on the port side of the bridge encouraging others to jump into the sea. *Ashanti* was not immediately able to place herself in a favourable position to rescue survivors, most of whom abandoned ship on *Somali's* lee side. Astern of *Somali* was the *Lord Middleton*. Her captain very gallantly went close in under the after portion of *Somali*. The *Lord Middleton* rescued an officer and seventeen ratings. *Somali's* stern had capsized quickly and was in a vertical position as it disappeared completely around 0250. The sinking of the forepart enabled the destroyers to windward to drift down over the position in search of survivors. A heavy snow-storm and the increasing gale greatly hampered the rescue work. It was feared that many of *Somali's* crew were killed when caught under the bilge keels of rescuing destroyers. *Ashanti* rescued Colin Maud and a rating, the latter dying later. In such awful conditions the destroyers picked up four men, the rescuers holding onto scrambling nets, with lifelines secured to their waist, trying to make a grab at survivors in the sea. At 0445 the search was terminated, the ships, with the exception of *Eskimo*, leaving to rejoin QP14.

Ashanti and *Somali* deserve credit for a tow which lasted 240 miles. Those of *Somali's* crew who had remained on board had carried out their duties with cheerfulness for four nights and three days without lighting or heating and in freezing temperature. Kapitanleutnant Bielfeld had been born in China. He had been in the navy 5 years at the outbreak of war. In July 1944 he was lost when the U1222 was sunk by the RAF.

HMS *Achates*

Achates was sunk when the Germans decided to attack convoy JW51B with the *Admiral Hipper* and *Lutzow*. The convoy of fourteen merchantmen to north Russia put to sea from Loch Ewe on 22 December with an escort of eight ships. After 2 days the convoy met up with Captain Robert Sherbrooke's 17th Destroyer Flotilla, five destroyers plus the attached *Achates*. Sherbrooke's task was to get JW51B to its destination.

On 30 December the *Hipper* and the pocket battleship *Lutzow* sailed at 1800 from their anchorage at Altenfiord, each in the company of three destroyers, to attack JW51B. The intention was that on locating the convoy *Hipper* would attack from the north, drawing off the escorts and forcing the convoy to turn south towards the waiting Lutzow. It was on 31 December at 0915 that *Hipper's* destroyers sighted and opened fire on *Obdurate*. The battle for JW51B had begun.

On sighting gun flashes Captain Sherbrooke turned towards them. *Obedient*, *Obdurate*, and *Orwell* were ordered to follow suit. In *Achates* the ship's company was piped to action stations. When *Obdurate* reported three enemy destroyers Lieutenant-Command Arthur Johns of *Achates* altered course and speed as necessary to screen the convoy with smoke. Almost immediately *Achates* was straddled. At 0945 a near miss to port holed the forward shell room, magazine, and stokers' mess deck, the latter having to be abandoned. Efforts to pump out the shell room and magazine came to nothing as a steam-line had been shattered. All available hands between decks set to work plugging the innumerable small holes in the ship's side and the forward mess deck. A portable pump was taken aft, hopefully to keep down the water-level in the ERA's and stoker petty officers' messes, which were slowly flooding. *Achates* continued to lay smoke until 1110 when she was signalled to proceed to the head of the convoy. She had no sooner proceeded as ordered when she again came under fire. Despite increasing speed and zigzagging, *Achates* was hit on the fore-end of her bridge. With the exception of two men, all present were killed on the bridge and in the wheelhouse. B gun was put out of action and a cordite fire was started there, though this fire was quickly extinguished by the seas breaking over the fo'c'sle as *Achates* turned into the wind. When Lieutenant Peyton Jones arrived on the bridge he found that *Achates* was circling to starboard under 20 degrees of helm and speeding at 28 knots, giving the ship a 20 degrees list to port. All bridge and wheelhouse instruments had been wrecked, but the wheel and engine room telegraphs were intact. To raise the damaged port side higher out of the sea, speed was reduced to 12 knots. *Achates* was steadied on a mean course roughly to that of the convoy. The signal ordering *Achates* to the head of the convoy was disregarded; instead she was manoeuvred as required to keep the convoy screened with smoke.

No communication could be established with Y gun. A verbal message ordering Y gun to open fire apparently did not reach the gun. A few minutes later the enemy was lost to view. There was a short respite, and then *Hipper's* guns roared once more. *Achates* was hit port side and another shell near missed, holing a boiler room which then had to be abandoned. Even proceeding at 12 knots *Achates* had a 15 degrees list to port. The list, and her being down at the head, made her difficult to steer. Nevertheless she was kept steaming across the stern and starboard quarter of the convoy in an attempt to maintain a smoke-screen between the convoy and the enemy, whose gun flashes could be seen to the north and the north west. As *Achates'* list to port increased, more unplugged holes in her hull were submerged until by 1300 it was no longer possible to maintain steam in No.1 boiler room and *Achates* was stopped. '*Not Under Control. Please Stand By Me*', was flashed by lamp to HM trawler *Northern Gem*. Preparations were put in hand for *Achates* to be taken in tow stern first. The upper deck became awash as the list to port became more pronounced. The order was given to clear away boats and rafts and for all hands to muster on the upper deck. *Achates* then rolled alarmingly to port, continuing thus until she lay on her beam ends. Carley floats were got away from the starboard side, and a few floated to the surface from the port side and the ship sank soon after 1300.

About forty of *Achates'* hands were killed in the battle, and a similar number wounded. *Northern Gem* had stood off ready to take on board survivors. Coxswain Sid Kerslake of *Northern Gem* takes up the story.

Suddenly Achates rolled over on her port side. In the darkness we could see the red lights on the lifebelts of the men and the red-tipped cigarettes of some ratings who were even smoking as they clambered over the rail and on to the ship's starboard, which in a few seconds had become the 'deck'. Seconds later the ship's bottom started to rise out of the water as the superstructure vanished from view on the side away from us. The men began to slide into the water off the ship's bottom, laughing and joking as they did, then to our astonishment someone started singing 'Roll Out the Barrel' and soon, even above the noise of the wind and the sea, we heard them all singing as they fought their way over to us. Some men still smoked, or tried to, as they swam in the icy waters, others held up wounded shipmates or dragged them along. Gem acted as a kind of lee for them in the heavy sea and our skipper (Skipper-Lieutenant H.C. Aisthorpe, RNR), taking over the wheel, kept giving a touch ahead or astern if he spotted anyone in danger of floating past. In spite of this a few men did drift past, but they must have been dead, either from wounds or from the killing cold of the water; our main concern was for those who were now struggling for their lives. We had dropped our rescue nets over the side. We had no boats to lower, our port board had been washed away in the gales, while as for our starboard boat, none of its running gear would work – we hadn't been able to get it to clear it of ice, and everything was frozen solid. In the waist of the ship some of us dropped over the side and hung on to the rescue nets with one hand, pulling and pushing the frozen survivors up to where other willing hands could lift them on deck. As we clung on to the nets we would first be lifted right out of the water as the trawler rolled to starboard, then when she came back we would be plunged up to the neck in the freezing sea, but we managed to come up again each time clinging to a man and pushing up the ship's to those above. Every member of the crew was at Gem's side. Those not busy in the waist or on the rescue nets stood throwing out heaving lines to men still struggling in the sea. I left the nets and ran to the port quarter to help throw out these lines and tow in the men who caught hold of them. One very young sailor, scarcely more than a boy, began drifting past the stern. We threw him a line which he caught, but as we pulled at the rope it slid through his frozen hands. Again we threw the line, but as he grasped it he panicked and started to cry, 'Mother, Mother!' It was heart-rending. We yelled to him to hold his hand up so that we could get a turn or two of the line round his wrist, but he slid out of sight for ever with the rope still slipping through his fingers and still crying out for his mother. Our rescue work reached a point where we seemed to have saved all but a number of bodies floating by with no sign of life. At this moment there was a huge underwater explosion as the Achates'. depth charges went off, certainly killing anyone still left alive and lifting Gem almost out of the

HMS *Defender* finally slips below the Mediterranean Sea near Tobruk in July 1941. She was the victim of a 1,000 kilo delayed-action bomb. *(Courtesy Peter C. Smith)*

HMS *Kingston* was the victim of a Stuka attack whilst in dry dock in Malta in 1942. *(Courtesy Peter C. Smith)*

The last moments of HMS *Bedouin* after her engagement with the Italian Navy 30 miles south of Pantelleria in June 1942. *(Courtesy Peter C. Smith)*

The bow of HMS *Grenville* after hitting a mine off Harwich in January 1940.
(Courtesy Peter C. Smith)

HMS *Fearless* was attacked by Italian torpedo bombers in July 1941. Severely disabled and on fire, she was sunk by HMS *Forester*. *(Courtesy Peter C. Smith)*

At 1845hrs on 12 June 1942 HMS *Foresight* was torpedoed by an Italian aircraft. Despite valiant attempts by HMS *Tarter* to save her she was eventually sunk by torpedo. *(Courtesy Peter C. Smith)*

HMS *Quail* was under tow in the Gulf of Tarranto when she struck a mine in June 1944. *(Courtesy Peter C. Smith)*

At the time of her sinking in October 1941, HMS *Cossack* was famous for her rescue of prisoners from the *Altmark*. She was the victim of a torpedo from *U563*. *(Courtesy Peter C. Smith)*

HMS *Mashona* having been hit by bombs from a Heinkel 111 in May 1941. *(Courtesy Peter C. Smith)*

The second destroyer loss of the war was HMS *Gipsy* which hit an air-dropped mine off Harwich in November 1939. *(Courtesy Peter C. Smith)*

HMS *Swift* struck a mine off the Ouistreham lighthouse in June 1944. *(Courtesy Peter C. Smith)*

HMS *Swift* was on her way to the Sword area of the D-Day landing zone to load ammunition.
(Courtesy Colin Henderson)

HMS *Legion* seen here when first completed. She was sunk in Grand Harbour Malta in March
1942. *(Courtesy Peter C. Smith)*

Seen here in August 1941, HMS *Laforey* after her completion in August 1941. She was to fall victim to *U223*, when torpedoed in The Mediterranean Sea in March 1944. *(Courtesy Peter C. Smith)*

Seen here at full speed, HMS *Lively* was sunk by a Stuka attack whilst trying to intercept an enemy convoy en route between Taranto and North Africa in May 1942. *(Courtesy Peter C. Smith)*

HMS *Lightning* was the first Mediterranean casualty of 1943 when sunk by a torpedo fired from an E-boat. *(Courtesy Peter C. Smith)*

HMS *Lance* was bombed in Malta in April 1942. She was eventually repaired and towed to the UK where she was scrapped. *(Courtesy Peter C. Smith)*

water. So great was the blast that we thought at first that we had caught an enemy torpedo on our starboard side; pots were smashed to pieces, cupboards thrown open, clocks stopped; but she didn't take any water and luckily escaped damage to the hull, so we turned again to help our survivors.

At great risk to his own life, Surgeon-Lieutenant Maurice Hood actually jumped from *Obdurate* onto *Northern Gem's* ice covered deck. Once in the trawler he performed outstanding work on the *Achates'* survivors. His skill as a doctor won the admiration and respect of all. Under the most difficult conditions, for almost 30 hours the doctor worked on and operated on survivors. Regrettably, he lost his life a year later in another Arctic convoy.

The German ships failed miserably in their attack on JW51B. Apart from *Achates* the sloop *Bramble* had been sunk and a few other vessels damaged. Captain Sheerbrooke was awarded the Victoria Cross, his defence of the convoy having so successfully frustrated German intentions.

HMS *Belmont*

Torpedoes fired by Kapitanleutnant Siegfried Rollmann sank the *Belmont*, ex-USS *Satterlee*, on 31 January. She was the first of three destroyers to meet misfortune in Canadian waters in 1942. At 2000 on 30 January convoy NA2 (North America-UK) left Halifax for the Clyde. It consisted of the *Largs Bay* and *Volendam*, escorted by *Belmont* and *Firedrake*. At 2212 the next day when NA2 was in approximate position 42.08'N/57.26'W two explosions near *Belmont* was seen by *Volendam*. *Firedrake's* captain reports events:

Convoy in line abreast, ships approximately 1 mile apart. Destroyers were zigzagging independently, and this line was approximately 3 miles apart. The convoy immediately altered course, by signal from commodore, 45 degrees to starboard. Firedrake *assumed position ahead. The commanding officer did not see initial explosion and assumed from the subsequent flashes and depth charge explosions at 2216 that* Belmont *was attacking a submarine. There was a smoke cloud that cleared away. This was taken to be funnel smoke caused by a sudden increase of speed.*

Between 2220 and 2240 flashes were observed drawing away to the rear of the convoy, which tended to confirm the CO's assumption that *Belmont* was in contact with a submarine on the surface. At 2250 the convoy assumed the previous course of 118 degrees. A signal was then made to *Largs Bay*, who was the nearest ship to *Belmont*. *Largs Bay* replied that she had seen explosions and smoke. This reply, together with the fact that no signals by VS nor WT had been received from *Belmont*, and that she had not rejoined, led to doubt as to whether CO's initial decision was correct. In fact, *Belmont* had gone down with the loss of all hands.

U82, which had sunk *Belmont,* was on her third patrol. It is known that apart from *Belmont* she had sunk two tankers, *Athelcrown* and *Leiesten.* She had lost contact with NA2 on 3 February but three days later picked up convoy OS18. That day she was sunk by two escorts of OC18. There were no survivors.

HMCS *Ottawa*

The C class destroyer *Crusader* had been completed for the Royal Navy in 1932. On 15 June 1938 she was purchased by the Royal Canadian Navy and commissioned as HMCS *Ottawa.* At the time of her loss in September 1942, *Ottawa* was captained by Lieutenant-Commander Clark Rutherford, RCN, who did not survive the sinking. He had been ten weeks in command. The rapidly expanding Royal Canadian Navy supplied much the greater part of the escort for ON127's (UK–North America) thirty-two merchantmen. Though the RCN was growing at a fast pace, it lagged behind in fitting ships with the most modern equipment. Unfortunately ON 127's escort lacked 10 cm radar, a vital piece of apparatus.

The convoy was first sighted by the U584 on 5 September. That night contact was lost and was not re-established until the 10th. Over the next three days a dozen U-boats attacked the convoy. Seven merchantmen were sunk and four more damaged. In one of the last attacks *Ottawa* was sunk to the west of Newfoundland by U91, Kapitanleutnant Heinz Walkerling. A week after the sinking an inquiry was held at St John's Newfoundland, to determine the cause of *Ottawa's* loss. The Board's findings are reproduced in part.

The Board is of the opinion that HMCS *Ottawa* was lost at about 2330 on 13 September 1942 due to enemy action, being hit by two torpedoes at 2305 and 2320, the first torpedo striking the ship between 28 station and the stem, port side. 28 bulkhead held. The second torpedo struck in No.2 boiler room, starboard side. The ship then listed to starboard, broke in half, and sank bow and stern up. Weather: moderate sea, wind force 3, very dark, no moon.

Reconstruction of the action

HMCS *Ottawa,* stationed 5,000 yards ahead of convoy between 1 and 2 columns, obtained two RDF contacts about green 20, 8,000 yards and 6,000 yards; turned towards and increased to 12 and then 15 knots, and set a shallow pattern. HMS *Witch* and HMCS *Annapolis,* in company, were expected to join convoy. *Witch* had made a signal to *Ottawa 'Am joining and taking station 8,000 yards ahead of convoy.'* This was intercepted in *St Croix* but there is no evidence that *Ottawa* received it. When RDF range had closed to about 2,000 yards and an object was sighted fine on the starboard bow and challenged. No reply was received. Commanding officer appears to have been satisfied that object was HMS *Witch* as he did not order the challenge to be made again. *Witch* then called up with shaded light using 'A's. *Ottawa* replied *Ottawa,* and received

Witch back. The range at this time was approximately 1,000 yards closing fast. *Ottawa* altered to port using 20 degrees of rudder. A/S cabinet, who had reported HE on *Witch's* bearing, was ordered to disregard and carried out an all round sweep for HE. After the ship had swung some 20 degrees, the first torpedo struck. The Commanding officer stopped engines, gave orders for examination and report of damage and to prepare for abandon ship, prepare for destruction of confidential books, and for signal *Have Been Torpedoed. No Immediate Danger Of Sinking* to be passed by RT to *St Croix*. It is not clear if this signal was made. It was not received by *St Croix*. Depth charges were set to safe and primers withdrawn by order of the first lieutenant. It is considered that the ship continued to swing to port and lost way after turning 180 degrees, when the U-boat, without changing position appreciably, fired the second torpedo. When this torpedo had struck, the ship started to list to starboard and break up. The order to abandon ship was given.

Contributing factors

The commanding officer had in mind the possibility of getting stern-way on his ship but was waiting reports on damage. He appears to have expected a second torpedo. It is considered that under these circumstances it would have been better to risk going astern in order to present a more difficult target. Had action stations been sounded when RDF contacts were reported, the loss of life would have been considerably less. It is estimated that approximately half the casualties were due to the explosion of the first torpedo, many of the ship's company being turned in on the mess decks at the time. The Board does not attach blame to the commanding officer for not sounding off action stations under the circumstances. The RDF contacts were obviously not a U-boat. Two destroyers were expected from ahead, and the ship's company had had little rest for some days. Had HMCS *Ottawa* been fitted with Type 271 RDF the U-boat would probably have been picked up in the sweep as well as the two destroyers. The fact that a dark object was sighted to starboard and that an exchange of signals took place diverted most of the lookout to starboard. Signals made by *Witch* were probably seen by the U-boat and assisted her in her attack.

U91's attack on *Ottawa*, which took the lives of 114 crewmen was her first attack of the war. She was sunk by three of HM ships in February 1944. Heinz Walkerling's only other sinkings came the following March when he sank five merchant ships of convoy HX229. He then left seagoing service.

HMCS *Saguenay*

Two months after the loss of *Ottawa* the *Saguenay* became a constructive total loss. HMCS *Saguenay* and *Skeena* were the first warships designed and built specifically for the Royal Canadian Navy. Specially strengthened to contend with floating ice, they had an unusually large margin of stability against accumulation of ice on their upper works. They also possessed elaborate heating systems. *Saguenay* was commissioned at Portsmouth on 22 May 1931. Two months later she was in Canada.

She became a war casualty on 1 December 1940 when at 0500 the Italian submarine *Argo* scored a torpedo hit near her bows. *Saguenay*, was to the east of Newfoundland when she was caught in one of the worst hurricanes to strike the area for decades. Raked from stem to stern by merciless seas, and with frames and plates buckling from a terrific pounding, it at times seemed as if she would go down. Leaking badly she put into harbour. Three months passed before she was able to resume duties.

On 15 November 1942 *Saguenay*, Commander Dickson Wallace, RCNR, sailed from Halifax on her last operational duty. Detailed to escort the liner *Lady Rodney* to St John's, Wallace was that night about 10 miles south of Cape Race when a suspended U-boat contact was made. Visibility was reduced by the blackness of the night and not infrequent rain–squalls, so that when the port bow light of the Panamanian freighter *Azra* was sighted at two cables it was too late to take effective avoiding action. *Saguenay* had crossed the track of convoy WB13 which was proceeding in the opposite direction. *Azra's* bow cut into *Saguenay's* starboard quarter, slicing deep into the stern. Depth charges stowed on her after deck exploded, tearing away her stern and so badly holing the *Azras* bow that in 5 minutes she had sunk. *Azra's* crew was rescued by *Saguenay*, which had to be towed into harbour.

It was estimated that more than a year would be required to make *Saguenay* fit for service. Since she had already undergone two major repairs and some 80 per cent of her expected life had passed, it was decided to withdraw her from service and convert her to a training ship. For several years she gave new entry seamen their first taste of naval gunnery aboard ship.

* * *

The Japanese had spectacular success against the Allies in Malaya, the Philippines, and the Dutch East Indies, though the forces employed were not large in number. Only eleven of Japan's fifty-one divisions were utilized when from December 1941 to May 1942 the Japanese strove to fulfil their desire to establish a New Order in the form of a 'Co-Prosperity Sphere consisting of free and equal nations', under Japanese rule of course.

On 26 January, when the Japanese were less than a week from completing their consequent conquest of Malaya, air reconnaissance reported two Japanese transports off Enday, to the east of the Malay Peninsula. A cruiser and several destroyers were in support. Troops and stores were being landed. HMAS *Vampire* (Commodore W. T. A. Moran, RAN) and HMS *Thanet* (Lieutenant-Commander B.S.Davies) were ordered to proceed to Endau.

HMS *Thanet*

By 0115 on the 26th *Vampire* and *Thanet* were off Siribuat Island. Course was then made towards Burong Island. Around 0215 they moved to close the mainland in search of the enemy. Twenty-five minutes later Commander Moran sighted a destroyer right ahead. He passed about 600 yards from it and then fired two torpedoes. Indications were that one torpedo passed close ahead and the other beneath the target. To Moran's surprise the enemy proceeded quietly on his way. *Vampire* and *Thanet* continued towards Endau. By 0313 Moran was satisfied that there was nothing at Endau. A return to base was in order. Within 5 minutes of making this decision he sighted a destroyer astern of *Thanet*. His report states what next took place.

As I fired my torpedo the enemy destroyer altered course towards, and afterwards came in astern, of *Thanet*. He then challenged with what appeared to be red-shaded Aldis, and then with it unshaded. When he received no answer he put a searchlight on *Thanet*. The destroyer astern went off to starboard. A third destroyer abaft the port beam then switched on its searchlight and shortly afterwards both opened fire. Both *Vampire* and *Thanet* were proceeding at full speed and making a considerable amount of smoke. *Vampire* opened fired simultaneously and the first salvo hit. This salvo seemed to land over the starboard bow. The destroyer abaft the port beam fired at *Vampire*, and the destroyer astern at *Thanet*. *Vampire* collected most of the overs which were falling pretty close astern. After about three salvos from *Vampire*, *Thanet* opened with midship and then after guns, a large column of sparks – not funnel spark – shot up from the vicinity of her tubes. Great clouds of black smoke issued from her and she sheered off to starboard at a reduced speed and presumably to take cover in *Vampire's* smoke.

Thanet had been hit by gunfire. Basil Davies, her captain, recorded that when the Japanese destroyers were sighted Moran ordered an attack with torpedoes, and then altered course to bring both enemy ships to port. Davies reports:

I followed in line ahead and after he had fired I turned outside his wake to starboard to carry out my own attack. We had evidently been sighted, as I saw the flash of one destroyer's torpedo discharge. I fired all torpedoes and returned to the retiring course and went on to full speed. At this time I was slightly on Vampire's *port quarter, distance about 5 cables. Shortly afterwards I was challenged from astern and realized that enemy craft were coming up. I ignored the challenge, and the enemy switched on searchlights. There were, as far as I can remember, about four searchlights. In order to avoid them I commenced a zigzag, but with so many lights it was almost impossible to remain undetected. By this time I had opened out from* Vampire *and was under fire from ships astern and the enemy were overhauling me rapidly. I opened fire with guns which would bear and altered course a little to port, and then commenced to lay a smoke-screen. My idea was to cover* Vampire*'s retirement and, if possible, later to make a bold alteration to starboard to get behind my own screen as the breeze was fairly light. Unfortunately I was not permitted to execute this manoeuvre as I had only laid smoke for about one minute when I was hit on the port side, the shell penetrating the engine room and severing both main and auxiliary steam-pipes. The ship gave a violent lurch and swung to starboard, and became unmanageable. The only guns that would bear were X gun and pom-pom, but the whole of the after part of the ship became enveloped in steam, thus rendering it practically untenable. The lights then faded and the ship seemed to settle lower in the water. As no useful purpose could be served by remaining on board, and as she was under very heavy, though not very accurate, fire I gave the order to prepare to abandon ship. With the decrease in range, enemy gunfire became more accurate. I ordered to abandon ship. I remained on board and to the best of my ability ascertained that everyone had left. I was walking forward from the engine room hatch and had arrived abreast B gun on the starboard side when a salvo hit somewhere near the port side and I found myself in the water. The enemy then approached to concentrate heavily on the ship, judging by the number of salvos that pitched in the water while I was swimming away, and she sank shortly after. Actually I think she went down 15 to 20 minutes after the commencement of action.*

Lieutenant-Commander Davies managed to get aboard *Thanet's* motor-boat. He and some of the hands were picked up by a Royal Navy patrol boat. Four officers and more than sixty of *Thanet's* ratings made it to Singapore, some by overland routes.

* * *

The Japanese advance in Malaya was so rapid that it even surprised the War Lords in Tokyo. By early January 1942 preparations were well in advance for the invasion of the Dutch East Indies. On 18 February two Japanese transports sailed from Mando for the coast of Bali, on the doorstep of eastern Java. The invaders landed without resistance and the seizure of Bali's airfield on the afternoon of 19 January not only served the air link between the Dutch East Indies and Australia but also open the way for an assault on Java.

The Battle of the Java Sea was fought 30 miles north of Toeban, Java, on 27 February. It lasted from approximately 1615 to midnight. At 1430 on the 27th news was received at Surabaya that a Japanese invasion force of forty-one transports had been sighted *en route* for Java on a southerly heading. Consisting of American, British, Dutch, and Australian naval units the Combined Striking Force had been formed in February 1942. Part of the force was termed the Eastern Striking Force, under Rear-Admiral Karel Doorman, flying his flag in the Dutch cruiser *De Ruyter*. This force at once left to intercept. At sea the

Allied cruisers formed into line ahead (*De Ruyter, Exeter, Houston, Perth, Java*) accompanied by destroyers, of which *Electra, Encounter,* and *Jupiter* were British.

HMS *Electra*

At 1620 *Electra,* 4 miles ahead of the line, signalled that she had sighted the enemy. Four minutes later the heavy cruiser *Nachi* (flagship) and *Haguro* appeared on the horizon. At 30,000 yards they opened fire. *Exeter* was soon hit, an 8-inch shell putting six of her eight boilers out of action. A few minutes later the Dutch destroyer *Kortenaer* was hit by a torpedo. She capsized and then broke in two. To cover the crippled *Exeter* the British destroyers were ordered to counter-attack. Commander Cecil May in *Electra* moved into action with *Encounter* and *Jupiter*. As they were by then too far apart to make a divisional attack they attacked independently.

Drifting smoke hung over a large area and visibility was considerably reduced. *Electra* raced into a smoke-screen. As she emerged the other side, she encountered three large Japanese destroyers steaming to enter the same smoke-screen from the opposite direction. Six thousand yards separated the adversaries. Both opened fire. The leading Japanese ship took four hits from *Electra's* 4.7s. As the Japanese disappeared into the smoke a shell from one ship hit *Electra* in No.2 boiler room, port side. This wrecked the boiler and telemotor pipes from the steering-gear. Steam was lost and *Electra* came to a stop, listing slightly to port. Soon after this a lone Japanese destroyer returned through the smoke to resume the fight. *Electra* immediately engaged. But unable to manoeuvre, *Electra's* guns were silenced one by one. Large fires broke out forward and her port list grew more pronounced. When only one gun was left in action, the order was given to abandon ship. Elsewhere the *Encounter* and *Jupiter* were attacking enemy ships.

This engagement prevented the Allies from making contact with the massed transports. Towards dusk Admiral Doorman elected to try and shake off the Japanese naval force in the approaching darkness, and then set a course for the most likely position of the convoy. But his attempt to work his way round the enemy fleet failed, mainly because a Japanese aircraft shadowing his every move dropped flares to indicate the Allied force's changes of direction, thus allowing the Japanese fleet to stay between the transports and Allied ships. Later that night the cruisers *De Ruyter* and *Java* were sunk. Also sunk were the *Electra* and *Jupiter*.

Petty Officer Charles Braley had been serving in *Electra* since her commissioning at Chatham in July 1939. In the Java Sea engagement his station was at the 3-inch AA gun. Petty Officer Braley:

The strange noise as the salvo approached was like a train in a tunnel. Then the whistle as they passed overhead. I remember the tummy all knotted up and each of us looking at each other, silent and wondering. The relief was almost tangible as each salvo fell over or short, but the near misses – they really were frightening. The uncanny way our skipper twisted and turned gave us such relief that we all felt like yelling and cheering, but we remained quiet. Then the range closed and the destroyers opened up on us. We had retaliated, and our nerves then relaxed. At least we were 'having a go'. No aircraft were taking part to our knowledge, so we were able to watch X gun, just above us, doing their stuff. With all the tension gone, the tummy knots became undone. It was a huge relief.

Exeter was hit about 1700. She stopped and hauled out of line. We were ordered to make smoke and to screen her from Japanese. Then an attack was anticipated by Jap destroyers and we were ordered to counter-attack. The other boats had for some reason fallen astern of us so on we went into the smoke. We suddenly emerged, into dazzling brightness, beyond the screen and alone. We were face to face with the enemy: the light cruiser Jintsu *and at least six of the biggest destroyers I had ever seen. It was, I have since learned, the 4th Destroyer Flotilla. We were immediately engaged. We retaliated, and all hell was let loose. We were hit repeatedly. One salvo came inboard between the funnels, destroying the 0.5 inch AA gun platform before exploding in No.5 boiler room, killing all the crew of the 0.5 and those in the boiler room. We stopped dead, losing all power. One Japanese ship remained to engage us while the others steamed on. We fired our four 'fish' at the* Jintsu *as we stopped, but there was no spread on the running 'fish' so we missed. We were repeatedly hit, causing fires forward. Of our two forward guns, A gun had been hit and B gun had had to be abandoned because of fire. X gun was hit, causing a fire in the after superstructure. The after magazine was evacuated with the loss of supplies to Y gun. As the ship was sinking by the head, so the angle increased, making it impossible to work the one remaining gun. We were then ordered to abandon ship.*

Those who were able lowered the starboard whaler, which was the only remaining boat, and helped the wounded into it. When loaded the boat moved away, but was hit almost as it cleared the ship's side. The boat was smashed and those in it killed or wounded. The Japanese didn't let up shelling. Shrapnel was making it almost impossible to move about the upper deck, yet men still went about doing what they could to get wounded into the first Carley raft we lowered. Leading Seaman Barrett, I well remember, calmly went around and set all the depth charges to safe. The Carley raft was hit and destroyed and so many people were being wounded or killed that it really was time to go. Three of us unlashed the last raft on the searchlight platform. As we were lifting it up over the guard-rail Able Seaman Castle, standing next to me, was hit in the back and badly wounded. The other chap, Leading Seaman Perkins, and I managed to get the raft over the side. Having secured the raft we lowered Fred Castle into it. We called the hands round and then left the ship.

Leading Seaman Perkins recalled his experience.

The battle was fierce. Electra *was straddled by bursting shells of different colour.* Electra *was shooting back at a very fast rate. Destroyers had laid a smoke-screen, thus it was difficult to see what was going on except for one's own ship. Knowing the position of* Exeter, Electra *entered the smoke-screen to counter-attack as* Exeter *was under heavy fire and torpedo attack. We too came under heavy fire. The first salvo to hit us was on the port side of the low power room. It damaged the wireless room, wheelhouse, and shot quartermaster, working spells of steering and telegraphs with the coxswain. As it was out of action, we abandoned the wheelhouse to man the secondary position on the searchlight platform. The coxswain never made it, so I was alone up there.* Electra *had stopped. There was no response to my shouts, down the voice-pipe to the engine room, to connect up secondary. I heard only a loud hissing of steam. Then I tried the bridge, but without success. All this time the Japanese ships were appearing through the smoke and giving us a full broadside at point-blank range. The casualties began to mount. My own position was pretty hopeless so I followed the drill and made my way towards the tiller flat. I never got there as I was informed that abandon ship had been ordered. I bumped into Charlie Bradley and Fred Castle. The three of us launched the last Carley Float. While doing this Fred Castle was hit in the small of his back, later dying from the wound. The Japanese were firing point-blank until* Electra *sank. In the meantime the float being pushed by Charlie and me had drifted well astern. Swimmers from all directions made it to the raft many of them were wounded. Room in the raft was made for the wounded, the remainder taking it in turns to hang on to the ropes on the outside or swim around.*

Thirty-two years old Able Seaman Frederick Potts was with Petty Officer Braley at the 3-inch AA gun. He recalls:

Amid all the fire and confusion I left my station. I saw 'Polly' Perkins. He said that we must go down to the after steering as the wheelhouse was destroyed. More shells came flying by and I lost contact with him. I went straight to X gun. After rendering assistance to no avail, most of the crew had gone, suddenly there was a huge yellow flash. It seemed to engulf me. I remember jumping from the gun platform into the drink and landing alongside a floating oar. Swimming around I saw a Carley float. I swam to it and managed to get inside with many others; but I had to get off as she was sinking. I just hung on to some grappling ropes and prayed and hoped some kind of survival was possible.

Able Seaman James Prett was a leading torpedo operator. His action station was Number One on the torpedo tubes with a crew of five men. He remembers that:

The shells came into Electra *fast and furious. Our guns were firing as fast as they could, but my big day was shattered by* Electra's *switchboard being out of action. Also, a shell had found the fore engine room and stopped the ship, so that all I could do at the tubes was to wait to see if the ship would veer enough for my sights to get on to the Japanese. But no such luck. So I asked the torpedo gunner, Tim Cain, if he would put W settings on the torpedoes, which would have given a zigzag one side of the date line, as I thought at that moment that there was a slim chance of a hit. But he said 'No', as we might hit the* Jupiter, *but she was nowhere in sight. Then we got the message to abandon ship. I told the gunner that I was going to fire torpedoes. He said* Okay. *I pulled the firing levers on A, B, X and Y tubes, and away went the torpedoes. I don't think they hit anything. I then assisted to free the Carley raft near the tubes and helped to get it into the water.*

As the ship had taken a severe list to port I crawled up the starboard side. I thought then that it was about time I got swimming, so I made my way aft to the after screen, where there was a fire. I was wearing my lifebelt and a cork life-jacket, so I knew I would float all right. I slid down the side into the water and started to swim away from the ship. The shells exploding in the water really shook my body but I managed to keep going. I caught to a mate of mine. He said, 'This is a rum old do, Jim. Don't keep too close to me as they will drop a shell on us'. I then spotted a damaged Carley raft. I found that it contained mostly wounded, so I swam round with several others. Looking back at Electra *I saw she was almost sunk. About 8 to 10 feet of her was still above water. The time was then about 1815. A mournful cheer went up from what was left of her crew.*

The shelling soon finished. The light was fading fast. I settled down to swimming and floating around the raft. I could still hear and see the gun flashes as the battle raged on, going away from us. During the night we were kept fairly busy as the sea was phosphorus and sea-snakes decided to have a go. By plenty of feet and hand splashing they were kept in their place. As time went on, someone in the raft saw an object in the darkness. He shouted, 'Hey! There's something that looks like a sub over there'. After some consultation, I believe it was Charles Braley who said, 'If it's a Jap, it would be better on there than treading water here'. So it was decided to give a shout as loud as we could.

Fortunately for the *Electra* survivors the submarine was the United States Navy's S38, Lieutenant H. G. Munson, USN. The S38 had sailed from Surabaya for a patrol in the Java Sea. Lieutenant Joseph Secl, USN, recalls the rescuing of the survivors:

We were in our assigned patrol area when the bridge reported flashes and booms coming from the horizon. The captain assumed that a battle must be going on and was anxious to go there, but as we had our assigned area we couldn't leave.

It was about 0200, the morning of 28 February that flickering lights and sounds were heard in the water. Uncertain what was going on, the captain called down into the boat for two men with flashlights and 0.45 automatics to come up on the bridge. Willie Sinks and I got the gear and went to the bridge. We were briefed on what was going on and told that the boat would close the area of the lights and sounds, when we were then to throw a light on whomsoever was in the water and: 'If they are Japs – shoot them'. *But, as we closed the area, we heard the cry* 'Hey, Yanks!' *We passed the word to the bridge:* 'They must be Limeys'. *And then the 'fishing' started. One of us would swim out to the raft or float and the other would pull it to the boat and get it unloaded. We had picked up quite a few of them and were near one lone man who shouted,* 'Get the others before me'. *We notified the captain. He said we should make sure we got him. We picked him up. I learned he was Able Seaman B. V. Roberts. One man in a life-raft could not stand up, so Willie jumped into the raft and lifted his arm to me so that I could yank him aboard. He gave a horrible moan. He had a life-jacket on. As we were walking him towards the conning tower to get him inside the boat, he went limp. His head fell back and he muttered* 'Mother'. *I told the captain I believed he was dead and asked if we should put him back in the sea. He said,* 'No', *so he was brought aboard. On our way with this man I had my hand on his back and Willie had his hand on the man's stomach. Willie told me the man had a hole in his gut and I said he had one in his back the size of my fist. Once on board, the captain asked him what he would like. The man answered,* a drink and a cup of tea. *He got his shot of brandy and was handed a cup of tea. But he never drank it, as he dropped the cup and must have died just then. This was Able Seaman Fred Castle. The last survivor we brought on board was Leading Seaman R. Excell.*

Fifty-three survivors had been rescued by Lieutenant Munson. *Electra* had left Surabaya with a ship's complement of 178. Commander May did not survive. A survivor recalls:

Once clear of the ship I saw someone, presumably the captain, come to the starboard side of the bridge and wave to the men in the water, who cheered lustily. The captain then appeared to leave the ship by the port side. The Electra *then settled more steeply, turned over and slowly sank until her screws and about 6 feet of the quarter-deck were showing. She remained in this position for some time before finally sinking slowly out of sight about 6 pm.*

Until his death in June 1975, Lieutenant Henry 'Hank' Munson maintained contact with *Electra* survivors. Chief Machinist Mate Willie Sinks died in September 1978. Commander Joseph 'Jumbo' Secl is still in contact with the men he 'fished' from the sea.

HMS *Jupiter*
Six officers and 161 ratings were lost or taken prisoner when *Jupiter* was sunk about 7 miles north of Toeban. At about 2115 she had formed astern of the Dutch cruiser *Java*. Lieutenant Thomas Martin of *Jupiter:*

> *The four American destroyers had been following the cruiser all the time and they formed about 1 mile astern of* Jupiter, *whilst on course of about 280 degrees.* Jupiter *followed* Java *at a gentle zigzag. Occasional green starshell was sighted well to the northward. At 2125 Jupiter, when in position 06.45'02"S/112.05'05"E, was torpedoed from the starboard in No.2 boiler room. The ships way was taken off almost immediately. A VS signal* Jupiter Torpedoed *was made to* Java. *The signal was not acknowledged.*

When it became apparent that *Jupiter* was not going to sink quickly, the boats were lowered into the water and secured alongside. As the ship was drifting shoreward, additional rafts were constructed to replace boats and rafts damaged by the explosion and the day's action. When 3 miles from the shore, *Jupiter* was brought to anchor in 8 fathoms. It was hoped that when scuttled, at a depth of 8 fathoms she would not easily been seen for salvage. Lieutenant-Commander Norman Thew, *Jupiter's* captain, planned to dispatch the motor-boat, with the whaler in tow, towards Java. The two boats were then to return for a repeat journey. When totally abandoned *Jupiter* would be scuttled. In accordance with this plan the two boats set off for *Java* at around 2215. The journey took just under 2 hours. *Jupiter's* armament, equipment, and instruments were damaged as much as possible by the hands still with the ship. By 2345 Thew was satisfied that nothing further could be done. Scuttles were then opened on the port side to ensure *Jupiter* sank on her side. More than eighty of the crew landed safely. But not Lieutenant-Commander Thew. He never reached the shore as he was taken prisoner by the Japanese.

With the Combined Striking force having fared so badly it was no longer a question of whether the waters off Java could be disputed but how fast the surviving ships could escape the closing net. The cruisers *Perth* and *Houston* were speedily got away, they leaving Batavia at 2100 on 28 February. Two hours later they ran into Japanese ships at the entrance to the Sunda Strait and were sunk. Four of the five American destroyers cleared Surabaya and on 4 March arrived at Freemantle. The USS *Pope* and the *Exeter* and *Encounter* were sunk.

HMS *Exeter* **and HMS** *Encounter*
At 1900 on 28 February the cruiser *Exeter,* the *Pope,* and HM destroyer *Encounter* left harbour for Colombo by way of the Java Sea and Sunda Strait. At 0845 a large enemy destroyer was engaged by *Exeter* and *Encounter* but it escaped when two 8-inch cruisers were seen to close HM ships at speed. *Exeter*

altered course with *Encounter* and *Pope* conforming. It was then seen that another enemy force closing in consisted of two more 8-inch cruisers accompanied by four destroyers. In order to prevent *Exeter* from being engaged on both sides, *Encounter* laid a smoke-screen to shield her from this second force. The enemy destroyers closed until about 16,000 yards, at which point they fired on *Pope*. As this range was too great for *Encounter's* guns, and as *Pope* appeared to be drawing all the fire, *Encounter* closed the range and opened fire. Fire was returned but by zigzagging she avoided trouble. *Encounter's* target appeared to sustain hits.

The action continued until 1140 when Lieutenant-Commander Eric Morgan, *Encounter's* captain, observed *Exeter* to have stopped or slowed down. With the object of circling round and laying a smoke-screen Morgan turned towards *Exeter*. No sooner had he done so when he was informed that *Encounter's* main engines were out of action. He soon came under intense and accurate gunfire. Lieutenant-Commander Morgan:

I received the report that both suction pipes to the forced lubrication pumps had fractured due, it was at first reported, to shell splinters and that this damage had not been discovered until all the bearings had gone. I learnt, further, that it would take at least 20 minutes before the bearings would have cooled sufficiently for anything to be done to them.

Unable to manoeuvre, for *Encounter* it was the end. The situation presented to Morgan left him little choice but to abandon ship: his main engines could not be used, his main armament was out of action, and there was a possibility that the ship could be boarded. On receiving reports that all confidential papers and material had been destroyed., he ordered the ship sunk. The ship, still under fire while being abandoned, heeled over to starboard then capsized and sank. It was 1210. At ten next morning Lieutenant-Commander Morgan and other survivors were picked up by a Japanese destroyer. He had commanded *Encounter* since November 1939. *Exeter*, of River Plate fame, did not survive the engagement. The USS *Pope* was sunk by dive-bombers called to the scene.

HMS *Stronghold*
Encounter's crew was already suffering Japanese hospitality when on the following evening the *Stronghold* was sunk to the South of Java. *Stronghold*, Lieutenant-Commander Giles Pretor-Pinney, sailed from Tjilatjap in southern Java in the evening of 1 March. She carried out an A/S sweep until midnight, speed then being increased to 22 knots for the return to harbour, which in this instance meant a 1,500 miles journey to Onslow in Western Australia. The night passed quietly with no sign of the enemy.

Between 0800 and 0900 the next morning, an aircraft was sighted. It flew off without making an attack. Around noon speed was reduced to 15 knots to conserve fuel. At about 1705 splashes were observed to starboard. An 8-inch cruiser was seen about 30,000 yards on the starboard quarter. The cruiser was part of a Japanese force sweeping south of Java to prevent the escape of ships from Tjilatjap. Action stations was sounded as *Stronghold* increased to best speed and began zigzagging. A thick smoke-screen was ineffective, the cruiser's superior speed allowing her to edge round the screen and force *Stronghold* to take avoiding action to port. At about 1815 two destroyers were sighted on *Stronghold's* port quarter. Pretor-Pinney altered course to engage. The destroyers, thought to be 5-inch, were first to open fire. Range was down to 10,000 yards when *Stronghold's* guns began returning fire, reducing gradually to 4,000 yards. With a main armament of two 4-inch guns *Stronghold* was greatly outranged and outgunned and stood no chance whatsoever. She was first hit aft. A fire broke out but did not interfere with the gun action. Later, fires started in the forward mess deck and in the engine room. The engine room and boiler rooms had to be abandoned. A direct hit on the pom-pom abaft the torpedo tubes caused the torpedo heads to ignite and prevented the tubes' mountings from being trained. Then came a hit just below the bridge, a steel splinter killing Pretor-Pinney. Shortly after this the order was given to abandon ship. *Stronghold* at this time was still underway with both guns firing but she was clearly doomed. With boats damaged beyond use, the crew had only Carley floats to release into the sea. *Stronghold's* way caused the four floats to be separated, though two of them stayed within hailing distance. Around 1900 *Stronghold* was sunk by gunfire and a torpedo.

The lightening sky in the east heralded the dawn of 3 March. During the forenoon they saw a ship approaching. It turned out to be Dutch – but with a Japanese crew. The survivors on the two floats which had remained in contact were picked up. No attempt was made to rescue the occupants of the other two floats even though the ship passed within 150 yards of them. Soon after this a Japanese force of three cruisers and some destroyers was joined. The fifty *Stronghold* survivors were transferred to a cruiser. Two days later they were landed at Macassar in Celebes.

Lieutenant-Commander Pretor-Pinney had been captain of *Stronghold* for almost a year. Nine officers and sixty-one ratings failed to survive the action. A further five hands died in captivity.

On 1 March Japanese troops landed in Java. By the afternoon of the 8th the Allies on Java had agreed to surrender unconditionally. The fighting in the East Indies had been at great cost to the Allies, with many ships sunk. Japanese losses were insignificant. Furthermore, the Japanese had taken 3 months to accomplish what they had envisaged would take six.

HMS *Tenados*

HMS *Tenados* was sunk at Ceylon (Sri Lanka) and the Australian *Vampire* off the island's coast. On the afternoon of 4 April a Catalina reported a strong force of Japanese warships 360 miles south-east of Ceylon heading towards the island. All ships capable of leaving Colombo harbour were ordered to sail. At dawn on 5 April air reports placed the Japanese carriers 120 miles away. At 0800 ninety-one bombers and thirty-six fighters began to attack Colombo. The *Tenados* was at anchor in the harbour with her stern secured to the wharf for refitting ship's head. The harbour came under attack from down sun by planes bombing from about 5,000 feet. *Tenados* was hit aft by a 250 lb bomb. Two more bombs fell within 50 feet. Badly holed, her stern sank too quickly for observation as to the full extent of the damage. The bomb which hit *Tenados* was released from a flight of six aircraft in tight formation. Lieutenant-Commander Richard Dyer, her captain, stated later that he thought the real target had not been *Tenados* but the main lock gate which was about 100 yards from the ship. Three officers and twelve ratings were killed and a further three officers and eight ratings wounded.

HMS *Vampire*

Though Colombo had sustained heavy damage its harbour was not put out of action. After this attack the Japanese carriers withdrew eastward to prepare for an attack on Trincomalee, on the other side of the island. On 8 April the enemy carriers were sighted 400 miles east of Ceylon, steaming towards the island. That night the harbour of Trincomalee was cleared of shipping. *Vampire* and the old carrier *Hermes* left harbour round 0100 and by 0600 were about 40 miles south of Trincomalee. At 0900 course was set for a return to harbour. An hour later the two ships were 10 miles off Batticaloa. They were signalled that they had been sighted by enemy aircraft and that they were to proceed with utmost dispatch towards Trincomalee. Fighter assistance would be sent. Before any fighter support could reach the ships, Japanese aircraft were seen to be closing at 1035. *Hermes* was at once attacked. Diving from out of the sun, in 10 minutes the two-man Aichi D3As scored about forty hits on *Hermes*. She turned on her beam end and at 1045 sank with a loss of 302 hands. The aircraft then turned their attention towards *Vampire*. About fifteen of them attacked and at first there just some near misses. However, bomb hits then followed in quick succession. Badly sagging and barely moving, and with a heavy list to port, the order was given to abandon ship. While the crew was taking to the water *Vampire* was continually bombed. A direct hit was made on the torpedo tubes. The warheads did not explode but the ship broke in two with the forward section going under almost immediately. The aircraft retired only when the after magazine exploded and the stern sank, at 1105.

Vampire had stood little chance against one of the heaviest air attacks on HM ships during the war. One of her officer states that, *Aircraft went into the sun in Vic formation, formed line astern, banked and followed each other down in very steep dives of between sixty and seventy degrees, attacking in waves of four. It is estimated that at least sixty aircraft took part, forty-three were counted forming up and retiring after having delivered attacks; this was before* Hermes *sank. Aircraft machine-gunned on the way down and in general carried out their attacks in a very determined manner. Two, however, were observed to break off the attack on the way down when Oerlikon tracers were going round them. The dive was so steep that the 12-pounder gun could not elevate sufficiently to engage aircraft on their way down and consequently did not fire much in the second stage of the action. Vampire* shot down one plane and had one probable. Hits were observed on other aircraft.

The survivors began to head for the coast, about 10 miles away. Around 2 hours later the hospital ship *Vita* was sighted. They made their way towards her. As they were rather scattered, it took more than an hour to pick them up but by 1800 all had been rescued. Two ratings had been killed outright and four others died later from burns. One man drowned. Commander Moran, *Vampire's* captain, had been seen to go aft and abandon ship over the stern, but soon afterwards the magazine blew up, and then the depth charges. He was not seen again. The attack had been carried out by aircraft of Vice-Admiral Chuichi Nagumo's First Carrier Strike Force, the *corps d'elite* of the Japanese Navy.

HMAS *Voyager*

HMAS *Voyager* was another Australian destroyer lost during the Far East war. She was sunk at Timor, an island to the north of Australia. It was on Timor in 1789 that Captain Bligh of HMS *Bounty* made landfall after his 3,600 miles journey in an open boat. In February 1942 the Japanese made their landing on Timor.

The supplying and reinforcing of Allied troops on Timor was undertaken by the Royal Australian Navy. The first run to Timor with supplies was made in May 1942. Troops of the 24th Independent Company were scheduled to relieve the 22nd Independent Company on Timor sometime between the middle to the end of September. At Darwin on 22 September 250 officers and men boarded the *Voyager*, Lieutenant-Commander R. C. Robinson, and RAN. At 1800 that evening *Voyager* left Darwin with the troops, 15 tons of stores, eight barges, and a 14 feet motor skiff.

At 1545 the next day Timor was sighted through a heavy haze. Landfall was made to the east of Betano Bay, situated roughly midway along Timor's southern coast. It is a wide bay some 2 miles across but it offered little in the way of anchorage or harbourage. The only sheltered anchorage for small craft is in a channel between two reefs in about the centre of the bay. Around 1830 *Voyager* entered the bay. There were no navigational aids or marks on the shore to help Lieutenant-Commander Robinson in anchoring, and he had only a very rough sketch plan devoid of soundings, plus his echo sounder and lead. He dropped anchor when about 500 yards from the beach and between 700 and 800 yards from the main (seaward) reef. All boats were ordered out for the disembarkation of troops. *Voyager* had been anchored about 5 minutes when Robinson realized that she had swung to her anchor port side parallel to the shore, with the main reef of the starboard bow, and appeared to be closing the beach. He decided to move to deeper water. The best way to get out was to swing the stern out by going astern on the port engine. The official history (Royal Australian History 1942-1945) states:

> *Unfortunately by now disembarkation boats had been lowered, and two army barges, half-full of troops, were immediately over the port propellers. Robinson could not get the troops to understand the necessity to move the barges quickly. There was a considerable amount of loud talking, cat-calling, etc., taking place, and I found it extremely difficult to get my orders through and obeyed.* He was in a taxing dilemma. *By going astern on the port engine and ahead on the starboard to endeavour to get the stern out into deeper water, I should have upset the boats and army personnel.* He decided, therefore, to turn the ship to starboard and proceed ahead. *The starboard propeller was clear and I decided to head the ship clear of the reef by moving the engines slow astern.* For some 16 minutes Robinson manoeuvred *Voyager* slowly round, using his starboard propeller only. Then at 6.50pm he ordered, 'Half ahead both. Starboard 20degrees. Ship's head clear of reefs'. *Less than a minute later, and only 23 minutes after he had anchored and started disembarkation, Voyager took the ground aft.*

Everything possible was done to re-float *Voyager*, but at moon on the 24th the attempt to salvage the ship without further aid was abandoned, as her propellers were firmly embedded in the sand which was over the shafts. At low water she was high and dry with a bank of sand piled high on the seaward side. The beach was in the process of being cleared of boats and material for hiding in the vines when at 1330 a Japanese reconnaissance plane with a fighter escort appeared. This was shot down by *Voyager*. With an air attack almost certain to follow, and with an attack from landwards also a possibility, Robinson ordered the wrecking and destruction of *Voyager*. Just after 1600 the Japanese contributed to the ship's destruction when they bombed her with high explosive, incendiary, and anti-personnel bombs from about 3,000 feet. That evening demolition charges were fired in the engine room, both sides of which blew out and broke her back. At 0430, Friday 25th, *Voyager* was set ablaze fore and aft. She burnt fiercely all day, accompanied by ammunition explosions.

Three days later 152 *Voyager* survivors were landed at Darwin from HMAS *Kalgoorlie* and *Warrnambool*. Seven of the crew sustained minor injuries from the bombing.

*   *   *

HMS *Heythrop*

Heythrop was torpedoed and sunk in the Mediterranean. She was a Type II Hunt class completed on 26 June 1941. Under Lieutenant-Commander Robert Stafford she arrived at Gibraltar on 30 August. Seven months later she was sunk by the U657. George-Werner Fraatz was born in Hamein. In 1933, when he was sixteen, he joined the German navy. When war broke out he was serving in U3. In April 1941 he was given his first command, the U652 and *Heythrop* was his fourth sinking.

By early March the Allies had decided to fight a convoy (MG1) from Alexandria through to Malta. The convoy of four merchantmen had an escort of four cruisers and sixteen destroyers. It sailed on 20 March. Six Hunt class destroyers, one of which was *Heythrop*, put to sea earlier to carry out an A/S patrol between Alexandria and Bardia on the night of 19th/20th. Oberleutnant zur See Fraatz was already at sea with U652, having left the Greek island of Salamis on the 18th for a patrol in the area of Tobruk. U562 was 40 miles north east of Bardia when her bridge party sighted *Heythrop* on her A/S search. Fraatz dived and manoeuvred for an attack. At a range of little more than 1,000 yards he fired four torpedoes. *Heythrop* was proceeding at 14 knots when towards 1100 on the 20th a torpedo struck to port. An immediate ten degrees list to starboard took place. She had been almost severed at No.3 mounting, which was blown overboard. Her after portion was only connected by the starboard side plating. It was thought worthwhile to make an attempt at towing, and *Eridge* closed for this purpose. The tow had been underway for several hours when at 1400 the port grand plate in *Heythrop* fractured. The pumps called not cope with a heavy list to starboard. Around 1600 Lieutenant-Commander Stafford and his towing party were transferred to *Eridge* by boat. Fifteen minutes later *Heythrop* turned over to starboard and sank by the stern.

Fatal casualties numbered fifteen. The hunt for U652 went on for 6 hours. Fraatz recorded seventy-nine depth charge explosions, and no damage. He continued his patrol.

HMS *Jaguar*

The loss of the J class destroyer *Jaguar* came less than a week after the sinking of *Heythrop*. She had been awarded six Battle Honours: Dunkirk, Atlantic, Spartivento, Matapan, Crete, Mediterranean, Libya and the Malta Convoys.

On 25 March the Greek destroyer *Queen Olga* and the British A/S whaler *Klo* left Alexandria at 0630 as escort to the Royal Fleet Auxiliary oiler *Slavol*. At 1300 the convoy was joined by *Jaguar*, Lieutenant-Commander Lionel Tyrwhitt. The *Queen Olga* attacked a contact when the convoy was in the area of Ras el Knais. A few minutes later a periscope was reported and at 1750 a second attack was undertaken. No further contact was made and so she rejoined the convoy. The small group settled down for the night.

Oberleutnant zur See Fraatz had not sunk anything since torpedoing *Heythrop*. At 0228 on 26 March he fired four torpedoes at *Jaguar* from a range in excess of 3,000 yards. *Jaguar* was zigzagging at 15 knots across *Slavol's* starboard bow when a torpedo struck to starboard between the funnel and bridge. This hit was followed immediately by a second hit, between the funnel and the pom-pom gun. Taking a heavy list to starboard she broke in two. A large fire started in the vicinity of the galley. The fire spread at once to the fore mess deck, passage, and the entire bridge structure. *Jaguar's* forepart sank within a minute of the ship being hit. The stern portion remained afloat for three minutes. Around 2 hours after sinking *Jaguar*, Fraatz also sunk the *Slavol*. She was his last success as a few months later he took command of U529. Before he could sink anything he was lost with his new boat when in February 1943 she was sunk by the RAF. Eight officers and forty-six ratings were saved from *Jaguar*, but almost two hundred were lost.

HMS *Southwold*

The naval supply ship *Breconshire* and the merchantmen *Clan Campbell*, *Pampas*, and *Talbot* sailed from Alexandria on 20 March in another attempt to get supplies through to Malta. Though subjected to attacks, the *Pampas* and *Talbot* arrived at Malta around 0930 the next morning. *Clan Campbell* was bombed when 20 miles from the island and she sank. The *Breconshire* was hit and disabled when only 8 miles from Malta. The cruiser *Penelope* tried to take her in tow but in the prevailing heavy sea the attempt failed. Next day the *Southwold* was making ready to pass *Breconshire* a line when the destroyer was mined. It was *Southwold's* first lieutenant, Lieutenant D. V. Macleod, who was on her forecastle preparing to pass the line. *Southwold* was going astern when, just as she was gathering headway, the mine exploded under her engine room. For some time the great heat of steam that filled the engine room prevented entry. Later, when the engine room had cooled, Macleod entered and he found:

The compartment was quite light inside owing to a very large hole in the approximate position of the starting platform. As far as I could see, all ladders and machinery were totally wrecked. The only body I could find, although unrecognizable, was so badly mutilated that I decided not to recover it from the compartment.

Another of the Hunts, *Dulverton*, stood by to render assistance while a tug took *Southwold* in tow. Lieutenant Macleod:

> *As soon as we got under tow there was a further crack in the ship's side plating abreast the engine room split right up to the upper deck on both sides. The ship then took up a considerable sag with a slight list to starboard. At this stage all confidential books were thrown overboard in weighted bags. All life-saving apparatus was cleared away ready for use. The ship's company was kept up to port to counteract the list. The whaler was turned out and lowered to take off two ratings who had been wounded in action on the previous Sunday. They were embarked in the whaler and subsequently transferred to HMS Dulverton. The crew was divided up with about thirty aft and the remainder forward.*
>
> *When HMS Southwold was under tow for the second time, the midships section gradually sank lower in the water and the list to starboard slowly increased. The two ends of the ship worked a great deal in the swell that was running, hinging on the upper deck plating on the port side. The plating was split and to starboard but on the port side the bend unfortunately came in the middle of a large plate when the strength was not prejudiced by a line of rivets. While the ship was under tow she was attacked by a JU88 who straddled her with a stick of bombs. The closest one fell on the port side, a considerable quantity of water falling inboard. Surprisingly little shock to the hull was experienced from the explosions.*

The situation became increasingly grave, the midships sinking lower into the water, and she had to be abandoned. Her captain, Commander Christopher Jellicoe, later took command of *Jackal*.

HMS *Maori*

The early months of 1942 saw a marked increase in the bombing of Malta with the naval harbours as main target. The *Maori*, Commander Rafe Courage, was the first of five destroyers to be lost in this phase of the bombing. The *Maori* was moored to a buoy in Grand Harbour when at 0115 on 12 February she was hit in the after end of her engine room by a bomb which probably struck slightly to port of the centre line. The attack took *Maori* by surprise, no ships or shore-batteries having engaged the raiders, with the result that nearly all the officers and ratings were asleep. The explosion opened the bulkhead between the engine room and the gearing room. Lubricating oil in the gearing room, about 2,000 gallons, caught fire. Oil fuel from one of the tanks later added to the blaze. The fire spread to the ready use ammunition lockers on the after superstructure, causing continuous explosions which flung jagged splinters round the deck. A large explosion was thought to be the depth charges in the warhead magazine. The position in *Maori* became untenable and she had to be abandoned. Boats in the harbour took off most of the crew. Soon after this there was heavy explosion, believed to be the 4-inch magazine blowing up. *Maori* settled by the stern and remained at an angle with her forepart out of the water up to the break of the forecastle. Three hands had been killed and six wounded.

HMS *Legion*

By March the bombing of Malta was rapidly moving towards it peak with more than 2,000 tons of bombs being dropped that month. On 26 March waves of bombers attacked Grand Harbour, sinking a number of ships. One of them was *Legion*, which was hit simultaneously on the forecastle and B gundeck by two bombs at least. The bombs passed through to the lower mess deck before exploding. Another bomb struck the jetty close alongside. *Legion*, split open forward, went down by the bows. When her forefoot touched bottom she turned over to port until her bridge and funnel lay on the jetty. Her fighting days were at an end.

HMS *Gallant*

Gallant was bombed at Malta a few days after *Legion*, but she had been out of action for a considerable time. And she was in fact at Malta for damage repair, having been mined off Pantelleria at 0830 on 10 January 1941. Her 15 months under repair at Malta had much to do with the need to repair less seriously damaged ships and the bombing of harbours. By April 1942 *Gallant* was near to completion of repairs and was afloat at a wharf when on 5 April she was holed and subsequently beached. After this she became useful as a supply of spare parts for other ships.

HMS *Lance*

Another casualty of the bombing was *Lance*. She was a hard working ship and had accomplished much in her year's service. *Lance* was in dock at Malta for war damage repairs when on 5th April and again on the 9th she was bombed. Her stern was under water but her bows were well up. Eventually she was repaired sufficiently to be towed home and scrapped.

HMS *Kingston*

Kingston was the last destroyer to be lost during the bombing of Malta. She had taken part in the Second Battle of Sirte. During this action she was hit by a 15-inch shell of the Italian battleship *Littorio*. Able Seaman George Sear recalls:

We managed to make it to Malta but owing to the devastation to the dockyard during the intensive bombing of the island, we could not get the necessary repairs done to enable us to leave. Most of the ship's company was drafted to army units and put under canvas for preparation for an invasion. I returned to the dockyard

as one of a party to manhandle the ship hawsers (there was no power of any kind)
into No.4 Dry-dock, where shortly after she was blown in half by Stukas.

Kingston was in fact bombed at Malta on two occasions, on 5 April and 11 April.
The second attack caused the greater damage. Lieutenant-Commander Philip
Somerville, the captain of *Kingston*, did not survive the bombing.

HMS *Havock*

Under Lieutenant-Commander George Watkins the *Havock* fought with
distinction in the Mediterranean. During the Second Battle of Sirte she
narrowly escaped disaster when emerging from a smoke-screen a 15-inch shell
exploded alongside. Several hands were killed. At reduced speed she struggled
through to Malta.

More than 6,700 tons of bomb fell on Malta in April and because of the
heavy bombing ships' crews obtained what rest they could by sleeping in
underground rest stations. Watkins was so concerned for the safety of his ship
that after each lull in the bombing he would rush out of the shelter to see if
Havock had survived. To Watkins the sound of every big explosion seemed to
indicate that she had been hit. But *Havock* survived, though at times all round
her had been devastated and she had been strew with chunks of masonry and
surrounding ruins. Though *Havock* had escaped being hit while alongside,
when she was declared fit for sea and was in the stream about four days before
leaving Malta when her after magazine and shell room were holed. She was
patched up with cement, which hardly had time to set before she sailed from
Malta for the last time.

On the night immediately preceeding *Havock's* departure Watkins took
charge of a flotilla of small craft with the object of taking a 500 tons oil-lighter
to offload a portion of the valuable oil from the sunken *Breconshire.* The task
was completed successfully and, after a short sleep, Watkins returned to
Havock. Later he reported to Vice Admiral Malta(VAM) the night's activities.
Returning to *Havock* at 1300, he gave the necessary orders for sailing at
1900 that evening. During the afternoon he again visited the VAM's office, this
time to collect his sailing orders. On this occasion he was accompanied by one
of his officers, Sub-Lieutenant Lack, RNVR. Lack had been in the navy for
almost 3 years but only a week of this had been spent in *Havock*, he being a
replacement for an officer killed in the Sirte action. Before leaving the VAM's
office Watkins corrected his charts up to date from the latest information.
Lieutenant-Commander Watkins' orders stated that he was to set course from
the Malta swept channel to a point of Kelibia Light. He was to pass the light at
a distance of not more than 3,000 yards off the coast and continue at such
distance until Cape Bon. *Havock* was to proceed at maximum speed till passing
Galite Island, at which point speed would be reduced so as to have sufficient
fuel to reach Gibraltar.

Owing to air raids Watkins was unable to return to *Havock* until 1830. He found that an air attack had severed current to the gyro. This was quickly sorted out, and the gyro was reported as running correctly. With the assistance of Sub-Lieutenant Lack and his first lieutenant, Lieutenant John Burfield, Watkins made out an intended track of the ships and checked the course and bearing of Kelibia Light. At Kelibia Light a course alteration would be made. Burfield and Lack worked out the time distance at 30 knots between the points on the chart marked by the captain. *Havock* cast off around 1930 and made to seaward. She had on board a number of passengers for Gibraltar. George Watkins and his officers were very weary. Although morale was as high as could be expected, months of constant strain of battle had produced a general tiredness among the overworked Mediterranean destroyers. After navigating the swept channel Watkins left the bridge for a couple of hours rest. He returned to the bridge when Pantelleria was sighted. *Havock* was in second degree of readiness but Watkins allowed half of his officers at a time to sleep at their quarters.

Shortly before the first turning point Watkins 'took' the ship and altered course to pass 1 mile off Kelibia Light. Sub-Lieutenant Lack was at the chart. The range-finder appeared to be working correctly. Glancing at the chart Watkins saw that *Havock* was being set in, and so altered course 10 degrees or more to seaward. Lieutenant-Commander Watkins:

The night was clear, no moon, but with patches of mist over the land. I asked Lack whether we were being set in, or were heading for my turning point. He replied we were a little inside, but quite all right. I glanced again at the chart and considered it all right to steer in a bit, and I did so. I had instructed Lack to inform me when I was about to come on for bearing before making an alteration, and then give me the time for each run. Everything had been tabulated on the chart previously to avoid error. There were some alterations to make round the corner of Kelibia Light. Havock was racing along at 30 knots.

The ship went to the first degree of readiness before the first turn round the point. Lieutenant-Commander Watkins states,

I constantly asked Lack whether we were all right. I was still passing ranges and bearings which he was plotting. The last leg of the turn looked strange to me and I hung on a bit longer after he told me it was time to alter. The time was then about 0350. I saw what looked like a white wave ahead. We were being plotted by range and bearing straight on to the shore. I immediately altered out a little and rushed to the chart-table and ordered full speed astern and hard starboard, but it was too late. We had run on to a sand-pit and were hard-and-fast aground.

When the blackness of the night had paled a little, the shore was seen 100 yards off. All ammunition was thrown overboard to help lighten ship. Torpedoes were fired to seaward. When it became clear that these measures were insufficient to re-float the ship, Watkins ordered his passengers ashore and prepared to destroy *Havock*. All confidential papers and secret equipment was destroyed. The spaces and cabins were strewn with cordite strips and oil fuel. When almost everyone was ashore the cordite was ignited. The fuse of the depth charge in the asdic compartment was then lit. The last whaler to go ashore was well clear when the depth charge blew out the sides of the fo'c'sle. *Havock* was seen to be well ablaze fore and aft. At about 1400 a huge explosion took place and a column of smoke hundreds of feet high was seen. This was *Havock's* after end blowing up. The hot sun, together with the fires below deck, had caused the depth charges to explode. The after magazine might also have been blown up. The British were taken prisoner by the French, who kept them under the most wretched conditions until the Torch operation of November 1942 liberated them.

HMS *Lively*
On 10 May information was received that four enemy merchantmen with escort were in passage between Taranto and North Africa. Acting on this information Captain Albert Poland in *Jervis* sailed from Alexandria that evening with *Lively*, *Kipling*, and *Jackal* to intercept the convoy off Benghazi around dawn of the 12th. Captain Poland's orders were that he was to abandon the operation if he was sighted by the enemy during daylight on 11 May or if unable to reach a position some 90 miles north west of Benghazi by 0600 on the 12th.

Early on the morning of 11 May the British force was sighted by enemy aircraft. In accordance with orders Captain Poland abandoned the operation. He turned round and made for harbour, requesting fighter cover. At 1620 the ships took up a diamond formation against possible air attack. In view of expected fighter protection the *Lively* was detailed fighter direction ship. At 1633 the British planes were picked up on radar. A few minutes later two Beaufighters appeared overhead. Just a few minutes after this, the ships' radar indicated aircraft, range 8 miles. The Beaufighters raced away to engage. No sooner had they left when on *Lively's* bridge was heard the cry, '*Aircraft diving on starboard bow*'. Eight Stukas were seen diving from 3,000 feet. The Beaufighters were called immediately by *Lively*. This was the last communication between ships and Beaufighters, for within seconds a salvo of bombs hit *Lively* forward, wrecking all apparatus on the bridge.

The Stukas dropped four bombs towards *Lively:* three appear to have hit or near missed on or about the water-line abreast A gun, whilst the fourth bomb penetrated B gundeck abaft the gun and exploded on the lower mess deck. A violent explosion was followed by a tremendous shaking of *Lively*. Everyone on the bridge was thrown to the deck and for several seconds water beat down solidly onto the bridge. By the time the bridge party had regained its feet *Lively* was well down at the bows and beginning to list to starboard. Down at the head, *Lively* ploughed through the sea for 30 seconds or so. During this period a second salvo of bombs entered the sea about 200 yards to starboard and abreast the after tubes. Then, and quite suddenly, *Lively* began to heel over rapidly to starboard. It took only a few seconds for her to go onto her side. *Lively* heeled over so quickly that only one of the port side Carley floats was released, almost everyone having to jump into the sea. *Lively's* Gunner (T), John Jones, states:

> *The captain, Lieutenant-Commander W. F. E. Hussey, and myself were the last two men to leave the ship; we were blown out when A boiler room's lateral bulkheads collapsed and the boilers exploded. When HMS* Jackal *came to pick us up, another wave of JU88s attacked her. One of the bombs which missed her hit the water and exploded close to us and seriously damaged us both internally, causing bleeding from the nose, ears, and mouth. Picked up by* Jervis *about two hours later, we were laid out together on the wardroom floor, where William Hussey died during the night.*

About a minute after the last man cleared *Lively* an explosion near her bow caused injury to a number of swimmers. A further minute passed and then *Lively's* stern sank with propellers turning. The whole ship had disappeared by 1640, about 3.5 minutes after being hit. Enemy aircraft caused some delay to the rescue of survivors but, while *Jackal* provided A/S cover, *Jervis* and *Kipling* were able to close and pick them up, *Kipling* taking on board six officers and 111 ratings.

HMS *Kipling*

Jervis, *Jackal*, and *Kipling* were heading eastward at best speed when around 1830 nine Stukas attacked. Though four bombs fell close to *Kipling* she was undamaged. The first Beaufighter patrol had to leave before the heaviest attack. Four more Beaufighters arrived at about 1845, but one of these left almost an hour later to return to base. At 1955 radar picked up a formation of aircraft approaching from the north-west. Before the Beaufighters could reach a position to intercept, ten Stukas were seen closing with the setting sun almost directly behind them. The destroyers put up a fierce barrage of fire and performed some drastic manoeuvres. *Kipling* was attacked from astern. A Stuka released four bombs; one bomb hit the ship and another near missed, probably bursting under the ship. *Kipling's* side was gashed open on the starboard side and split port side, the damage probably extending to the ship's bottom. She took on a heavy list to port and consequent flooding broke her back. Despite the port list, the pom-pom and starboard 5-inch gun kept firing until abandon ship was ordered. Very soon afterwards, *Kipling* sank by the stern.

HMS *Jackal*

Jervis and *Jackal* were also under attack. *Jackal*, Commander Christopher Jellicoe, was proceeding at 30 knots when a Stuka released four bombs. One of the bombs passed through the upper deck, starboard, above No.2 boiler room, through which it then passed before penetrating the ship's bottom and exploding almost beneath the keel amidships. The shock of the explosion lifted *Jackal* bodily. Two other bombs were near misses and probably caused underwater damage port side, while the remaining bomb fell short of the starboard side. The engine room and both boiler rooms were flooded. Within an hour the gearing room had flooded. The *Jervis* had been near missed by several bombs but had received no serious damage. Captain Poland, recognizing that *Jackal* was not about to sink, made towards *Kipling's* survivors intending to pick them up, but he called this off when a bomb fell close to *Jervis* and the survivors in the sea. His decision was then to leave the area until darkness. He steamed northward until 2100, then turned south to return to the scene of the action. At 2134 he stopped among the *Kipling* survivors, which had of course many of *Lively's* survivors among them. Thirty minutes later he secured alongside the damaged *Jackal* embarked those of her crew not required for towing. At 0053 *Jackal* was taken in tow by *Jervis*.

About 20 minutes after the bomb had hit, an oil fuel fire had started in *Jackal's* No.1 boiler room. At times the flames issuing from the funnel reached a height of 20 feet. The towing at once revealed an unforeseen problem: as soon as *Jackal* began to move, the increased draught over the top of the funnel increased the fire considerably. The upper deck in the vicinity of No.1 boiler room was kept fairly cool by a chain of buckets, but the interior of the ship became very heated. When the after bulkhead of B magazine became hot the magazine had to be flooded. This had the effect of bringing the ship nearly upright but at the same time reduced the fo'c'sle's freeboard to about 8 feet. Around 0200 *Jackal's* stern began to settle. She took on a six degrees list to starboard, so that the starboard side of the quarter-deck became awash. Flames from the funnel were by now occasionally rising to a height of 50 feet, illuminating *Jackal* and *Jervis* clearly. Water was entering through the ship's side plating. Taking everything into consideration, including the fact that Alexandria was still some 200 miles off and that *Jackal* was settling slowly, it was decided that she would not remain afloat long enough to reach harbour. At 0306 *Jervis* slipped the tow and 2 minutes later secured alongside *Jackal* to take off the towing party. She remained alongside until 0435. Ten minutes later after drawing away, *Jervis* fired two torpedoes at the derelict. One torpedo broke surface and missed the target, but the other struck home and the *Jackal* went down. Of the four fine destroyers that had left Alexandria on the evening of 10 May, *Jervis* alone returned to harbour. She had on board 630 survivors.

HMS *Grove*

When thirty-one years old Kapitanleutnant Heinrich Schonder of U77 sunk *Grove* it began a period in which seven destroyers were sunk in less than a week. Lieutenant-Commander James Rylands' appointment to *Grove* dated from 12 December 1941. *Grove*, named after a hunt in Nottinghamshire, was at that time under construction at Swan Hunter's Tyne yard at Wallsend. Two months later she was ready for her work-up at Scapa Flow. *Grove* arrived at Alexandria on 18 May 1942, where she joined the 22nd Destroyer Flotilla. Less than a month later she was sunk. In the early hours of 12 June *Grove* sailed from Tobruk to Alexandria in company with *Tetcoot*, another Hunt. At 0124 *Grove* briefly touched ground, damaging her port propeller and shaft. This damage reduced her speed to 8 knots, and played a part in her eventual loss.

Kapitanleutnant Schonder put to sea from Messina on 8 June for a patrol, his sixth with U77, in the Central Mediterranean. On the morning of the 12th, U77 sighted *Grove* and *Tetcott*, north of Bardia and still on their eastward heading for Alexandria. Schonder fired four torpedoes at *Grove*. At 0654 *Grove's* bow and stern were each blown away by a torpedo. Fourteen minutes later she sank. *Grove* had sighted the torpedoes and a change course had been ordered, but at her slow speed the ship did not respond to the helm quickly enough. Six officers, including James Rylands, and seventy-three ratings were picked up by *Tetcott*. Five days after the sinking the U77 was alongside at Salamis. *Grove* had been her only sinking of the ten days patrol. In December 1942 Heinrich Schonder took command of U200. He was not a survivor when a year later U200 was sunk by aircraft of the United States Navy.

* * *

Five destroyers were lost in the June 1942 attempt to provision Malta. The plan was that two convoys (Harpoon and Vigorous) would converge on Malta simultaneously: Harpoon from the west of Vigorous from the east. Under the command of Rear-Admiral Philip Vian eleven merchant ships made up the Vigorous convoy. Its escort of forty-seven ships included eight cruisers and twenty-six destroyers. As no aircraft carriers were available, air support was restricted to what could be provided by land-based aircraft. On the evening of 13 June Admiral Vian left Alexandria to overtake the merchantman ships and close escort off Tobruk.

By nightfall of 14 June the convoy had been attacked seven times by a total of seventy aircraft. With the coming of darkness the attacks ceased, though enemy planes were repeatedly illuminating the convoy with flares. However, the darkness helped protect the E-boats lurking on the fringe of the convoy waiting for an opportunity to attack. By 2315 Admiral Vian was aware that Italian heavy ships were at sea. Possible contact with these ships could be made by 0700 next morning.

HMS *Hasty*

Shortly before 0400 15 June an E-boat of the 3rd Schnellboot Flotilla, operating from Derna, hit the cruiser *Newcastle* with a torpedo. Soon after this an E-boat made an unsuccessful attack on the *Hasty*, Lieutenant-Commander Nigel Austen, one of the destroyers screening *Newcastle* and the cruiser *Arethusa*. By 0440 *Hasty* had taken a position off the starboard beam of *Newcastle* was able to increase speed, she ordered her screening destroyers to take up an alternative screening formation. Austen was almost at his new position, with starboard wheel on to put *Hasty* on the same course ahead of *Newcastle*, when he saw the track of a torpedo approaching *Hasty* on the port quarter. He ordered hard astarboard. The torpedo, by then too close to avoid, struck *Hasty* port side in the vicinity of A gun. An E-boat had fired the torpedo from abaft *Newcastle's* beam. The torpedo had approached *Hasty* at an angle and in the process passed close ahead of *Newcastle*, for which it had undoubtedly been intended. Austen reports:

> *It was some seconds before I recovered from the explosion and torrent of water, but it was by then obvious that the ship was crippled, as from A gun forward had been blown away. The engines were stopped, and I ordered all officers and men off the bridge. I ordered* 'Prepare to abandon ship'.

It was then nearing 0530. Austen and his engineer officer together carried out an inspection of the ship. *Hasty's* condition and the certainty of further attacks decided Austen to abandon ship. *Hotspur* made an alongside and took off the crew. *Hasty* was then sunk. Twelve ratings had been killed, and a wounded man died later in *Hotspur*. It is believed that the S55 had fired the torpedo that struck *Hasty*. Her captain, twenty-two years old Oberleutnant zur See Horst Weber, survived the war.

HMS *Airdale*

At 1525 that afternoon twelve Stukas were observed approaching the convoy from the starboard quarter where Lieutenant-Commander Archibald Forman was stationed with *Airedale*. Forman at once increased speed and altered course to bring all guns to bear. He opened fire with main armament. When the four leading aircraft were seen to begin their dive, full speed ahead was ordered and fire was opened with pom-poms and port Oerlikons. Restricted by the close proximity of other ships, no further course alteration was made. The Stukas took only 6 seconds to complete their attack on *Airedale*. Bombs were seen hurtling towards the ship. Two large bombs near missed to port, a third bomb entered the sea close to starboard. Then another large bomb, and probably several smaller ones, struck *Airedale* in the vicinity of the after gun mounting. A violent explosion aft shook the ship, leading those on the bridge to believe that the 4-inch magazine or the depth charge magazine had blown up. *Airedale* immediately began to sink by the stern and take on a slight list to port. The bombs had blasted away everything abaft the searchlight platform, a third of the ship. The forward end of the after superstructure was curled back of the searchlight superstructure, and the ship's side abreast this position was folded back towards the bow. The upper deck amidships was badly buckled. Splinters and debris, and 4-inch ammunition, had showered the bridge, mortally wounding the chief yeoman. The pom-pom and port Oerlikon were put out of action and, with the exception of an officer and two ratings, the crews of both weapons killed. Fire broke out in No.2 boiler room.

At 1545, 20 minutes after sighting the aircraft, Forman ordered the ship abandoned, his engineer officer having reported that he considered *Airedale* could not be saved. Two other Hunts, *Hurworth* and *Aldenham*, were ordered to stand by. *Airedale's* boats received splinter damage, but the whaler was lowered and sent across to *Hurworth*. *Airedale's* crew was ordered over the starboard side and told to swim to the rescue ships. While this was taking place the badly wounded were lashed to lengths of timber and ferried to *Aldenham*. When *Airedale* was clear of all hands she was sunk by gunfire from *Hurworth* and a torpedo from *Aldenham*. Three wounded died next day.

HMAS *Nestor*

Air raids on the convoy lasted from 1720 to around 1930. During a high-level bombing attack the Australian destroyer *Nestor*, Commander Alvord Rosenthal, RAN, was, at 1806, straddled by two heavy bombs, one falling to starboard abreast the bridge at a distance of 500 feet and the other falling to port abreast the motor-cutter and close alongside. The shock to *Nestor* was so severe that the ship in the vicinity of the bridge the mast and the funnel flexed violently and, apart from throwing everyone to the deck, caused considerable damage to fittings in the structure. The most serious damage was to the hull port sides, which was extensively distorted and holed. The damage caused the immediate flooding of No.1 boiler room with the consequent total loss of steam, and also electrical power as the two diesel dynamos were located there. Because of damage to the bulkhead separating this boiler room from No.2 boiler room, the latter subsequently flooded. The bulkheads between No.1 boiler room and three and four oil fuel tanks were also damaged, allowing oil fuel to escape into the boiler room and a fire started in this compartment. *Nestor's* damage caused her to settle by the head with a list to port. *Javelin*, detailed to assist her, closed and at 1850 took her in tow. The towing had scarcely got underway when shortly after 1900 the bombers attacking the convoy switched their attention to *Nestor* and *Javelin*. A stick of bombs fell close to *Javelin*.

Around 0500 on 16 June serious consideration was given to scuttling *Nestor*, and the reason for such an action was strong: owing to her trimming down at the head, the 4 inch wire had twice parted under ideal conditions and the only towing-gear now available was the 3 inch towing-wire of the Hunts, or the hurricane hawsers and inadequate manila carried by *Nestor* and *Javelin*. And as towing would have to be at a very slow speed, both ships would be an easy target for aircraft or U-boat attack, particularly as Alexandria was still some 200 miles away. It was felt most strongly that an attempt to reach Alexandria was inviting the loss of both ships. *Nestor*, only completed in February 1941, was therefore sunk.

* * *

The escorts had been too short of ammunition to continue battling through to Malta and had had to call off the effort. The cruiser *Hermione* was sunk on the morning of 16 June. That evening the battered ships of the Vigorous convoy arrived in harbour, greatly disappointed in having failed to get through to Malta.

The Harpoon convoy of five freighters and a tanker sailed from the United Kingdom on 5 June and passed into the Mediterranean on the night of 11th/12th. The convoy consisted of the British *Troilus*, *Orari*, and *Burdwan*, the Dutch *Tanimbar*, the American *Chant*, and the tanker *Kentucky*, also American. By dawn of 14 June the convoy was about 120 miles south west of Sardinia. At 2130 that night its strong covering force, detailed to support the close escort as far as the Skerki Bank to the north-west of Cape Bon, left the convoy, which was now the sole care of the AA cruiser *Cairo* (Captain C. C. Hardy), the fleet destroyers *Bedouin*, *Partridge*, *Ithuriel*, *Marne* and *Matchless*, the Hunts *Badsworth*, *Blankly*, *Middleton*, and *Kujawiak* (Polish), the minesweeping sloops *Hebe*, *Hythe*, *Rye*, and *Speedy*, and half-dozen motor-launches.

HMS *Bedouin*

At first-light on 13 June the Harpoon force was 30 miles south of Pantelleria. Malta was about 12 hours away. Around this time a Beaufighter from Malta reported to Captain Hardy that enemy cruisers and destroyers were 15 miles north of the convoy. At 0615 the Italian cruisers *Raimonde Montecuccoli* and *Eugenio di Savoia* with four destroyers were sighted 12 miles off. When the range had closed to 22,000 yards the Italians opened fire, the first salvo falling astern of *Bedouin*. At 0627 *Bedouin*, Commander Bryan Sccurfield, opened fire at 17,400 yards, straddling one of the destroyers. Ten minutes later fire was shifted to the leading cruiser at a range of 13,000 yards. By this time *Bedouin* had been hit several times and communication by flags and W/T was impossible. The action as observed by *Bedouin's* first lieutenant, Lieutenant Errol Manners, reveals how this Tribal class destroyer met her end:

Bedouin was being hit a good deal, particularly about the bridge structure, and at 0650 the director was put out of action. Being by then within 5,000 yards of the enemy cruisers, who were firing close-range weapons at us, it was considered advisable to turn and fire torpedoes before the ship was brought to a standstill. Lieutenant J. Reeve-Moller, RNR, the torpedo control officer, although wounded made his way to the tubes and, as the ship turned, fired all four torpedoes as the sights came on. The ship was hit in the engine room while turning and was stopped. The enemy made a drastic alteration of course to the northward and broke off the action shortly afterwards, disappearing from view. No torpedo hits were seen. The situation on board Bedouin *after this action was that the main and steering engines were out of action, there was no electric light, the primary fire control system was out of action, but all guns were ready for further action and the ship was seaworthy.* Partridge *had one engine out of action.* Marne *had suffered damaged. After an examination of damage* Marne, Matchless, *and* Ithurial *left to rejoin the convoy.*

By 0930 Partridge *had the* Bedouin *in tow. It was decided to steer for the Tunisian coast to avoid saddling Malta Dockyard with a crock. Later in the afternoon the convoy passed us on an easterly course. The tow proceeded westward at some 5 knots. The ship's company were employed in repairing damage and attending to the dead and wounded. Depth charges were jettisoned to lighten the ship aft, ammunition was redistributed, and all confidential matter destroyed. The engineer officer and his staff were working feverishly to get things in order again and it was hoped to have the main engine working in a few hours, though it was feared that the gears would strip before long.*

At 1300 Stukas were observed and Partridge *was ordered to cast off the tow in order to give her freedom of manoeuvre. No attack developed but an hour later, when* Partridge *was preparing to resume tow, the Italian cruisers hove in sight to eastward. They began to fire at us so* Partridge *was ordered to withdraw and return for us later if she could. She made a smoke-screen round us and then made off to the westward. In the* Bedouin *we ignited all remaining smoke-floats, the enemy for some reason did not close in but once again withdrew.*

At 1415 a Sovoia 79 appeared through the smoke on the starboard beam and dropped a torpedo at a range of 400 yards. The plane was fired on by every gun in the ship. We subsequently heard that it had crashed. The ship had actually begun to move ahead at 4 knots, and the engineer officer was on his way to the bridge to report, but there was nothing to be done but get the men clear of the expected point of impact. The torpedo hit on the bulkhead between the engine room and the gearing room, and the ship at once took a heavy list to port. It was clear that the ship was going to sink so all rafts and float nets were put over the side and the wounded put into them. The order to abandon ship was given and a few minutes later she went down. The motor-dinghy was the only serviceable boat, and with it and the rafts there was just enough to accommodate the survivors.

An officer and nine ratings were rescued by an Italian seaplane. A large number of the crew was picked up by an Italian ship. Among those taken prisoner was Commander Scurfield. After the fall of Italy Scurfield was among prisoners transferred to Marlag Nord at Westertimke near Bremen. On 10 April 1945 the camp, on the approach of the Allies, was moved east on foot. During the afternoon of the next day the rear of the PoW column was attacked by two RAF fighters. Commander Scurfield was among the casualties, losing both legs. He was taken to a hospital at Sven but was beyond help and died that evening.

Bedouin had survived just over 8 hours from the time she had sighted the enemy force. During this period the convoy had of course still been fighting its way towards Malta. There had been two casualties, the *Chant* being sunk and the *Kentucky* disabled. *Kentucky* was taken in tow. Shortly after this the *Burdwan* was disabled in a bombing attack. Both *Kentucky* and *Burdwan* were abandoned, Italian aircraft delivering the *coup de grace*. At 2040 the final aircraft attack on the convoy was beaten off. But the ordeal of the Harpoon ships was not yet over. In the approach route to Valletta the *Orari, Badsworth, Hebe, Matchless,* and *Kujawaik* were mined, but of these only the *Kujawiak* failed to enter harbour.

(Polish) HMS *Kujawiak*

The *Kujawiak* (laid down as HMS *Oakley)* was still under construction at Vickers-Armstrong (Tyne) as a Type II Hunt when on 3 April 1941 it was agreed that on completion she would be handed over for service with the Polish Navy. Command of the new ship, completed the following June, who had been first lieutenant of the *Grom* when she left Gdynia on 30 August 1939 in company with the *Burz* and *Blyskawica.* The three destroyers arrived at Leith two days later for operations with the Royal Navy.

Loss of life was not great when in the early hours of 16 June *Kujawiak* were mined off Malta. At 2240 on the 15th the destroyers were ordered to form single line ahead: *Marne, Middleton, Matchless, Blankney, Badsworth, Ithuriel, Kujawiak.* Six vessels had entered harbour ahead of the destroyers when at 0042 on the 16th a signal was received in *Kujawiak* stating that *Badsworth* had struck a mine. Lieutenant-Commander Lichodziejewski states:

Ithuriel altered course to starboard, to leave Badsworth *on her port side, and resumed her station astern of* Blankney. Kujawiak *asked whether she required assistance. The reply was* 'Yes. I have 120 survivors on board'. *A few seconds later, at 0053/16, a mine exploded on the port quarter of* Kujawiak *under*

No.2 gun platform. The ship immediately listed to port but main engines continued to turn at slow ahead. Engines were stopped. Collision stations were piped. When the ship lost steerageway, the anchor was dropped, the ship bringing up in position 35.52'2"N/14.38'2"E. Depth 40 fathoms. Wind NW force 3, sea and swell 21. A large collision mat was secured on the port side but was not large enough to cover the hole. A small collision mat was secured satisfactorily over the hole on the starboard side. Four after compartments were damaged and oil and water poured in. Steam-ejectors were insufficient to cope with the inrush of water. All guns were trained to starboard, and disengaged personnel ordered to side. The list to port continued to increase quickly, however. All possible lifebelts, rafts, and floats were cut adrift. Depth charges were set to safe and steam safety-valves were opened. All confidential books were dropped overboard in sea-safes and weighted bags. It was not possible to lower boats owing to the degree of the list. The order to abandon ship was given at 0108/16, the angle of list then being over 35 degrees.

Twenty-two-year-old Petty Officer Mieter Muszynski (now Michael MacLean and settled in Scotland) recalls:

After being at action station for many hours, I felt very tired; so, when I saw the shores of Malta, I thought we were safe and I went down to my accommodation to have a sleep in my hammock. I was only there a few minutes when I heard a loud bang and then felt my face hit the deck-head above me. I managed to get out to the upper deck. My face was cut below my right eye, and my right leg was torn below the knee.

Muszynski jumped into the sea.

Kujawiak's captain was fortunate to survive the mining. On the day prior to the Harpoon convoy leaving Britain, General Sikorski in a visit to *Kujawiak* had decorated him with the Virtuti Military, the Polish equivalent of the Victoria Cross. A fellow officer of Lieutenant-Commander Lichodziejewski had recorded:

After his abandon ship order a sudden flash reminded him of his decoration by the Commander-in-Chief only 12 days ago. Without thinking, Commander Lichodziejewski rushed to his cabin, got hold of his most precious order and rolled scroll diploma and then found he couldn't get out. He was on the port side of his quarters and as ORP Kukawiak was heavily listing to port it was not possible to get to the door located on the starboard side. There were no convenient projections to help him climb up the steeply sloping floor. At this moment Chief Petty Officer Moszczynksi (died in ORP Orkan) checking that no wounded crew members were forgotten anywhere in the ship, glanced into his commanding officer's cabin. To his amazement there was his CO unsuccessfully trying to reach the door. Moszczynski called for help and with the last available seaman on board lifted Commander Lichodziejewski off his cabin. 'Thank you, chief', said the CO officially, 'Now jump!'

Ninety seconds after they jumped into the sea, *Kujawiak's* bows reared up and she sank stern first. Just over 27 minutes had passed since the mine exploded. Thirteen of the crew were lost.

Lieutenant-Commander Lichodziejewski, who had been decorated with the British DSO by Admiral of the Fleet Sir Andrew Cunningham, took command of the destroyer *Blyskawice*. After the war he settled in America. He died in April 1974, aged sixty-nine, and the following month was buried in Poland. A gallant officer.

HMS *Wild Swan*

The last of the seven destroyers lost between 12 and 17 June was *Wild Swan*. Her captain, Lieutenant-Commander Claude Sclater, had been her CO since August 1940.

Convoy HG84 sailed from Gibraltar at 1930 on 9 June. Escort to the twenty ships was the sloop *Stork* and corvettes *Gardenia*, *Convolvulus*, and *Marigold*. *Wild Swan* and *Beagle* sailed from Gibraltar at 1800 the following evening to join HG84. It was the intention of both destroyers to detach from the convoy after a day and proceed to England where a refit awaited them. They met up with the convoy at 1100 on 11 June. The following afternoon three merchantmen joined the convoy from Lisbon. At 2000 that evening Sclater left HG84 and proceeded independently for home, arriving at Plymouth on the morning of the 15th. *Wild Swan* had been away for a year. It was good to be home.

When on the 15th the convoy came under U-boat attack the ability of its escort to protect their charges fully was stretched to the limit: at one time the convoy had only the *Convolvulus* as close escort, the other ships being engaged elsewhere. The first torpedo to strike hit the *Pelayo*. Four other merchantmen were hit in quick succession. Rescuers picked up 172 survivors. All five ships had been sunk by Korvettenkapitan Erich Topp of U552.

Wild Swan had no sooner arrived at Plymouth when, to the dismay of all hands, she was ordered to prepare for a return to HG84. Seven hours after having gone alongside, *Wild Swan* had refuelled, rearmed, and had taken on some provisions. She sailed as ordered, rejoining the convoy around mid-afternoon on 16 June. More reinforcements joined later. The night passed without incident.

At 1600 on the 17th *Wild Swan* left the convoy for a return to Plymouth. Later, a Kondor reconnaissance plane was seen heading towards the convoy and the drone of more aircraft was heard by *Wild Swan* at 2115, 90 minutes after the Kondor sighting. These were twelve JU88s in search of the convoy. Just at this time *Wild Swan* was passing through a formation of about a dozen Spanish trawlers, each of about 150 tons, at a point roughly 230 miles west of the Isles of Scilly. Sighting what they assumed to be ships of the convoy they were seeking, the JU88s prepared for an attack.

At 2131 two JU88s suddenly appeared from out of the clouds. During their run in towards a target the planes collided, one diving into the sea and the other crashing onto a trawler. From another attack four bombs exploded close to *Wild Swan*, breaking her back and bringing down the mast. The after boiler room and engine room were flooded and her engines stopped. *Wild Swan* gradually lost way as she circled with her rudder jammed hard to starboard. She had slowed to about 5 knots when, still out of control, her bows struck the trawler *Nuevo Con*. The trawler's crew were taken on board *Wild Swan* as their boat sank beneath them. An attack by two or more planes ended with both of them being hit by gunfire and crashing into the sea. Another plane was shot out of the sky. *Wild Swan* was seriously damaged by another bomber, which was hit by gunfire and crashed into sea to become the last of six aircraft destroyed in the battle. Satisfied that *Wild Swan* was sinking, the remaining aircraft terminated the 45 minutes engagement.

The Spanish fishing fleet had lost four of its number. *Wild Swan*, sagging amidships, made an SOS and prepared to abandon ship. She had broken in two and at 2315 sank in two parts, the after part sinking a little ahead of the upturned bows. The following day the destroyer *Vansittart* rescued 144 survivors, including eleven Spaniards from the *Nuevo Con*. Thirty-one of *Wild Swan's* crew did not survive the action.

A vital convoy to Malta, codenamed Pedestal, assembled in England during August. The convoy was considered so important that at times the escorting warships outnumbered the merchant ships by four to one. Big gun protection came from two battleships and seven cruisers. Twenty-four destroyers were also in the show. Air cover was provided by the carriers *Furious and Eagle*. As well as protecting the convoy *Eagle* was at sea to fly Spitfires to Malta. The convoy entered the Mediterranean on the night of 10/11 August. Five of the fourteen merchantmen fought through to Malta. Not being the main target, the escorts fared better: the *Eagle* was sunk almost as soon as she entered the Mediterranean and the cruiser *Manchester* was badly damaged and had to be sunk. The destroyer *Foresight* was another fatal casualty.

HMS *Foresight*

Foresight, Lieutenant-Commander Robert Fell, was to the north of Galite Island when at 1845 on 12 June an Italian aircraft released a torpedo at her during one of the many air attacks on the convoy. The torpedo hit to starboard abreast the steering compartment. *Foresight's* back was broken and her stern dropped 7 feet. Her main engines were still workable but only with a strong vibration even at the slowest speed. *Tartar,* Commander St John Tyrwhitt, was detached to stand-by *Foresight:*

> *It was my intention to tow* Foresight *to the westward in the dark and rely on the attention of the enemy being drawn to more valuable targets.* Foresight *could not steer and could only steam at about 2 knots. The flooding situation aft in* Foresight *seemed to be in hand. The tow was passed by 1930, the commanding officer of* Foresight *having been informed that in the event of a heavy attack I should slip the tow. Unfortunately when taking the weight of the tow at about 1935, a group of five Beaufighters (which were not recognized) dived at the ships.* Foresight *thought I would slip and went ahead. I did not slip, not having seen them, and* Foresight, *who was broad on my starboard quarter, rode up alongside and the towing wire fouled my starboard propeller. This caused considerable delay. The tow was passed for the second time at about 2040. During the operation one JU88 dived low over the ship and dropped two depth charges which landed about 50 feet on the starboard quarter but no damage was sustained. At about 2030, just as the westerly course was attained, one cruiser and two destroyers were sighted against the light, bearing 320 degrees about 1,000 yards distant. Having no up to date knowledge of friendly forces and an enemy report having been received of a similar force which could possibly have attained this position, the tow was parted and* Tartar *remained between* Foresight *and the approaching forces until ready to engage. By this time it was thought that it might be a 5.25 cruiser, but the speed was increased to 30 knots, the attack commenced and the challenge made. The force eventually proved to be friendly. A considerable amount of time was wasted trying to get into touch with the force so that another destroyer could take* Foresight *in tow,* Tartar's *wires being now depleted, but, this being unsuccessful, at about 2230* Foresight *was in tow alongside and course set to pass south of Galite.*
>
> *At 0515/13 the tow-spring parted and with it the preventer which had been rigged in case this occurred.* Foresight *was taken in tow astern again at 0610, it being considered that the risk of towing alongside could not be accepted in daylight owing to the difficulty in getting clear in the event of attack. At 0815 in position 218 degrees Galite 13 miles a seaplane thought to be a Cant shadower was sighted. At 0930 another was sighted and at the same time a periscope seen on the port beam. The tow was once again parted, and a counter-attack commenced. No contact was made but the area was liberally covered with depth charges. It had been my intention to continue towing during daylight providing this remained feasible and that I was not continually shadowed. The low risk of an attack appeared to be acceptable in view of the more attractive targets elsewhere. The risk of surface attack, though negligible, and that of submarine attack, though considerable, was acceptable in the flat-calm weather conditions prevailing and with the efficient*

lookout expected after a submarine salvo had been avoided the previous day; on the other hand Foresight *could not steer. The little movement of the engines possible increased the flooding of her engine room, which was barely being kept in check. The remainder of the after part was flooded. Even in light airs her list forced her to be far out on my starboard quarter, and to tow her in any wind would have been impossible, 7 knots being the maximum speed attained in calm weather. At this juncture two shadowers had appeared in an hour and a quarter. A submarine was suspected to be in the vicinity and it had become clear that towing was dependent on there being no wind during the passage to Gibraltar. Consequently the decision was made to sink* Foresight *and clear the danger area at high speed.*

Commander Tyrwhitt went alongside *Foresight* and eight officers and 173 ratings were transferred to *Tartar*. At 0955 *Foresight* was torpedoed and sunk. Tyrwhitt set off at 27 knots to rejoin the convoy. Shadowing aircraft were engaged frequently. At 1735 the cruiser *Nigeria* was sighted. *Tartar* joined the cruiser's screen.

Two weeks after the loss of *Foresight* an Italian torpedo also ended the active service days of *Eridge*. She became a constructive total loss in August following an attack by the famous Italian special forces unit Decima Flottiglia MAS.

HMS *Eridge*

In the early hours of Saturday 29 August the *Eridge*, Lieutenant-Commander William Gregory-Smith, was bombarding in company with other destroyers the area of El Daba, 35 miles west of El Alamein. *Eridge* was just over 2 miles from the shore, and had completed her bombardment, when at 0456 she was hit to starboard by a torpedo while proceeding at 20 knots. The ship came to a halt.

The Italian MAS unit had only recently arrived in the vicinity of El Daba and was encamped in tents with their motor torpedo boats moored near the shore. The destroyers were still bombarding when Sottotenente di Vascello Piero Carminati and his fellow crewman swam out to the only motor-boat available. He then made towards the destroyers, guided by gun flashes. Selecting *Eridge* as target, Caraminati fired a torpedo from 170 yards, scoring a hit. The small motor-boat came under fire from the ships and as it sped away the boat was attacked by an aircraft. A Fire broke out in the motor-boat. The two-man crew was hurled into the water by a bomb exploding a few feet from the boat just as they left their seats to try and put out the flames. Both swam ashore.

Caraminati's torpedo blew a 20 feet hole from the keel up to within 3 feet of *Eridge's* upper deck. The engine room and gearing room flooded to about a foot of the upper deck port side. All electric power was lost. *Eridge*, with a heavy list to port, was taken in tow for Alexandria by *Aldenham*. Damage to *Eridge* was so extensive that she was made an accommodation ship at Alexandria, where she was scrapped in 1946.

HMS *Berkley*

The 19 August assault on the French port of Dieppe (Operation Jubilee) was to establish whether it would be possible to capture a port during the Allied invasion of Normandy. The Jubilee force had a strength of just over 6,000, of which almost 5,000 were Canadian troops. Of the eight Hunt class destroyers in the force only the *Berkley* failed to return. Supply Assistant Thomas Hare served in *Berkley:*

> Berkley *sailed from the south coast with the rest of the assault force on the evening of 18 August. It was a relatively quiet crossing until the early morning skirmish with a small German coastal convoy. This incident seemed to be the prelude of the frightening hours that lay ahead, hours which were a living nightmare to the 5,000 or so men of the armed forces who fought that day in and around the town of Dieppe. The surprise element which undoubtedly was the mainspring of the attack had been upset by the coastal convoy, and Hitler's reception party awaited our arrival.*
>
> *Very soon after the* Berkley *reached the coastal waters of Dieppe we suffered our first casualties when the for'ad twin 4–inch gun was hit by shore batteries and most of its crew were injured. But throughout the morning and early afternoon we kept up a steady bombardment with the rear gun of strategic targets in Dieppe and attacked as best we could the many enemy aircraft in the skies above. After the order for the withdrawal from the beaches had gone out,* Berkley's *last mission, I understand, was to penetrate Dieppe harbour and capture one of the barges that, it was thought, Hitler was at that time preparing for his invasion of Britain. But* Berkley *never reached the harbour. Landing craft loaded with Canadian troops were making their way back from the beaches and* Berkley *stopped to take on board men from the four regiments that had taken part in the frontal attack on the town. Some forty to fifty men of these famous regiments came on board happy in the thought that soon they would be on their way back to England. Of the men we took on board many were badly wounded and all were suffering from shock and exhaustion from a battle far more horrible than anything for which they had been prepared, or the top brass had led them to believe. The walking wounded and a handful who had miraculously escaped injury ashore were shepherded down to the ratings mess decks. We tried to make them as comfortable as possible. Cigarettes were handed round and I can remember one Canadian soldier declining to be third to light a cigarette from one match with the remark,* 'We've pushed our luck to the very limit today. Let's not push it any further'. *But even the avoidance of the third light was not to save him when in the next few minutes the German Air Force struck.*

The *Berkley* was Jeffrey Knight's first ship and by August 1942 he had been serving in her 16 months. He recalls:

At the time of the Dieppe raid I was the leading signalman on board the Berkley and together with the yeoman and signalman was at action station on the bridge from the early part of the middle watch. On arrival off Dieppe each destroyer, having been given a target on which to concentrate its fire, took up its appointed station. Unfortunately during the forenoon our twin 4-inch AA for'ad guns were put out of action by enemy shore batteries, thus making the forecastle area vulnerable. However, we were still able to continue firing with our twin AA 4-inch guns aft. During the operation we had the heart-rending job of rescuing many Canadian soldiers, many severely wounded. With the forward guns out of action no ammunition supply party was needed, so the soldiers were taken to the forward mess deck until it was filled to capacity. Soon after this the flotilla received orders to return to Portsmouth, but before Berkley could carry them out disaster struck.

Scanning the skies for enemy aircraft, as is a signalman's duty, in reporting the approach of enemy aircraft I actually saw two bombs leave the plane. With Berkley having no forward guns in action, the plane scored a hit on the forecastle with the blast penetrating the bridge. All the Canadians on the mess deck were killed. We had a Major Hillsinger of the American Army on the bridge as an observer; he had his foot cut off by a part of the metalwork of the director. An RAF officer was also on the operation as an observer. The state of his internal parts indicated there was no hope for him. His life was ebbing fast. In an attempt to alleviate his pain the first lieutenant administered a shot of morphine. The coxswain and quartermaster in the wheelhouse were literally blown to pieces. I considered myself fortunate in that I received a shrapnel wound just above my right eye and the signal table landed on my leg. It was rather difficult to see much in those circumstances but all the bridge personnel one way or another threaded their way through the chaos to the upper deck, with the exception of the RAF officer who had died.

A steam gunboat was laying alongside. Most of the ship's company was taken on board her. Some of the after gun's crew when the bomb struck the ship dived over the side and swam to the *Albrighton* where they gave additional help to the gunners.

The order had at 1240 been given for all ships to assemble 4 miles off Dieppe. It was about 1300 when three Dorniers had approached *Berkeley*. These were engaged by British fighters and during this action one of the Dorniers jettisoned its bombs, two of which hit *Berkeley*. As *Berkeley* remained stubbornly afloat, the *Albrighton* was ordered to sink her. A torpedo blew the bows off *Berkeley*. Another torpedoed was fired and *Berkeley* disappeared in a huge cloud of smoke. Her captain, Lieutenant John Yorke, later took command of *Tynedale*.

* * *

Within a month of Operation Jubilee the garrison of Tobruk also became the object of an Allied raid. The Allies at Tobruk had surrendered on the morning of 21 June 1942. Three months later British plans went ahead for a raid on Tobruk harbour which, if successful, would assist the British 8th Army's breakout and advance from El Alamein. The object of the raid was to take control of Tobruk for 12 hours and in that time to render it completely useless as a means of supplying the Afrika Korps.

Operation Agreement entailed the use of three assault groups: Forces A, B and C. Force A consisted of 380 Royal Marines. They were to go ashore from the Tribals *Sikh* and *Zulu* in crudely constructed plywood landing craft, hopelessly inadequate for the job. Force B consisted of more than seventy commandos. Masquerading as POWs they would at the appointed hour enter Tobruk from the desert in three-ton trucks. Their 'guards' were German Jews of the Special Identification Group working with the Allies. Force C, the Argyll and Sutherland Highlanders and the Royal Northumberland Fusilliers, would arrive in motorboats at a bay immediately south of Tobruk harbour. Forces B and C would link up in attempt to hold back the inevitable counter-attack. For this narrative only the activities of *Sikh* and *Zulu* are related.

HMS *Sikh*

On Sunday 13 September at 0545 the *Sikh*, Captain St John Micklethwait, and *Zulu*, Commander Richard White, sailed from Alexandria with the marines and their landing craft. By 0300 they were off the beach where the marines were to make ships appear to resemble Italian destroyers. After landing the marines *Sikh* and *Zulu* were to break through the boom at Tobruk harbour. They were then to destroy whatever they could in the way of shipping. After that they would list ship to 15 degrees, light fires on the upper deck, and make smoke. It was hoped that this ruse would lead enemy aircraft to believe that they were Italian destroyers in a sinking condition. By 0348 the first contingent of marines were heading towards the beach. *Sikh* and *Zulu* moved seaward for 25 minutes. They then closed the shore in readiness to meet the returning craft and send a second detail shoreward. An observer in *Zulu* comments:

> *Nothing much happened to us after that for almost an hour. Anti-aircraft fire ashore ceased and the searchlights went out after a last tired sweep of the sea and sky. Then Tobruk disappeared in utter darkness and became as silent as a dead city. We spent some time wondering what was happening to the boys in the landing craft. Suddenly, just after 0500, a searchlight or two flickered on and began waving across the sea as if seeking something. Apparently the alarm had been given on land. We had not long to wait for this to be confirmed. Bright flashes flickered against the blackness, followed by thumps, and then the eerie moan of shells came to us on the bridge. The shore batteries were firing at us.*

Sikh was the first to be gripped by the searchlights. She then came under fire. A hit damaged the forced lubrication system to the main engine gearing, making it likely that the main engines would seize. Further, her steering was put out of effective control. Fiercely ablaze forward, *Sikh* at 10 knots went round in circles. At 0250 Captain Micklethwait signalled *Zulu* that the *Sikh* had been seriously damaged. Twenty-five minutes later White was ordered to take *Sikh* in tow. The *Zulu*, herself damaged by gunfire, closed *Sikh*. Commander White, in a fine display of seamanship, brought round *Zulu's* stern to meet *Sikh's* bow. Unfortunately owing to a combination of factors the line from *Zulu* was not taken up. The two ships were by now easy targets for the shore batteries and were repeatedly hit. Another fire broke out aft in *Sikh*.

In the grey light of dawn the destroyers' activities were clearly visible from the shore as Commander White manoeuvred for another attempt at passing a line. Though the line was successfully passed it snapped after being made fast. White circled and came in to try again. A line was passed and the hawser that followed made fast in *Sikh*. Then by a cruel stroke of luck the hawser was parted by a shell which struck *Zulu's* quarter-deck. For *Sikh* the freak hit on the hawser spelt the end. Both destroyers had received considerable punishment and it was by then broad daylight. A fourth attempt by *Zulu* to pass a tow was forbidden by Captain Micklethwait. *Wait Ten Minutes*, was his reply to White's signal as to whether he should draw alongside the *Sikh* to take off the crew. In *Zulu* it was assumed that the order to wait ten minutes was to enable *Sikh* to make smoke to cover the transfer. *Zulu* was also making smoke when towards 0710 she was signalled by *Sikh* to leave the area. Coastal guns were hitting both ships with ease. It was now too hazardous for *Zulu* to remain within range of the enemy guns. Commander White with the greatest reluctance, turned away. *Goodbye. God Bless You*, signalled White. *Thanks. Cheerio*, was the brief reply. A *Zulu* eye-witness states:

With heavy hearts we turned out to sea and raced away. There were still a few landing craft round Sikh, *but it was impossible to tell whether those contained further installments of troops who were to land, or some who had returned from shore. For the next 10 minutes the batteries continued to fire at us and shells whistled down fairly close, but now we were moving at high speed and every second getting farther away. No further hits were scored on this ship, but I fear that Axis gunners had the easiest target of a lifetime in the* Sikh. *While we were racing away, and until she slipped out of sight behind the horizon, shore guns continued to fire at her. I could see the columns of water leaping up on all sides of the stricken vessel, and smoke pouring from her. But Sikh refused to give in. For every flash from the shore guns, I saw a defiant answering flash from the guns of the crippled ship. I could still see those flashes when she was nothing more than a tiny speck at the base of a huge column of dirty grey smoke.*

X gun, the last of *Sikh's* 4.7s to keep firing, fell silent only when its ammunition ran out. With *Zulu* having gone, *Sikh* took the full anger of every gun within range. Around 0800 Captain Micklethwait ordered abandon ship. *Sikh* had no boats, their place having been taken up by landing craft. Carley rafts were lowered for the wounded, and anything floatable was thrown overboard. Scuttling charges were detonated and Captain Micklethwait went below to check that *Sikh* was flooding. Satisfied with the result, he returned to the upper deck and jumped into the sea. Thirty minutes later he saw his command go down.

HMS *Zulu*
The cruiser *Coventry*, Captain Ronald Dendy, was on her way to meet *Zulu* when, at 1125 on 14 September, more than a dozen Stukas attacked *Coventry*, which had six Hunts in company. *Coventry* was gravely damaged. Too near a hostile coast and too far from a friendly harbour for towing, Captain Dendy ordered her sunk. As *Coventry's* scuttling charges had been removed, *Dulverton* was ordered to sink her with torpedoes. Unfortunately none of the Hunts were equipped with torpedo tubes. *Zulu* would have to sink her.

A little after 0850 a lone Stuka attacked *Zulu* but failed to hit her. At 1116 several planes attacked her but again failed to score. A third attack at 1234 was beaten off. Two hours later another attack also failed. Shortly after this White sighted the burning *Coventry*. He then came under attack by five aircraft. Still damage free, he reduced to 12 knots and positioned for sinking *Coventry*. White fired two torpedoes and hit with both. At 1505 *Coventry* was on her way to the bottom of the Mediterranean. Soon after this the *Zulu* was attacked by a half dozen Stukas, but again she escaped damage. At 25 knots the British raced eastward.

After almost an hour went by without being attacked, the situation began to be viewed with greater confidence. But at 1600 six JU88s and twelve Stukas found the ships. A determined and concentrated attack was thrown at *Zulu*. The planes attacked from every quarter, allowing *Zulu* little room for manoeuvre. For much of the attack Commander White was able to keep *Zulu* out of harms way. Then a bomb hit the ship. The bomb passed through to the engine room where it exploded, causing such damage that the engine room, a boiler room, and the gearing room became flooded. *Zulu* came to a stop and settled 2 feet deeper. *Croome* was ordered alongside to take off marines and all hands with the exception of a towing party. *Hursley* took *Zulu* in tow.

Aircraft again attacked but it was a small raid and was driven off without difficulty. Around 1900 there came the final attack of the day. No bombs were dropped, but *Zulu* was strafed. It soon became evident that *Zulu* would not remain afloat long enough to reach Alexandria, about 100 miles away. *Zulu* was well down in the water and sinking rapidly when *Hursley* was ordered to release the tow. *Croome* was closing to take off White and the towing party when *Zulu* suddenly began to sink at a rate which took everyone by surprise. She rolled to starboard. Those still on board *Zulu* were hurled across the deck and into the sea. They were rescued by *Croome*. Captain Micklethwait was taken prisoner. He retired from the navy in December 1953 as a rear-admiral. Commander (later Captain) Richard White retired from the service in 1955.

* * *

HMS *Veteran*

Returning to the Atlantic theatre of operations, the convoy, which in September assembled at St John's, was not quite the usual assortment of shipping that made up an Atlantic convoy. It was in fact a special convoy. Designated RB1 it consisted of Coast Line ships from Canada's Great Lakes. The ships had been disguised to resemble troop transports. Their escort was the old V class destroyers *Veteran* and *Vanoc*. Almost a year had passed since they had been in a home port. They had been working out of Nova Scotia, escorting convoys halfway across the Atlantic and then returning to harbour for further duties. The crews of both ships were delighted to be going home. Leading Seaman James Reed was serving in *Vanoc:*

> *Our shore clothes were neatly stacked away in lockers until the next leave, we could never tell when that would be, and out came out sea gear. What a strange assortment! Civilian shirts and jackets, fur and woollen headgear, miles of scarves, sea-boots, and socks in every colour of the rainbow, representing football clubs back home. In oilskins and duffle coats, no two men were dressed alike, but all were wrapped up against the bitter cold and fury of those angry, menacing seas. Warmth and comfort was preferred to smartness on these little ships. We often wondered what our mates on the big 'uns would say if they saw us.*
>
> *One other destroyer was making the same preparations. HMS* Veteran*; a name that could not have suited her better. A great comradeship existed between this ship and ours. We always seemed to fight our way through together. With the good-hearted remarks from other escorts ringing in our ears, the two destroyers slipped away, cleared the harbour and headed for the open sea. In the distance we could see the dim outline of the assembled ships that we would have to nurse all the way across the Atlantic. They did not appear to be the usual cargo vessels. There was something different about them. Some looked remarkably like troopships, and a few resembled some of our more famous liners. As we came closer I blinked and rubbed my eyes in amazement. They were in fact, old ships of the steamboat type one would expect to see on the Mississippi. I counted fourteen ships, all with superstructure jutting from the water, false funnels and dummy fittings.*

James Reed may have counted fourteen ships but only eight of them comprised the special RB1 convoy. At 1400 on 21 September the convoy sailed from St John's. The eight merchantmen were deployed in four columns. There was no attack on the convoy until 1400 on 25 September when the *Boston* was hit and sunk by two torpedoes from U261. Around nine that night, the *New York* was sunk by U96. The convoy had come under attack by boats of the Vorwarts group. U404 of this group had been five weeks out of St Nazaire on her fourth patrol. She has been one of ten boats that had just attacked convoy 127. In these attacks her captain, Korvettenkapitan Otto von Bulow, had torpedoed two Norwegian tankers, though one had eventually made harbour. He had been ordered to close RB1.

On 26 September U404 was surfaced when, at 1035, her captain fired a spread of three torpedoes at *Veteran* from seven hundred yards. *Veteran* was steaming to rejoin the convoy after rescuing survivors from *New York*. In the U-boat three explosions were heard in the U-boat during the next 2 minutes. As U404 retired after the attack, and as there was no survivors from *Veteran*, there was no witness to the destroyer going down. *Vance* received no communication as to what was taking place aboard ship.

Veteran had been attacked roughly 650 miles to the west of Ireland. On learning of the sinking the C-in-C Western Approaches directed two corvettes to make a search, but nothing from *Veteran* was discovered. Apart from *Veteran's* eight officers and 151 ratings, there was on board fifty survivors from the *Boston* and another thirty from *New York*. All had perished.

After one further loss the RB1 convoy arrived in the United Kingdom. The special convoy had crossed the Atlantic without cargo or passengers, leading those who had taken part to assume that RB1 had been a decoy convoy which had sailed to enable a fast troop convoy, well to the north, to make the crossing safely. Lieutenant-Commander Trevor Garwood, *Veteran's* CO, was the son of an engineer rear-admiral. He had entered Dartmouth in 1928. Garwood had at one time served in the boys' training establishment HMS *Ganges*. Korvettenkapitan von Bulow had taken command of U404 in 1941 following a period as captain of U3. The war was near its end when he became commander of the 1st Naval Armed Battalion, North Germany.

*   *   *

In November 1942 the Allies carried out Operation Torch: an Anglo-American force invaded the Vichy-French colonies of Morocco and Algeria in North Africa with the object of seizing the ports of Casablanca, Oran, and Algeria. For the assault on Algiers it was envisaged that twenty thousand troops would be needed to take the town and the airfields at Blida and Maison Blanche. Among the sixty-seven warships taking part were thirteen destroyers, and of these the

Broke, Lieutenant-Commander Arthur Layard, and *Malcolm,* Commander A. B. Russell, are involved in this narrative.

In the early hours of Sunday 8 November three task forces were in their area of operation. At 0140 Rear-Admiral Harold Burrough ordered *Broke* and *Malcolm* to begin Operation Terminal, a plan to prevent the enemy at Algeria from scuttling ships and destroying harbour installations. The operation involved *Broke* and *Malcolm* entering harbour via its southern entrance. After securing at a jetty the ships would prepare to land three companies of American troops.

HMS *Broke*

By 0435 the *Broke* and *Malcolm* were in the vicinity of the harbour's southern entrance. The dark background of hills, the strong dazzle of searchlights, and enemy gunfire, made finding the entrance very difficult. Starshell was fired but still the entrance remained undetected. At 0407 the *Malcolm* was hit by gunfire. Damaged in her boiler room, she withdrew. Another attempt by *Broke* to find the elusive entrance ended in failure. Then at 0520 more than 90 minutes of frustrating search came to an end when just as dawn was breaking, the entrance was sighted. Ordering full speed ahead Layard made a dash towards the entrance boom. Bursting through he pushed on towards a jetty 600 yards ahead. An enemy minesweeper fired at *Broke* but this did not prevent her from securing alongside to land her troops. Though enemy snipers and machine-gunners made conditions uncomfortable, the situation for a while was not untenable. However, during the next 2 hours Layard had twice to change berth because of fire from a harbour battery 1 mile away at the northern entrance. Around 0915 *Broke* came under fire from another quarter. Facing gunfire from several directions greatly increased the danger of *Broke* becoming seriously damaged, and possibly sunk. Captain H. ST J. Fancourt, who commanded Operation Terminal from *Broke,* decided to withdraw the ship, the troops were recalled. Casting off, *Broke* proceeded across the harbour against strong enemy fire. She was being hit repeatedly and sustained heavy damage. On clearing harbour, which she had entered four hours earlier, *Broke* took a north–east course. The *Zetland,* one of the Hunts, took *Broke* in tow, both ships at one stage colliding with each other. The situation was held more or less in hand until the following day when a deterioration in the weather, together with the extensive damage of the previous day's action, caused *Broke* to founder. Those still on board were rescued by *Zetland.*

HMS *Martin*

Operation Torch was into its third day when the *Martin* was sunk by U431. *Martin* had been in commission about 6 months when on 2 November she arrived at Gibraltar for Torch. The *Martin* was Signalman George Parker's first ship:

We anchored in the bay. Not since before the war had such a fleet been assembled at the Rock: battle-ships, carriers, cruisers, destroyers, and supply vessels. Strict security was in force. No shore leave was granted. We left Gibraltar and steamed into the Med. When we had formed up it was a sight to see: as far as the eye could see there was a vast collection of steel and firepower. The odd air attacks were driven off, but compared to the Russian runs this was a picnic, and warm weather as a bonus. We steamed west to east, east to west, and it would have become rather boring had not the admiral been obsessed with flag exercises at sea, the flagship making sure that we were awake. The admiral's favourite exercise was to quote passages from the Bible by lamp. Ships had to give the answer by flags, and woe betides any ship that didn't know their Bible. Geordie Newton and I had the middle watch, that is midnight to 0400. On 9/10 November Martin's position at this time was approximately 200 miles off Algeria. At about 0255 the OOW called down the voice pipe to inform the captain that we were to execute an alteration of course at 0300. The captain acknowledged and said he was coming up to the bridge. Normally the OOW would make any small alteration of the course, but any major alterations were the captain's responsibility. About 1 minute later there was an enormous explosion astern on the starboard side. By this time the captain had joined us on the bridge. Seconds later there was another explosion amidships. Martin listed violently to starboard. I was thrown against the Oerlikon (AA gun) platform. Before I could catch my breath a third explosion in the bow nearly turned her over. This third and last explosion lifted me bodily and blew me into the sea. Having my life-jacket inflated I popped to the surface like a cork. There were flames everywhere from burning oil. I heard cries for help, and men screaming in the dark. I swallowed quite a lot of oil (we had only topped up with a fuel oil the day before). A Carley float was near-by. It must have been torn free. I grabbed it and hauled myself inboard. In between coughing and choking on the oil, my shipmates and I tried to locate men in the water. Bodies floated by. The red lights attached to life-jackets were bobbing in the distance. The Carley float was soon full. To my recollection we did not appear to have any maimed or torn limbs among the survivors. Martin was gone in a flash and soon all that remained of her was oil and debris. A sad end to a fine ship and an excellent crew. Sometime later, after trying to identify voices in the float, one could not recognize faces as we were all covered in oil, one wit remarked, 'Well, I got out of the morning watch'.

Dawn came. Thank God the water was warm; I shudder to think what would have happened had we been in Arctic waters. We had an officer in the float with us; I don't recall him, but he was probably Lieutenant Cavanagh. After being adrift for some 6 hours or more, I spotted a mast on the horizon, the sea being very calm. I suppose that being trained in visual signalling, and being blessed with good eyesight, it was not unusual for me to spot the mast first. 'A ship, a ship', I shouted, upon which everyone started jumping and shouting, and nearly capsized the float. In all this excitement very few of us shared the officer's concern that the ship might be the enemy. But this was no enemy; it was the destroyer HMS Quentin *which had been detached from the fleet to search for survivors.*

Martin had been sunk while proceeding at 16 knots to the north-east of Algiers. Lieutenant Charles Cavanagh reports:

At 0259 on the morning of 10 November a violent explosion occurred. This was followed almost immediately by a second and a third explosion. It is though that the explosions were caused by three torpedoes, the first of which struck the ship abaft the forward cabin flat approximately abreast of No.86 bulkhead. The cabin flat and wardroom immediately burst into flames. A second torpedo struck between 20 and 27 bulkheads, blowing off A turret and the forecastle and causing extensive fires in the remaining mess decks. Flames were observed coming up B turret's hoists. It is estimated that the third torpedo struck abreast the gearing room. All lights were extinguished with this explosion. Approximately 30 seconds elapsed between the first and third explosions. All torpedoes appeared to come from the starboard side. Shortly after the third explosion the ship listed heavily to starboard and stated to settle by the bows. It is estimated that the bridge was under water within 2 minutes of the first explosion. The ship eventually settled with the stern floating at an angle of about 60 degrees and remained in that position for about 20 minutes. On finally sinking at least one depth charge exploded.

The *Quentin* picked up a sixty-three survivors. Commander Charles Thomson and six of his officers and 154 ratings had perished. The attack on *Martin* had been made by Kapitanleutnant Wilhelm Dommes of U431. Dommes, serving in *Scharnhorst* when war broke out, had been in the navy 12 years and in command of U431 for 19 months. He survived the war.

HMS *Ithuriel*
Operation Torch was a resounding success, all objectives quickly falling to the Allies. On 12 November British parachutists supported by commandos landing from seawards occupied Bone, 3 miles east of Algiers. Two weeks later the *Ithuriel* was bombed in Bone harbour. On the night of 27/28 November the *Ithuriel* was Emergency destroyer, and hence at immediate notice for steam. She was on slip-wires, berthed alongside the merchant ship *Cartland* on the north quay of the large basin at Bone. *Ithuriel* was at action stations for air attack. Main armament and close range weapons were intermittently in action. At about 0050 on the 28th two bombs fell, within seconds of each other, close to *Ithuriel*. The first bomb plunged into the sea a few feet from the ship and exploded beneath the after magazine and shell room. The second bomb fell abreast the engine room and closer to *Ithuriel* than the first. This bomb exploded under the ship. Reports of flooding were soon received on the bridge.

All available pumps were brought into operation. When it became clear that the pumps were not coping, her captain, Lieutenant-Commander David Maitland-Makgill-Crichton, requested pumping assistance. The *Quentin* was ordered alongside *Ithuriel* to fulfil this need. A collision mat was placed over the hole in the ship's bottom and the starboard side of the engine room. Damage parties were employed in shoring up bulkheads.

It was decided to move *Ithuriel* to a berth where shore pumps could be made available. *Quentin* towed her to another quay and pumps ashore were connected. As the day wore on, the extent of the damage was determined. It was apparent that her back was broken in two places and that her stern was sagging more and more. After consultation with his engineer officer and shipwrights Maitland-Makgill-Crichton was of the opinion that he should beach the ship, reasoning that she could be salved when and if required, and in little worse conditions than now she was. Apart from the sagging stern which was growing worse by the minute, to tow *Ithuriel* to a repair port would be hazardous operation with repairs taking at least 18 months. Another point for consideration was that she was now occupying a valuable berth, alongside which she must on no account be allowed to founder. So, on the afternoon of 29 November a tug beached *Ithuriel* on a sandy, shelving bottom. As many fittings as possible were disembarked. *Ithuriel* was declared a constructive total loss and was reduced to care and maintenance. She was later towed to the United Kingdom and broken up.

HMS *Quentin*

It was from Bone that the *Quentin* sailed on her final sortie. Fighter protection over Bone having been strengthened, Admiral Cunningham was, on 30 November, able to base at Bone ships that made up Force Q, the cruisers *Aurora*, *Argonaut*, and *Sirius*, and the destroyers *Quentin* and *Quilberon* (RAN). On the night of 1/2 December Force Q was sweeping the waters between the western end of Sicily and the north Tunisian coast in search of an Italian convoy comprising two troop transports and two supply ships. Three destroyers and two torpedo-boats made up the escort. The convoy had been attacked the previous day by a British submarine. Although this had failed, the submarine had signalled the convoy's position. The RAF located the convoy and after dark worked at keeping it illuminated with flares until Force Q could intercept, which it did around 0030 at a point 60 miles north-east of Bizerta. As the British ships wanted to attack out of the darkness with the use of radar, the aircraft ceased to illuminate the convoy.

The British guns opened fire. In a gallant attempt by the Italian destroyers to cover the fleeing convoy, the *Folgore* was sunk and another destroyer damaged and forced to withdraw. A German munitions ship erupted in a deafening explosion. One of the transports was hit and sunk, while the other drifted away on fire and belching smoke. A merchant ship made an effort to escape into the darkness. She was pursued and shelled. Cables securing tanks to her deck snapped as she heeled over and tanks went sliding into the sea among the swimmers. By 0130 the fighting was over. Force Q emerged from the encounter undamaged, but did not return to harbour without loss.

The five ships were proceeding in line ahead when, at 0615 at a point 50 miles 048 degrees from Cape de Garde, an enemy aircraft released a torpedo which struck *Quentin* to starboard. Visibility was about a mile. The torpedo hit *Quentin* about 8 feet forward of the after bulkhead of the engine room, blowing the forward torpedo tube mounting overboard and collapsing the starboard Oerlikon platform. The after boiler room, engine room, and gearing room were at once flooded, as were the shaft tunnels and gland spaces. Owing to damage, no means of pumping was available. Soon after the attack, and as *Quentin* was so gravely damaged, the *Quiberon* secured alongside and transferred the crew. Around 30 minutes later *Quentin* again came under an aircraft attack. Approaching port side, an Italian plane released a torpedo which struck amidship. *Quentin* appeared to break in two and there was a heavy explosion. Debris fell almost a mile from the ship. About 15 seconds after this hit, *Quentin* sank by the stern, a sad sight for her captain, Lieutenant-Commander Allan Noble. The ship was almost new, having been commissioned the previous April.

HMS *Porcupine*

A week after the loss of *Quentin* the *Porcupine* also fell victim to a torpedo, but in this case it was a U-boat that scored the hit. *Porcupine, Antelope,* and *Vanoc* were escort to the important submarine depot ship *Maidstone* and the steamer *Tegelburg* when on 9 December at a point between Gibraltar and Algiers *Porcupine* was hit by a torpedo. The convoy, zigzagging to specific patterns and had been at sea for most of the day when at 2210 *Antelope* reported having obtained and HF/DF bearing of 251 degrees, believed to be a U-boat transmitting a first-sighting report. One hour and 20 minutes later *Porcupine* was hit to port by a torpedo from U602. Her engine room and gearing room were completely wrecked. All power failed but both diesel motors were immediately started and power was restored. Although the torpedo had struck port side, *Porcupine* at once took on a starboard list. *Vanoc* closed and took off most of the crew. *Porcupine* was later taken under tow. It was the intention to tow her to Oran but her starboard list became so alarming that course was promptly changed for Arzew, much closer than Oran. *Porcupine* berthed at Arzew at 2015 on the 10th. By that time she had a 28 degrees list and was drawing 25 feet aft. Six ratings had been killed, and another died later from burns. *Porcupine,* her captain was Commander George Stewart, RAN, was deemed a constructive total loss and in May 1946 she was scrapped at Plymouth.

HMS *Blean*

The Type VIIC U-boat U443 and the Type II Hunt class *Blean* were launched within a few days of each other. On 11 December the two met in the Mediterranean. *Blean*, in service only three months, was sunk. She had left Algiers the previous day to escort MKF4 to the UK. The U443, Oberleutnant zur See Konstantin von Puttkamer, had sailed from Brest on 29 November. She was on her way to the Mediterranean, patrolling *en route*. *Blean*, Lieutenant Norman Parker, was about 60 miles west of Oran when von Puttkamer fired three torpedoes at a range of 2,000 yards. Two torpedoes hit to starboard, one striking forward and the other blasting off the stern. *Blean* rolled onto her side. Four minutes after being hit she sank by the stern. The U-boat rescued ninety-two survivors. Eighty-nine of the crew were lost. On 22 December U443 put in at La Spezia. Two months later she was sunk with the loss of all hands.

HMS *Firedrake*

The Atlantic theatre claimed its last destroyer of 1942 on the night of 17 December. *Firedrake, Chesterfield,* and the corvettes *Pink* and *Snowflake* sailed from Moville, in the north of Ireland, at 1100 on 12 December. Within hours they joined up with the escorts of ON153. Suitably reinforced ON153 settled down for its passage to New York. After little more than a day at sea, the indications were that U-boats were concentrating for an attack.

At 0740 on 16 December the convoy came under direct attack when U610 sank the Norwegian tanker *Bello*. Further attacks followed and a number of ships were sunk. Around 1800 Commander Eric Tilden, *Firedrake's* captain, took station about 4 miles on the convoy's starboard beam. It is believed that Tilden wanted to avoid the probable track of a U-boat closing the convoy to attack from north-wards, there being a bright moon to the south at the time.

Kapitanleutnant Karl Hause of U211 was among those showing an interest in ON153 and it was Hause who attacked *Firedrake*. Survivors report that it was soon after 2200 on the 16th that the ship was torpedoed to starboard in the vicinity of No.1 boiler room. *Firedrake* listed to starboard then righted and broke in two about a minute after being hit. The bow portion floated away vertically with about 20 feet showing above water. After 30 minutes this forward portion sank. Up to the final moment a number of hands were seen on it. As almost a full gale was blowing and the sea was very rough, none could be rescued and all perished. The stern portion, with thirty-five survivors, remained afloat on an even keel. This stern portion lay constantly with the sea pounding against the forward engine room bulkhead. Three of the hands were able to shore this bulkhead. Lieutenant Denis Dampier realized that none of the ships were aware that *Firedrake* had been torpedoed. Beginning at 2335 starshell was fired at intervals. Dampier states that:

At 0015 HMS *Sunflower* was sighted ahead. She was contacted by torch flashing. As it was impracticable for her to come alongside, it was decided to wait till daylight, but at 0045 the wind increased and heavy seas struck the forward bulkhead, which collapsed, and the ship, which was rapidly settling, was abandoned. In the extremely rough sea existing at that time, twenty-five survivors were picked up by HMS *Sunflower*.

Kapitanleutnant Hause did not survive the war. In November 1943 U211 was sunk off the Azores by the RAF. There were no survivors.

HMS *Partridge*

Of the fourteen destroyers sunk by U-boats in 1942, the Mediterranean boats claimed eight of them. U565, Kapitanleutnant Wilhelm Franken, sailed from La Spezia on 23 November for her tenth war patrol. There was little activity until the morning of 18 December when a lookout sighted a number of destroyers to the west of Oran. In good visibility U565 closed to within 1,000 yards and fired one torpedo. At 0806 it struck the *Partridge* port side and in the vicinity of the wardroom. In *Partridge* there had been no indication of a U-boat in the area, nor of the approaching torpedo. On the morning of the attack *Partridge*, Lieutenant-Commander William Hawkins, was carrying out an A/S sweep with *Penn*, *Milne*, and *Meteor*, the ships being spread in that order in line abreast from port to starboard wing ship. Speed was 16 knots. Hawkins had left the bridge a few minutes previous and was in the process of washing in his sea cabin when the explosion occurred, Lieutenant-Commander Hawkins:

> *On reaching the bridge I observed that the forepart of the ship was developing an increasing list to starboard and there appeared to have been a large explosion in the after part of the ship. The flames and smoke which had been visible quickly subsided, but as the list on the forepart seemed to be increasing I decided that the end could not be long in coming. The memory remains, the impression only, that the after part of the ship from 78 bulkhead had broken away from the forepart and was righting itself. This impression however is not confirmed definitely by other of the ship, I gave orders to abandon ship and to cut away as many life-saving and Carley rafts as possible. In addition all and any woodwork that could be removed was thrown overboard. A large majority of the ship's company were able to scramble down the now almost horizontal side of the forecastle. Having reached the water by this time, in company with a stoker who could not swim, my impression was that the ship settled amidships, probably through the flooding of the gearing room and the engine room (there is no confirmation of this actually happening), righted herself, and then proceeded to lift her stern and forefoot almost vertically in the water, finally submerging with the forepart of the keel still vertical. Being almost ahead of the ship at this moment, my chief concern was in which direction the forepart would fall. I was unable to see the after part of the ship at all.*

Four days after torpedoing *Partridge* the U565 sank a merchant ship. By 1 January she was trying up at La Spezia. Wilhelm Franken did not survive the war. Promoted to korvettenkapitan on 1 January 1945, he was killed in an air raid a few days later.

Another destroyer that never saw the year out was *Campbeltown*. In March she had been expended as an explosives vessel to destroy the Normandie Dock at St Nazaire in France, and her employment as such does not warrant her inclusion in this narrative. The sinking of *Achates*, the account of her loss appears elsewhere, on New Year's Eve brought a miserable year to a close.

Note
1. PQ15 of twenty-five ships (Author).

Chapter Five

1943

The battle of the Atlantic was the dominating factor all through the war. Never for one moment could we forget that everything elsewhere depended on its outcome.

Winston Churchill

In the early weeks of 1943 the Battle of the North Atlantic was every quiet. Raging storms made U-boat operations extremely difficult. With stars and sun obscured by thick cloud, celestial navigation was not possible, so keeping an accurate track of their own position was out of the question. Even with 164 U-boats operational in the Atlantic, for the first two weeks of 1943 not one convoy was seen. But by March the battles were as fierce as ever, with the U-boats gaining the upper hand; in fact so complete was their triumph that when the Admiralty later evaluated the significance of the March losses it was concluded that:

The Germans never came so near to disrupting communications between the New World and the Old as in the first 20 days of March 1943.

One of the March convoys was HX228. This convoy escaped serious loss because the Germans redirected U-boats away from the convoy's actual course by sending them to the northward, expecting the convoy to have been informed where the U-boats would be waiting, and so would move north. The outcome of this cat-and-mouse affair was that the convoy maintained its original course and so passed to the southward of the U-boats. When the wolf-pack realized what had happened some of its U-boats were able to give chase and eventually make contact, sinking four merchantmen and the destroyer *Harvester*.

HMS *Harvester*

Lieutenant Derek Lukin Johnston, RCNVR, joined *Harvester* at Halifax, Nova Scotia, on 4 March 1943. It had been arranged for the lieutenant, a recently qualified signal specialist, to temporarily join *Harvester* 'for experience'. Lieutenant Lukin Johnston recalls:

Despite the tiredness of her crew after their previous crossing, Harvester *managed to look the image of a spick and span Royal Navy destroyer. As I stepped on to her quarter-deck, I was saluted by a quartermaster standing by a gleaming white lifebelt in whose centre was a ship's crest, a golden what-sheaf on a blue background. I was to see that lifebelt later under very different circumstances. The ship's officers made me welcome, and the captain, Commander 'Harry' Tait, DSO, insisted on showing me over his ship himself. He and his ship had an outstanding record, commencing with good work at Dunkirk, and had sunk or had shared in the sinking of seven U-boats. We sailed on Friday March 5, and next morning took over from the group which had escorted our 'flock' from New York.*

The flock was HX228 of sixty-one ships. Around 0315 on 10 March an aircraft from the American escort carrier *Bogue* unsuccessfully attacked a U-boat 10 miles off the convoy's port beam. The attack was on a boat of the 'Neuland' group which had been spread over a wide area in a search for HX228. Consisting of thirteen boats, the group was that night to launch its main offensive.

Kapitanleutnant Hans Trojer was the one who made contact with the convoy. Under cover of a snow-squall he torpedoed the British *Tucurinca*. Trojer reports that, *Hundreds of steel plates flew like sheets of paper through the air.*

The inactivity of U-boats over the previous 5 days led Lieutenant Lukin Johnston to believe that the danger from U-boats had been overrated. Then came the night of 10/11 March. Lukin Johnston had been preparing to bunk down when he heard a distant thud; at the same time *Harvester's* alarm bells sent hands scurrying to action stations. Lukin Johnston:

Like the others, I seized my inflated rubber ring that then served as a life-jacket and made my way up to the pitch-black bridge, where orders to gun and asdic crews were being calmly given by the captain. We were slipping back through the convoy. Two merchant ships had been torpedoed: one was on fire and sinking, and by this light we could see the bow and stern of another, as well as some Carley floats and men swimming in the water. Our captain reckoned that we were probably being followed by a wolf-pack, and he had himself decided to attack. After 2 hours we were well astern of the convoy, but there had been no further events, and several of us were ordered below to get some sleep. We were just swallowing some hot cocoa when the alarm bells rang again, and we dashed to out stations. As I reached the bridge an excited young signalman said: 'Did you see the sub, sir? She passed right down our side!' I had not, but my reply was drowned in the roar of exploding depth charges that Harvester had dropped. We had caught a U-boat on the surface and attacked immediately. Now we circled back, and in a few moments picked up the U-boat in our searchlight. She was underway but evidently could not dive because of damage done by the depth charges. Harvester's guns opened fire; but one misfired, the other failed to hit the target, and the captain decided to ram; an accepted Admiralty instruction. Harvester's *bow struck the U-boat abaft her conning tower at high speed; but this U-boat was new and of tough construction and she did not sink, or break, but to our astonishment, bumped along under our keel. The Germans decided to abandon ship and came on deck wearing full life-jackets, which shone a brilliant yellow in our searchlight's beam. As they were jumping into the water* Harvester *ground and scraped her way across the back of the U-boat and then disaster happened. The sub's wires and gear caught in the twin propellers of our ship. For some 15 minutes I watched the incredible sight of a U-boat conning tower bumping up and down* Harvester's *stern, doing irreparable damage, while the ship's executive officer and some petty officers and seaman tried without effect to part the two vessels.*

The U-boat was U444, Oberleutnant zur See Albert Langfield. Seeing U444 helpless on the surface the Free French corvette *Aconit* sped towards her and rammed, sinking her. After rescuing survivors *Aconit* rejoined the convoy.

Damage to *Harvester* was serious in that one of her two propellers was lost and the other damaged. She was immobile for several hours, eventually proceeding on her starboard propeller. At 5 to 7 knots she trailed astern of the convoy, by then 25 or more miles ahead. Lieutenant Lukin Johnston:

At 0730 I was awakened in my bunk in the after part of the ship by a terrific racing of the propeller shaft. Our second and only propeller had dropped off. As the executive officer now announced to the ship's company, we were derelict, and could only toss helplessly waiting for help to return from the convoy escort. It was a bright March morning, with little wind, and patches of sun and blue sky alternating with black clouds and cold rain. But the visibility was good, and we could be seen for 10 miles around. There was nothing to do but keep a futile watch for periscopes, eat some breakfast, and chat to pass the time, hoping that we should soon see on the horizon a mast of a returning corvette. Commander Tait was the first to sight a faint wisp of smoke on the horizon, some 12 miles away. 'There she is!' he said; but seconds afterwards there was a loud explosion from somewhere behind the bridge and a cloud of wood and steel splinters showered down on us. We had been torpedoed amidships. Without hesitation the captain shouted, 'Abandon ship!', and we all began to troop to our stations. Mine was a Carley float on the starboard side below the bridge. Some seamen cut the big raft away and it dropped into the water 20 feet below. With others I scrambled down to the next deck. I was preparing to jump into the float when a colossal explosion hastened my departure and blew me about 10 feet down in the water. The U-boat's captain, not able to see that Harvester was heeling over and sinking, elected to fire a second torpedo. I swam up towards the light until it seemed that my lungs would burst, and surfaced. The Carley float was nowhere to be seen. The ship had broken in two sections. I found myself swimming under the bow, which seemed to be bearing right down on me. Swimming as strongly as I could, I got away from the menace of the bow, and watched the bow section sink in a few minutes. Shortly afterwards the stern section, with little figures still clinging to it, went down.

'The sea was dotted with three or four Carley floats and many heads of swimmers as well as debris from the upper deck. The ship's boats had all been shattered by the second torpedo explosion. A white object came floating by me. It was spattered with oil, but still recognizable as the once-immaculate lifebelt that was placed by the gangway when Harvester *was in harbour. I held onto it for a while, but then relinquished it to a swimmer who had no lifebelt of his own, whilst I, at least, had my rubber tubing. The few Carley floats were filled with men, and round the sides of each of them clung other survivors in water up to their shoulders. Then, on the crest of a wave about 150 yards away, I saw an empty float net, a sort of mat consisting of several dozen large pieces of cork held together by netting. I decided to swim for it. Eventually I reached the float net and climbed on it, or rather pushed the cork matting under me, for it was a most inefficient piece of equipment, and I was constantly preoccupied with keeping myself from falling back into the sea. However, it did not keep about 60 per cent of my body out of the water, and this was important; for all those clinging around the floats died during the next 2 hours from being almost entirely immersed in cold water.*

Alone and surrounded by miles of grey ocean Lukin Johnston was feeling utterly miserable. Then about 200 yards away he saw a Carley float with survivors. He made his way over to the float.

The water was icy cold, and so was the wind, which was not high but which was strong enough to create long mountainous Atlantic rollers. The Carley float would surmount these and then seem to slide down an interminable slope into the deep gap between waves. At one point it snowed and I can remember vividly the snow on the heads of the men sitting upright around the rim of the Carley float. I reckoned I could last no more than half an hour, for my hands and feet were quite numb from cold, and I was exhausted by the effort of trying to keep balanced on the float net. Suddenly a cheerful, if weak, cry went up from the men. I turned to look behind me and there was another corvette bearing down on us. It was HMS Narcissus, *a Royal Navy Flower class corvette. Nets were rolled down the ship's side for us to scramble up, but we were rolled down the ship's side for us to scramble up, but we were all too weak and* Narcissus' *men had to come down the nets and literally drag us aboard the ship. I remember collapsing on the upper deck and being carried below to a bunk. From this ordeal I escaped with nothing worse than a feverish bout of flu. Others were not so fortunate and there were some traditional burials at sea.*

It had been the U432, Kapitanleutnant Herman Eckhardt, that at 1100 had fired two torpedoes at the stationary *Harvester*. But the French *Aconit* had arrived on the scene and had sunk the U-boat, rescuing twenty of the forty-six crew. Eckhardt, in command of U432 for less than 3 months, went down with his boat. He was twenty-six.

Thirty-nine years old Commander Arthur Tait did not survive the sinking. After serving from 1936 to 1939 in the cruiser *Suffolk*, he took command of the destroyer *Hesperus*. Then came *Harvester*. Convoy HX228 lost four merchantmen. Of *Harvester's* 192 crew only fifty-one survived.

HMS *Lightning*

The year's first destroyer casualty in the Mediterranean was the *Lightning*, Commander Hugh Walters. At 0700 on 12 March an Axis convoy left Naples for Bizerte. Shortly after 1800 that evening Force Q (*Aurora, Sirius, Loyal, Lightning*) put to sea from Bone. The squadron proceeded eastwards at 28 knots in search of the convoy. Between 1850 and 2050, enemy torpedo planes made several attacks. Hurricane fighters accompanying the squadron at this time went in pursuit. With the intention of preventing Allied interference of the Bizerte convoy, Axis MTBs were patrolling in several areas. Force Q had passed Galite Island and was some 40 miles to the north of Bizerte when at 2206 *Aurora* detected E-boats in the vicinity. Almost immediately some craft were observed off her port bow. She opened fire and the squadron turned 90 degrees to starboard by rapid manoeuvre procedure.

In *Lightning*, German RT conversation had been heard after passing Galite Island, and so a particular lookout for E-boats was posted. At 28 knots Commander Walters altered course directly towards the sighting. *Lightning's* main armament was on the target and fire was about to be opened when a torpedo from the S158 struck the ship forward. Main engines were ordered stopped, to lessen the danger of a breakdown of the watertight bulkheads forward. Walters ordered Carley floats on lines to be lowered and the lifeboats turned out. An attempt was being made to report the attack when a second torpedo hit *Lightning* amidships abreast the fore end of the engine room. Broken in two, *Lightning* settled very quickly. Commander Walters: *As I reached a Carley float the bow and stern were both standing vertically on end, stem and propellers both in the air, and they sank after a few seconds.* There was no time to launch the boats, so the half-dozen Carley rafts were soon crowded.

Meanwhile, an attack on *Sirius* failed narrowly, a torpedo exploding in her wake and then E-boat attacks tailed off. The squadron had resumed its easterly course when *Lightning's* signal was received. *Loyal* was detached to assist.

Flying his flag in *Aurora* was Rear-Admiral 12th Cruiser Squadron. His report of events states:

> *In view of the fact that we had now twice been attacked by the enemy I felt that any convoy which might be proceeding to the area north east of Skerki Bank would probably be turned back. Bearing this in mind I did not feel justified in proceeding further east without destroyers and decided to turn back. After the last engagement with E-boats neither* Aurora *nor* Sirius *was able to get in touch with* Loyal *with WT. I did not know what had happened to* Lightning, *and for a short while it appeared possible that both* Loyal *and* Lightning *had been sunk. I therefore decided to close the position where* Lightning *had last been seen.*
>
> *As we came up to the position, men, rafts and lights were seen in the water and men were heard shouting. We were proceeding at 25 knots at the time, so lights were flashed at the rafts to indicate that we had seen them. Just at this moment RDF reported three small echoes on the starboard beam. The area was searched with starshell with the gratifying result that* Loyal, *who had in fact been detected, flashed her fighting lights. Just at this time WT contact with* Loyal *was again established. By this time I realized that* Loyal's *report of a convoy in the vicinity was probably false.* Loyal *was therefore ordered to pick up survivors and the cruisers swept in the vicinity until the work of picking up survivors had well progressed. At 0035 the cruisers shaped course for Bone, being rejoined by* Loyal *at 0500.* Loyal *rescued 170 hands but 46 were lost.*

HMS *Derwent*

The 22nd Destroyer Flotilla was reduced by one ship when on 19 March a torpedo hit the *Derwent* while at anchor in Tripoli harbour, at the time crowded with shipping. Six of the crew were killed. *Derwent*, Commander Royston Wright, was anchored in 4 fathoms. At 1850 twelve JU88s swept in low over Tripoli harbour, roughly in line abreast, and proceeded to attack the shipping with bombs and circling torpedoes. Commander Wright:

> *About 1930 it was decided to move* Derwent *clear of a nearby merchant ship and, whilst the anchors were being weighed, a violent explosion occurred on the on the port side of the ship in the vicinity of her waterline and approximately abreast the junction of the two boiler rooms. A large number of personnel were thrown off their feet and a cloud of smoke and steam enveloped the funnel and bridge. The ship rolled first to port and then to starboard, where she remained listing at an angle of 5 degrees. All electric power and steam was lost and practically all communications failed, the latter being maintained by messenger thenceforth. At the time, it was thought that the explosion was due to an acoustic mine actuated by the noise of the cable rattling home; subsequently it was considered to have been due to a circling torpedo. Both boiler rooms flooded rapidly. Water also entered the low power room*

and the wardroom, as soon as the water in No.1 boiler room reached lower deck level. Some 5 minutes after the explosion the engine room commenced to flood slowly. Despite damage control measure the situation gradually deteriorated until a decision was made to beach the ship to avoid the possibility of her sinking in the harbour. The operation was carried out successfully by 2100.

The torpedo blew a hole 28 feet by 16 feet in *Derwent's* port side. Her two boiler rooms were severely damaged by blast and flooding. After undergoing temporary repairs she was towed to England. Permanent repairs were put in hand but were never completed. Declared a constructive total loss, *Derwent* was scrapped.

HMS *Beverley*

During 6 days in April three destroyers were lost: the *Beverley* was sunk by a U-boat, the *Eskdale* by an E-boat, and the *Pakenham* by a destroyer.

Convoy ON176 of around some forty ships sailed from Liverpool at about 1430 on 31 March. Escort vessels numbered eighteen. On 9 April the convoy ran into dense fog and, as a consequence, *Beverley* and the steamer *Cairnvalona* were in collision at 2205. *Beverley* was holed and her Asdics put out of action. The bulkhead forward and abaft the damage held and *Beverley* was able to remain with the convoy at 9 knots.

Lieutenant-Commander Rodney Price was from Hertford, about 600 miles from Neubrandenburg where Kapitanleutnant Siegfried Ludden was born. At about 0500 on the morning of 11 April the two officers were within a few hundred yards of each other; Price as captain of *Beverley* and Ludden as captain of U188. From the report of *Beverley's* few survivors and evidence of the nearest escort vessels it seems that *Beverely* sank at once after being hit by two torpedoes fired by U188. The explosions were very heavy and were followed by underwater explosions, presumably her depth charges detonating. The corvette *Clover* rescued three survivors. Although *Clover* and her sister ship *Abelia* searched until daylight, all they came across were dead bodies. Nine officers and 139 ratings had been lost.

Beverley, the ex-USN *Branch*, had been sunk about 700 miles north-east of Cape Race. She had been Ludden's first sinking. He had begun U-boat training in September 1939 after having been almost 2 years attached to the Luftwaffe. In January 1945 he was killed in an air raid. Rodney Price had entered Dartmouth in September 1925. He had served in the battleship *Ramillies* and the aircraft carrier *Eagle*. He did not survive the sinking.

(Norwegian) HMS *Eskdale*

The Hunt class destroyer *Eskdale* was nearing completion at Cammel-Laird when, on 8 June 1942, it was agreed that she would be taken over by the Royal

Norwegian Navy. On 20 July she was commissioned by her Norwegian crew. The following September she joined the 1st Destroyer Flotilla at Portsmouth. *Eskdale* served with the flotilla until her loss on 14 April 1943. In a calm sea and in bright moonlight convoy PW323 (Portsmouth-Bristol Channel) was, on the night of 13 April, making steady progress in the vicinity of Lizard Head. The convoy of six merchantmen was escorted by *Eskdale* and the Norwegian-manned Hunt *Glaisdale*, several trawlers, and an MTB. Some time around 0045 on the 14th a signal was received on *Eskdale*'s bridge to the effect than an unidentified vessel had been plotted to the east of Lizard Head, steering 300 degrees at 30 knots. Action stations was sounded and Commander Storehill, R Nor N, increased to 20 knots. From *Glaisdale* came the signal that the convoy was to put in at Falmouth. Soon after this, starshells were seen bursting to westward and indications were that E-boats were in the vicinity and about to attack. And this was correct, as seven boats of the 5th Schnellboote Flotilla was preparing for a strike against PW323.

Commander Storehill had increased to maximum speed when the wake of either an E-boat or a torpedo was seen off *Eskdale's* port bow and moving to the right. Helm was put to starboard and starshell was fired. *Eskdale* was then struck by two torpedoes from Oberleutnant zur See Stohwasser's S90. *Eskdale's* bow and stern were blasted away. As *Eskdale* had remained on an even keel, and as an investigation had revealed that she was not about to sink, the order to abandon ship was not given, though preparations were made in readiness to do so. About 20 minutes after being torpedoed, *Eskdale* attracted some E-boats away from the convoy. A torpedo was seen to break surface and explode off her starboard beam. ML180, Lieutenant Richard McCullagh, RNVR, at that time rescuing survivors who had been blasted overboard, motored alongside *Eskdale* to take off the crew. McCullagh continued with this task until he came under attack from E-boats. *Eskdale* was hit for a third time when a torpedo from the S112, Korvettenkapitan Karl Muller, struck amidships and sank her. The steamer *Stanlake* was also sunk by torpedoes. Without loss to themselves, the E-boats withdrew. Lieutenant McCullagh, his boat crammed with survivors, proceeded to Falmouth.

HMS *Pakenham*

Commander Basil Jones was *Pakenham's* CO at the time of her loss in the Mediterranean. On the afternoon of 15 April the *Pakenham* and *Paladin*, Lieutenant-Commander Lawrence Rich, were exercising off Malta when a signal was received from the C-in-C Malta that enemy units had been sighted off Pantelleria and that both destroyers were to investigate. At 1745 they proceeded as ordered.

Eight hours later Pantelleria was abeam. The destroyers were proceeding at 20 knots with *Paladin* 3 cables astern of *Pakenham*. At 0242 an object at a range of 7,200 yards was picked up by *Pakenham's* radar. The contact was temporarily lost to sight as *Pakenham* turned, but at 0245 it was again observed; this time the contact was made out to be two torpedo boats in line ahead on a nearly opposite course, range 6,000 yards. *Pakenham* and *Paladin* then altered to starboard in an endeavour to gain a down moon position. At 0248 *Pakenham* opened fire on the leading torpedo boat from a range of 2,700 yards, her searchlight illuminating the target. The torpedo boats *Cigno* and *Cassiopea* were both smaller than the British ships. *Cigno* was hit by *Pakenham*, then by *Paladin* when *Pakenham* shifted target to *Cassiopea*. The *Cigno* came to a halt enveloped in a high cloud of smoke and steam. *Paladin* fired four torpedoes at her. One hit *Cigno* amidships. She broke in two and sank with heavy loss of life. *Pakenham* scored hits on *Cassiopea*. Her captain, Capitano di Corvetta Virginio Nasta, returned fire, hitting *Pakenham* about six times. *Pakenham's* pom-pom and searchlight was put out of action and a fire started aft. But in *Cassiopea* two serious fires had taken a hold, one in the bow and one in the stern. These fires were so heavy that *Pakenham* observed her to be *blazing from stem to stern and blew up shortly afterwards*. Though badly damaged she survived the action, remaining active until 1959.

Pakenham and *Paladin* shaped course for return to Malta. It soon became clear that engine room damage sustained by *Pakenham* was serious, even though she was able to proceed at up to 25 knots. High-pressure steam was escaping from the engine room, where two hits had been taken port side: one at or below the water-line, causing the engine room to flood, and one higher which had cut both port and starboard main steam-pipes. High-pressure steam escaping in the engine room made it uninhabitable. One of several alternatives opened to Commander Jones was to shut off steam at the upper deck emergency valve and then to wait until repairs could be effected in the overheated engine room. This would entail being shut down for at least 2 hours. Alternatively he could continue until such time as the boiler feed-water was exhausted, *Pakenham* then coming to a halt. In view of his nearness to enemy airfields Commander Jones had no doubt that he should continue, and in fact *Pakenham* covered about 13 miles before she came to a stop at 0350. *Paladin* then took her in tow at between 4 and 5 knots.

At 0600 two enemy aircraft were seen. Dawn was breaking as the planes came in for an attack on *Paladin*. The tow was slipped and both ships opened fire. Two more planes attacked without success. At 0620 another tow was passed. After only a few minutes this parted. Enemy planes remained in the vicinity. When Italian and German fighters arrived Commander Jones decided to sink *Pakenham*, he being of the opinion that she was too far from Malta for Allied fighters to remain overhead when progress might only be 5 knots. And the increasing threat of air attack made it likely that *Paladin* would be damaged or sunk. Malta was aware of the situation and at 0630 ordered *Pakenham* sunk.

While RAF fighters were in combat with enemy aircraft, *Pakenham's* crew was transferring to *Paladin*. At 32 knots Rich headed for Malta, arriving without further incident. *Paladin* was free of damage and casualties, but *Pakenham* had lost nine ratings and had another fifteen wounded.

HMS *Puckeridge*

A hunt in the area of the Hertfordshire village of Puckeridge was taken as a name for the Hunt class *Puckeridge*. Her captain was Lieutenant-Commander John Cartwright. At 1800 on 6 September Cartwright sailed from Gibraltar and on passing Europa Point he set a course of 077 degrees. Owing to an increased temperature of glands which had been temporarily repaired at Gibraltar, Cartwright thought it imprudent to exceed 19 knots until a uniformed temperature had been reached. He had been at sea an hour when a signal was received ordering him to Algiers with all dispatch. Cartwright decided it would be nearing 2030 before he would be able to increase to 20 knots. In view of the U-boat situation report and his own feeling that is was unlikely that an enemy submarine would be active so close to Gibraltar, he altered to 083degrees and ceased zigzagging, intending to recommence on increasing to 20 knots. The OoW at 2015 was Lieutenant James Lyle:

> *I was just turning over to the new Officer of the Watch. I had just passed an order down the voice-pipe to increase to 268 revolutions (20 knots) and was standing on the port side of the bridge when I heard an explosion which shook the ship.*

A second or so later Lyle heard a deafening explosion, much heavier than the first, and looking aft saw *an enormous amount of debris going up in the air. Puckeridge* at once took on a list to port. Gibraltar was 40 miles to the west. The first lieutenant, Lieutenant John McKaig, states:

> *I was just taking over the watch when I heard an explosion aft about as loud as a depth charge set at 50 feet exploding. I turned aft, the interval was about 3 seconds, and there was another and much louder explosion. I immediately shouted 'Keep your heads down', and everyone got underneath the front of the bridge. The captain told me to get an Enemy Report away, and I shouted down to the officer to make an Enemy Report. I could not hear the reply at the time because of escaping steam. I told the boatswain's mate in the wheelhouse to pipe Stand-By to Abandon Ship as I could see that the list, which immediately went to 10 degrees, was rapidly increasing. I went on to the fo'c'sle and as far aft as I could and got the Carley floats out. The first time I went aft I could not see any farther than the forward depth charge throwers as the deck from there was curled up. The ship's list was increasing rapidly and, when I had seen that all the Carley floats were away, I did everything I could to get all the loose gear on the upper deck over the side and*

to turn out the motor-boat, which was not possible because the boat was secured for sea.

John Cartwright at once saw that *Puckeridge* would not remain afloat for long. Looking over the after end of the bridge he saw that the stern had been blown over the searchlight platform. He ordered abandon ship and reports:

Just before abandoning ship I noticed two large explosions which put up high columns of water about 2 miles on the starboard beam. About this time a Hudson aircraft on patrol was sighted about 5 miles away to the northward in good light. He appeared to notice nothing amiss. All power had failed in the WT office when the ship was struck and endeavours to get away an Enemy Report were of no avail. The ship must have in all lasted less than 6 minutes after she was originally struck. When she went her bows went up into the air and it was noticed that a large slice was missing from the stem.

Kapitanleutnant Albrecht Brandi of U617 had made the attack. Possibly four torpedoes had been fired: one might have hit the stem without exploding, one had struck aft (blowing up the magazine), and the other two had missed as after running on for 2 miles they exploded, as witnessed by Cartwright. Neither the U-boat nor the torpedoes had been seen or detected. By good fortune the Spanish merchantmen *Antiquers* was 5 miles off *Puckeridge's* starboard bow when she was attracted by the explosions. Her master, Captain Roman Guerequeta, rescued 128 survivors and provided them with tea, coffee, and blankets. Although he could have landed the survivors in southern Spain, where they would have been interned, he generously decided to pass through the Strait, knowing full well that his ship would be stopped and search by a British patrol from Gibraltar. At 0200 on 7 September the *Antiquere* was boarded by HM trawler *Anglia*. The survivors were transferred and taken to Gibraltar. Six of *Puckeridge's* crew had been killed in the explosion.

Within a few days of sinking *Puckeridge* U617 herself was scuttled off Spanish Morocco, where for several months her crew was interned. Brandi died in 1966.

HMCS *St Croix*

In September the Battle of the Atlantic claimed the Canadian destroyer *St Croix*. At the time of her loss the Allies were beginning to gain the initiative in the Atlantic. The war in this theatre is considered to have turned in favour of the Allies in the months of April and May 1943. This change of fortune was the result of several factors. Towards the end of March 1943 the Allies were able to include Merchant Aircraft Carriers (MAC) ships as part of North Atlantic convoys, and thus at a stroke the mid-ocean air-gap was bridged. Also, by March an adequate number of support groups were available. A support group was not a part of convoy's escort, but was at sea ready to reinforce a convoy escort under pressure from submarine attack. Also of worry to the U-boats was new asdic apparatus which could maintain contact with a deeply-submerged boat. Another new ant-submarine weapon was ten centimetre radar, undetectable by U-boats. These factors combined to make U-boat operations too hazardous and on 24 May 1943 Admiral Donitz withdrew all U-boats from the Atlantic convoy routes following a five days assault (15-20 May) by a large concentration of U-boats against convoy SC130 which failed to sink any ships, but which resulted in the loss of five U-boats. It was the beginning of the end for the U-boat Arm as it was never to regain the initiative in the battle for the North Atlantic sea-lanes.

In hope of redressing the balance the German Navy introduced several new innovations, one of which was the T5 acoustic torpedo, the zaunkoening (wren), known to the Allies by the acronym GMAT (German Naval Acoustic Torpedo). The gnat, which homed onto the noise of a ship's propellers, became available for operational use by mid-August 1943. By September, after an absence of 3 months, the U-boats were back in the Atlantic trusting that their new equipment: an improved radar receiver, a much stronger AA armament, and the gnat torpedo, would enable them to strike at the convoys on favourable terms.

On Sunday 12 September the slow convoy ONS18 of twenty-seven merchantmen sailed from Milford Haven. Three days after its departure for America and Canada, the fast convoy ON202 of forty ships put to sea from Liverpool and headed west.

On Thursday 16th nineteen U-boats formed a line roughly north-south and approximately on longitude 25 degrees. The exchange of radio signals required to form the U-boats into their operational line were intercepted. Before the day was over, the Canadian 9th Support Group comprising the destroyers *St Croix* and *St Francis*, the corvettes *Chamberly*, *Morden*, and *Sackville*, and the frigate *Itchen* was on its way to assist the convoys. On Sunday 19th first contact with the U-boats came at dawn when an RCAF Liberator sank the U341 several miles to the south of the convoys. By this time ON202 was rapidly gaining on the slower ONS18 and was some 30 miles to the north-east of it.

The battle opened at 0300 on Monday 20th when U270 fired a gnat at the frigate *Lagan*, blasting away 30 feet of her stern and forcing *Lagan* to return to harbour under tow. At 0540 a merchantman was damaged by a torpedo from U238, and soon sank. Around dawn Liberators from Iceland arrived, and just after 1000 one of them sank U338. By midday ON202 had almost caught up with ONS18. At 1220 the C-in-C Western Approaches ordered the convoys to merge. Five hours later they made contact with each other but soon after the convoys began to merge. At 1756 the *St Croix*, Lieutenant-Commander Andrew Dobson, RCNR, was hit by a gnat from U305. The gnat exploded at

St Croix's stern. Realizing that his ship could not survive in the conditions then prevailing, her captain signalled *Am Leaving The Office*. The *Itchen*, Commander C. E. Bridgeman, RNR, went in search of U305 and at the same time ordered the corvette *Polyanthus* to close *St Croix*. While these moves were underway, U305 sent another torpedo into *St Croix*. *Polyanthus* was closing *St Croix* when she was too hit by a gnat, from U592. Survivors from *St Croix* and *Polyanthus* were rescued by the corvette *Orchis*. *Itchen* was also able to rescue survivors. Sometime after rejoining the convoy, *Orchis* transferred her survivors to *Itchen*, which, being a larger ship, was better equipped to administer their needs.

On Wednesday 22nd a torpedo from U666 hit *Itchen* in the vicinity of her forward magazine. *Itchen* disappeared in *a tremendous, orange-coloured mushroom of flame and an ear-shocking explosion*. Only three hands survived from three ships' companies. A sad day. Andrew Dobson of *St Croix* did not survive. His appointment to the ship dated from 6 January 1942.

Kapitanleutnant Rudolf Bahr had torpedoed *St Croix*. He had joined the navy in 1935 when he was nineteen. In January 1944 the U305 was sunk by HM ships. There were no survivors.

(Polish) HMS *Orkan*

Apart from the Polish naval vessels that escaped to Britain in 1939, the Poles named a number of Royal Navy ships, submarines, and MTBs. In Glasgow on 18 November 1942 the Polish ensign was hoisted in *Orkan*, the ex-Royal Navy *Myrmidon*, a new M class destroyer. *Orkan*, the name means cyclone, was sunk on 8 October 1943 about 500 miles to the west of Ireland when escort to SC143 from Halifax to United Kingdom. She had been with the convoy only 2 days, having joined from another convoy. One of the few *Orkan* survivors was Konstanty Chropowicki, a radar operator who had been in the ship about nine weeks. At the time *Orkan* was torpedoed he was asleep in his hammock at the bow, suffering a high temperature, almost certainly flu:

The night was passing quickly and I went into a deep sleep; but then there was just a feeling of uneasiness, a discomfort rather than anything else. On opening my eyes for a few seconds, I noticed that the lights were unusually dimmed. There was something else: the electric generator, almost in the immediate vicinity of my hammock and usually a very noisy affair, was silent. I felt that none of this could really be true, and that I must be imagining it; even better, it was probably a dream. And so I closed my eyes, turned round, and continued with it. Then out of the corner of my eye I registered something new: a sailor running and then disappearing down a ladder leading to the lower quarters. As there was nobody around me (all on night shift) he had assumed that there was no one there and, without wasting valuable time, had hurried below to awaken those there. I could hear his distant but sharp calls. Something was happening and it was all true! I quickly jumped to the floor and grabbed my boots, only to find that they were now several sizes too big. I could not at the time understand why somebody else's boots were under my hammock. In hindsight it is obvious that they were shifted by the shock wave, the hammock performing a cushioning function admirably. I still had not spoken to anyone. In the dim but very efficient, and indispensable, emergency lighting I made my way to the adjoining mess room. I could hear a few rather garbled words and there were about fifteen people there. I wondered where they had come from. And why so many? And why were they all standing practically still? What was going on? I received my first answer: 'We have been hit by a torpedo. I don't know anything else'. *This was much more than I knew. I noticed a group walking towards the emergency portholes. Somebody suggested that we should blow up our lifebelts. I clearly remember how embarrassing this proved to be. We gazed at one another, no one wanting to be the first to do so. In the event, pride won over common sense and the belts remained empty, awaiting another time. I must have been in the mess room a full minute. I have often wondered how these people would have reacted had they known that they had less than 1 minute left. I could not understand the increasing activity at the stubborn portholes if one could jump from the upper deck. There was no one to ask, no officers or petty officers, and no intercom instructions. I learned later that at that time the commanding officer and everybody on the bridge was dead and that the officer who was second in command, Lieutenant Commander Michat Rozanski, had died in the officers' mess room at the stern where he had gone to have his coffee. The radio office was damaged and the senior operator was reported dead. I was told later that petty officers who were off duty in their quarters at the bows fought desperately to open the fireproof door to get into the open, which they never succeeded in doing.*

I decided to explore the situation on the upper deck as the two queues at the portholes each had about six people and even if the locks finally yielded under the strain, one was beginning to show some signs of movement, it would still have been a lengthy operation to get all of us through. I chanced my quick judgement and proceeded along the corridor on the port side. What I found at the end was worrying still further. On my left was a spiral staircase leading to the bridge. Fifteen or so people were crammed on it, stationary, desperately trying to open the trap-door above them. Having been jammed by the explosion, the trap-door resisted attempts to dislodge it. I should think that this group remained in there forever. On my right were washrooms. I did not think they had emergency portholes. At this moment the blackout curtain directly leading to the open deck swung open in front of me and someone really terrified jumped from behind it screaming at the top of his voice: 'Stop. Stop. Don't go on deck! Keep away from this curtain!' *He rushed past me into the corridor along which I had just come. But I was left with no option; I just had to go through the curtain to find out for myself what was happening. As I opened the curtain the picture in front of me was ablaze with burning oil, stored in the stern. The space I was standing in was probably aflame a moment earlier, but in that very instant it was clear, washed out by a wave. There was no sign of the lifeboats or rafts. On my left was something unusual: there seemed to be a big hole at the top of the deck superstructure. Something huge and familiar was no longer there, and I am almost certain it was the funnel itself. I later wondered if the ammunition magazine near it was caught up in the explosion. If so, that would have accounted for everybody on the bridge being dead. On the other hand, if that were the case I would find it difficult to understand why the ship did not break in two immediately. According to J. Pertck (author of* Great Days of a Small Fleet*) Orkan was struck by two torpedoes. The first hit the oil tanks in the stern and the second torpedo hit amidships and was responsible for blowing open the watertight door of the machine room, letting in the water which drowned the night-shift crew.*

I was on the deck no longer than ten seconds when something unexpected and scary happened. I looked at the sea and saw a wall of water, perhaps 30 feet high and still rising, approaching menacingly, and fast. There was something ominous about that wall. I knew in that instant that no matter what I did it would succumb me. I hurriedly grappled with the cord of my lifebelt and blew vigorously. It was almost too late. It was only half-full when the wall of water hit me. I remember that my last thought was to tighten and secure the cord. I then took a deep breath and awaited the inevitable. Orkan was capsizing to port and sinking rapidly. The huge wave struck the hull and the superstructure and bounced off with colossal speed, taking me with it. I was completely submerged, I dread to think to what depth. I pushed forward, away from the ship in some unknown direction. My oversize boots, so recently acquired, slipped off gently and I remember how grateful I was for instinctively I felt that a loss of even the smallest weight could help me. Quite suddenly and unexpectedly, my head was out of the water. I looked towards Orkan. *What a sight! That splendid ship was now in the last stage of her fight with the elements. Rapidly sinking by the stern, her bow was high in the air, surrounded and scorched by a pool of flames. It was quite a spectacle; like being shown suddenly a brightly illuminated obelisk or tower. Gun-turrets were still in position, although hanging vertically. Then they slipped, first turret No.2 then turret No.1. And then it was all over. The bow submerged and that beautiful and highly promising destroyer, with most of her crew still in her, was no longer there. Thoughts went to all those, who minutes earlier were still full of expectations, standing on the spiral stairs or queuing at portholes. Could they have survived? I did not see how. Perhaps only the first two at the head of the queues. As soon as* Orkan's *bow went under, the burning surface oil was extinguished by the waves. It was a pitch-black night.*

I was still on my own, and could not see or hear anything except the waves. The current that had supported me up till then had gone, and I had to rely on my own uncoordinated movements to keep afloat. The lifebelt, although only half-inflated was most helpful. The salty water probably helped too. I then spotted a dark shape, not too clear at first; but then I began to make out a figure, and what is more, it had a little raft with it. I mustered all my strength and hurried towards it. What followed was not without its comical side, although at the time we were far from laughing. The small (personal) cork raft was very inviting. One jump and I was at it, or perhaps even on it! In some most 'clever' way I managed to dislodge from its surface and sink myself, the raft, and my new companion. All three appeared on the surface again. It was not long before we could see some more shapes in the dark, some of the larger ones being Carley rafts holding several people. Also, quite a number of small red SOS lights appeared in the distance, virtually from nowhere. We could hear many voices, and had obviously been swept by the current towards a group. Just when we began to wonder if we could ever be found we heard a big yell of joy. Quite near to us, and just visible in the darkness, we saw the silhouette of a destroyer much like Orkan. *Emerging from the mist it appeared very large, particularly at the angle at which we were viewing. Some cries of Help were heard, but only very few as it was obvious the destroyer had seen us and was coming to our rescue. The destroyer positioned herself so that the current swept us right against her port side. Her preparations for rescue were already well advanced, as we could see rope-netting hanging from the deck all along her side. My companion became very excited. In his excitement he let go of our raft and grabbed the netting. Foolishly I did the same, that is I let go of my precious raft before first securing my hold on the netting. This proved at once to be the biggest mistake I made that night. As I was swimming towards the netting, I could hear the noise of the propellers. The ship having been practically still for quite some time, I presumed that our rescuer was losing her perfect position and had started the engines to make some adjustment. There may of course have been reports of more U-boat sightings in the vicinity. With what seemed to me a fantastic speed, I was swept along the hull towards the propellers. Someone seeing the straits I was in dropped a rope for me to grab. It was then, in the dim light of the early morning, that I saw oil covering all my body and, most importantly, my hands. I was already more than two-thirds the way along the ship. For the first time I must have screamed for help. Someone heard me, as suddenly a hand grabbed me at the collar and to my surprise and obvious delight I was pulled into a big raft which had several people on it. Hardly had I time to thank my rescuer when a new problem began to arise.*

Whether we had been swept out by the fairly choppy sea or whether the destroyer decided to change her location I do not know, but within minutes not only had we lost our immediate contact with the netting but somehow or other we had managed to lose the destroyer as well. She just disappeared. We became very uneasy but they must know where we were. Someone found an oar attached to the side of the raft. With this we tried to help ourselves a little by paddling in the direction from which we thought we had come. Then very suddenly our rescuer reappeared from over the horizon. Before we managed to exchange many words, everything was over. As I climbed up the netting an arm from the top reached down to help, and not a moment too soon. I suppose we were all quite exhausted by them. I cannot praise our rescuers enough. The destroyer turned out to be the sister ship of Orkan, HMS Musketeer. *The loss of* Orkan *in terms of manpower was the greatest single loss of the Polish Navy in the Second World War. Most of her splendid crew, many in their teens, went with her, never to see again their far distant native land. The Battle of the Atlantic and the war with Germany were soon brought to a successful end by the Allies. One still hopes they did not die in vain.*

The number of survivors picked up by *Musketeer*, Captain Edmund Currrey, was stated to be one officer and forty ratings. *Orkan's* captain, Commander Stanishaw Hryniewiecki, was not a survivor. Born in November 1896, he had started his naval career in the Russian Navy. In England he was appointed to command the Polish destroyer squadron. The attack on *Orkan* had been made by Kapitanleutnant Erich Mader in U378. Within days of the attack U378 was stunk by aircraft of the USS *Core*. There were no survivors.

* * *

On 3 September 1943 the Allies landed in Italy. An armistice with Italy was signed that day. Less than a week later the Italians surrendered. The weeks following the fall of Italy saw the struggle between the Allies and Germany for control of the Dodecanese and some islands to the north. The Dodecanese, a group of twelve major and numerous smaller islands, lie off the south-west coast of Turkey. Ceded to Italy in 1912 at the conclusion of the Tripolitan War, the islands' inhabitants are predominantly Greek. Rhodes, with two airfields, was the largest and most important island of the group. Scarpanto Island, 20 miles south-west of Rhodes, had an airfield suitable for fighter aircraft, as did the island of Kos 50 miles north-west of Rhodes. At Leros Island the Italians had turned Alinda Bay into a seaplane base.

As long ago as 1941 Britain had formulated plans for the capture of Rhodes. Only German success in North Africa had prevented the plans being put into operation. Prime Minister Churchill thought of the Dodecanese as a base from which to attack German communications and the Rumanian oilfields. If taken by the Allies, the islands could be utilized as a platform from which help could be directed towards Greek and Yugoslavian partisans. Another point not to be missed was that control of the Aegean would enable supplies for Russia to pass through the Dardanelles, thereby avoiding to a large extent the dangerous Arctic passage. And finally, the Dodecanese under Allied control might well be sufficient to persuade Turkey to foresake her neutrality and join the Allies. So there was much to be gained by the seizure of the Dodecanese.

With the one exception of Rhodes the Germans had no troops on any other islands. By the end of September they had occupied most of the smaller islands. On Kos, Leros, Salino, Kalymnos and Simi British troops had reinforced the Italian garrisons. The Germans recognized the strategic importance of the Dodecanese and set out to bring them under their control. That they succeeded in doing so was largely due to their having mastery of the air and the difficulty the British had in supplying the island garrisons. Submarines and destroyers were used to supply the island garrisons. For destroyers the operation was particularly difficult as only very limited air support was available, so much of their work was done at night. Another consideration was that the distance from their base at Alexandria to the Dodecanese meant that the fuel situation reduced the period they could operate in those waters.

HMS *Intrepid*

Kos Island was attacked at dawn on 3 October. The island quickly fell and then Leros and Kos were taken. But before Leros fell the Greek destroyer *Queen Olga* and HMS *Intrepid*, Commander Charles Kitkat, were sunk there by aircraft. Both ships had arrived at Port Laki at 0700 26th September. They secured to buoys about 2 cables apart. At about 0950 Commander Kitkat and his first lieutenant, Lieutenant Roland Roe, were on their way ashore in the motor cutter when enemy aircraft appeared flying up harbour at about 2,000 thousand feet. Bombs were seen falling among the destroyers. *Queen Olga* was hit aft, her depth charges or magazine exploding and blowing off her stern from the searchlight platform. Within minutes the fore-end capsized very suddenly. *Intrepid* received damage to No.3 boiler room. It was then decided to anchor *Intrepid* away from the readily visible mooring buoys that were highly visible to enemy reconnaissance aircraft. The new anchorage had a land background hence bomb-aiming would be adversely affected should there be a follow-up attack. Never the less at 1650 the harbour was again attacked. In this attack *Intrepid's* stern was blown off up to X gun. Commander Kitkat was wounded. The possibility of the ship capsizing like the *Queen Olga* was a matter for urgent consideration, as it was not then realized that *Intrepid* was aground. With this in mind Lieutenant Roe ordered all hands except guns' crews to muster on the upper deck and abandon ship. *Intrepid* had a port list of 10 degrees. After another air attack the ship was abandoned completely. Seven hours later *Intrepid* capsized and sank. Fifteen hands from *Intrepid* were lost and seventy from *Queen Olga*.

HMS *Panther*

The *Panther* was also lost by bombing in this theatre of operations. She had been completed in December 1941 by Fairfield's of Glasgow. Wilfred Sherwood was one of her hands:

I joined her as a telegraphist after serving for two years in the battleship Nelson. *I was a member of the stand-by party, joining her in mid-November. She was tied up in Fairfield's yard and as I walked along the dock I thought how untidy and rusty she looked. I wondered how many months it would take to have her ready for sea. In fact it was only two or three weeks.*

Telegraphist Sherwood was still serving in *Panther* when under Lieutenant-Commander Viscount Jocelyn the ship was engaged in an operation in the Dodecanese from 7 to 9 October, 1943, in company with the cruiser *Carlisle* and the destroyers *Petard*, *Rockwood*, and the Greek *Miaoulis*.

We were looking for invasion barges because it was expected that the Germans were on their way. We withdrew on the morning of the 8th, but went in again that night. On the morning of the 9th we failed to withdraw beyond Stuka range. They were taking off from Rhodes and waiting until the sun was high and for a gap in the air cover.

The squadron was returning to Alexandria and in a position north of Scarpanto when at about 1220 the Stukas attacked. Visibility at the time was excellent. The sea was calm and there was the usual Mediterranean glare. Lieutenant-Commander Viscount Jocelyn was concentrating *Panther's* Type 291 radar watch in the sun sector, on the starboard bow. The Stukas attacked from aft and were not detected by *Panther* until they were sighted when very nearly in position to attack. In his report of events *Panther's* captain states:

It is possible that my action in not keeping an all round Type 291 watch may be criticised but I have found from experience that with a fighter patrol in company the operators cannot complete an efficient 360 degree watch in time to detect a fast flying aircraft at reasonable range and if pressed to do this have a habit as classifying all fighters as 'Own fighters'.

The first attack was against *Carlisle*. About 5 minutes later the Stukas again struck. By this time *Rockwood* was standing by *Carlisle* and the other destroyers had started a circular patrol round the cruiser. *Panther* was to the northward, that is in the direction from where the Stukas were approaching, and had to remain steady while she tried to break up their attacks. At least five aircraft dive-bombed *Panther*. In one of these attacks she was hit just abaft the funnel by a bomb which must have exploded near her keel as it broke the ship's back. Another bomb was either a hit or near miss. Telegraphist Sherwood well remembers his experience of that day.

I was on the Panther's *flag deck with Graham Bowsher, a signalman. I heard the bombs exploding on the* Carlisle's *quarter-deck. This was the first anyone knew there were Stukas. I saw them streaking away, then raced to the WT office, my action station. Via the voice-pipe from the bridge, we were told that we were going across to take* Carlisle *in tow. We were actually on the way over when we were hit by the next wave. The first lieutenant, Lieutenant Hudson, was running aft on the port side to organize the tow when the bombs landed around him. With the ship beginning to list to port I took over the receiver and transmitter, whilst our petty officer telegraphist was packing confidential books into the disposal chest. I made the signal OEAB, meaning* Am Being Attacked By Enemy Bombers. *The yeoman yelled down the voice-pipe, 'Abandon ship'. Keith Pritchard and I left the WT office together. We were the last out. Pritchard decided to go forward and escape through the PO's mess on to B gun deck. I decided to go aft and out on to the iron deck. The list was around 45 degrees by then and I went aft along the starboard passage with one foot on the tilted deck and one foot on the inner bulkhead. When I got to the cross passage just inside the iron deck, the water was over the port and starboard engine room hatches, and the cross passage was like a deep well. I held on to the bathroom sliding door to help me shoot across, and as I did so I remembered that in a heaving sea we used to take the bathroom door off because it was loose and rattled. I prayed that it would hold, and it did. I can still hear the dreadful sounds from the trapped engine room staff as they breathed their last. Among them was 'Dusty' Miller who had joined with me in 1939.*

Once on the iron deck I found the Coder Head stuck in the top of the starboard guard-rail, which was under water, and the skipper trying to free him. Together we got him away. Being a stronger swimmer, and knowing Head was not, I gave him my lifebelt as he did not have one. The skipper was also a strong swimmer; he insisted on getting Head onto his back and swimming with him away from Panther, *which was following us round, though she was sinking fast. I remember seeing some splashes ahead of her. I never saw Keith Pritchard again. I don't know whether he was trapped up forward or whether bombs landed near him in the water. I can recall the survivors floating in a group a couple of hundred yards off the starboard waist. We kept together as we watched* Panther *sink. The stem and bow reared high in the air before slipping under, the stern disappearing just slightly ahead of the bows. Only one Carley float was available and this had some survivors, among who was Able Seaman Ray Leadbeater who was badly injured. He and I came from adjoining villages, just outside Wolverhampton. Ray lingered on for about 2 years before dying in Stoke Mandeville. We were eventually picked up by the Greek Hunt class destroyer* Miaoulis. *I can remember lying on* Miaoulis' *upper deck alongside the pom-pom and watching them firing at more Stukas. We were landed at Alexandria the next day.*

Panther broke in two near the middle, both halves sinking about 10 minutes later. Her captain says that he, *got the impression that the attack was on a scale too big for the defence, which included eight Lightnings. These intercepted part of the second attack.* Three officers and thirty-one ratings were lost with the ship. *Carlisle* had to be towed to Alexandria.

HMS *Hurworth* and (Greek) HMS *Adrias*

The island of Kos fell to the Germans in early October. Some thought was given to evacuating Leros but after due consideration it was decided to try and hold the island. On a night run to Leros with supplies, the *Jervis* and *Pathfinder* were supported by the Hunts *Hurworth* and *Adrias* (Greek) carrying out a diversionary operation. The Hunts joined the *Jervis* and *Pathfinder* to lay up for the daylight hours of 22 October at Yedi Atala in the Gulf of Kos. At 1915 the four ships slipped and proceeded on their respective duties. *Jervis* and *Pathfinder* went ahead at 28 knots. The Hunts followed at 20 Knots. At these speeds Captain John Crawford of *Jervis* expected to arrive at Leros at 2200, at which time the Hunts would be off to port Atki to begin a series of bombardments and make a general nuisance of themselves. In the same area on the previous night, as soon as *Hurworth* had switched on her searchlight the lights of Kos airfield had been seen and shortly afterwards she had been illuminated by flares and bombs. Commander Royston Wright, *Hurworth's* captain, believed that had he not given away his presence he would not have been detected.

Around 2130 *Hurworth* and *Adrias* were approaching the area of the previous night's activity. Twenty minutes later Commander Wright reduced to 15 knots and signalled *Adrias*, 5 cables astern, to do likewise. Wright planned not to make his presence known until he saw Kos airfield being operated, hoping that should this happen Captain Crawford would by then have begun unloading at Leros. *Adrias*, Commander J.H.Toumbass, RHN, was stationed on *Hurworth's* port quarter when at 2156 a heavy double tremor shook *Adrias*. Commander Toumbass felt himself being lifted off his feet. He fell face downwards on the deck with all manner of debris crashing down on him. At the same time a big explosion was heard, followed by a series of noises of rending mental. Battered and dazed Commander Toumbass staggered to his feet. The bridge appeared to be deserted. There was no response to his call to the wheelhouse. Then he saw the British Liaison Officer struggling to rise from the deck. A signalman was also tottering to his feet. Believing *Adrias* had been torpedoed Toumbass ordered that a signal to this effect be passed to *Hurworth*. He then went aft with the intention of steering the ship from there. The crew was put to shoring up bulkheads and repairing damage. *Adrias* quickly took on a 12 degrees list to starboard, and was sagging at the head. From *Hurworth* the *Adrias* was seen to be enveloped in smoke and steam. Wright saw that the bow had been blasted away as far back as the 4-inch gun. *I am coming alongside to take your crew and then sink your ship*, Wright called through a megaphone as he closed *Adrias*. Toumbass replied that he did not agree to the sinking of the ship, and that he intended to try and ground her in Turkish waters. He did agree to the transfer of superfluous hands. Wright was closing when the Greeks thought they saw a slow moving E-boat, but this turned out to be the broken off forepart of *Adrias*. Wright then lay 2 hundred yards off *Adrias*. By V/S he had just passed the first word of Report State when, at 2210, *Hurworth* struck a mine to starboard and probably just abaft the bridge.

The Greeks were stunned by *Hurworth's* misfortune. They heard loud whistling noises and a flash was seen to shoot hundreds of feet into the darkened sky. Burning oil fuel spread over the sea. Until this moment there had been no suspicion that they were in a minefield. Both ships had manoeuvred in this same locality the previous night when under attack from aircraft, so the likelihood was that the mines had been laid only a few hours previous. Commander Toumbass says of the event

> *I had no hope that anyone from the* Hurworth *had survived after the terrific explosion that had been witnessed. I tried though to get near the place of the explosion, which was completely in darkness.*

Steering by use of the engines Toumbass arrived at the point where *Hurworth* had struck the mine. With engines stopped, the Greeks peered into the darkness and listened for shouts of survivors. *Hurworth* had been blown in two at approximately the break of the fo'c'sle. The forward part had sunk in 3 minutes and the after part in less than 15. Most of her boats and floats had cleared the ship, and eighty-five of the crew were eventually rescued and taken to Turkey. But from *Adrias* nothing was seen or heard. As her list seemed to have increased to more than 15 degrees, Toumbass decided to make for the Turkish coast without delay. Lifebuoys and baulks of wood was thrown overboard to aid survivors from *Hurworth*. Despite the possibility of the forward watertight bulkheads giving way and new leaks developing, Toumbass proceeded bow-first rather than stern-first to allow the bow-wave to extinguish fires in wreckage below the bridge, and also to help minimize the prospect of striking a mine with the stern, which would have killed most or all of the hands were mustered on the quarter-deck. After little more than 2 hours of sailing without charts or compass, the entrance to a small bay was seen. Toumbass entered Gumusluk Bay, where he beached so gently that it was hardly felt. Throughout the passage *Adrias* had been in danger of capsizing and good seamanship had prevented her doing so. Six weeks later she entered Alexandria.

Adrias had spent the whole of her service with the Royal Hellenic Navy, to which she had been transferred in May 1942, 3 months prior to completion.

Under the White Ensign she would have commissioned as HMS *Border*. Declared a constructive total loss, she arrived at the breakers in November 1945.

HMS *Eclipse*

Because of an error in reporting the position of the minefield which had claimed *Hurworth* and damaged *Adrias*, the *Eclipse*, when under the command of Commander Edward Mack, was lost in the same field just over 24 hours later when she too was on a run to Leros with troops and supplies. On the afternoon prior to leaving Alexandria for her third run to Leros, *Eclipse* embarked about two hundred soldiers (mainly the 4th Battalion The Buffs) and their 40mm guns, and ten tons of stores. The destroyer *Petard* also loaded troops and stores. In addition *Eclipse* had on board Commodore Percy Todd and Brigadiers Stayner and Davies were to make a joint review of the situation at Leros. At 0030 on 23 October the *Eclipse* and *Petard* in company with the Hunts *Exmoor* and *Rockwood* put to sea for the run to Leros. The squadron was routed to pass east of Rhodes after dark, keeping in the Turkish waters as much as possible to minimize air attack.

At 1400 the *Rockwood* reported to Commander Mack that the oil fuel in her forward tanks was contaminated with water. This drastically reduced her endurance and made it imperative that she return to Alexandria. As *Rockwood* could not be left alone in such dangerous waters Commander Mack detached *Exmoor*, which had no troops or stores, to return with her. *Eclipse* and *Petard* raced on alone. They passed through Kos Strait at 2330 in line ahead at 20 knots, *Eclipse* 4 to 5 cables ahead of *Petard*. Commander Mack states that:

At about 2359 on 23 October in position 37.02'N/27.08'E a very violent explosion occurred apparently abreast No.1 boiler room, though possibly slightly further forward, under the ship on the starboard side. The ship quickly took a list to port which steadily increased until she lay on her beam and sank in about 3 minutes. Before sinking she was seen to break in two abreast the bridge, it appears there were two explosions with about 1 or 2 seconds between. The first was not as violent as the last. Neither magazine exploded, and men escaped from the immediate vicinity of both. From the rapid way in which the ship sank and the severe damage which must have been done, it seems possible that two mines may have been detonated almost simultaneously, one by antenna and one by contact. The majority of the men in the vicinity of the bridge were blown overboard, though not many survived. All three members of the rangefinder's crew left the ship in this manner, severely cutting their heads on the Type 285 serials in passing. The rangefinder was seen on the deck on the port side amidships by witnesses aft.

Seaman W. G. Bowden was in the rangefinder. He relates how fortunate he was to survive.

My action station was in the rangefinder, which is to the rear of and above the bridge. When I came to, the rangefinder was only a few feet above the surface. I didn't have time to recover completely and was still in the rangefinder when the ship rolled over. I had to struggle and kick quite a lot to get out and get back to the surface. When I arrived on the surface I was just in time to see the stern of the ship rise up and then plunge to the bottom. There was a lot of cries and shouting which went on for some 15 minutes or so. Then it went very quiet. I owe my life to the fact that in the darkness I came across a plank of wood, which I was able to cling to. It turned out to be one of the stages we used for painting the ship's side. I was picked up in the early hours of the morning by a boat from Petard. *It is hard to describe the scene on board* Petard *that night, or to describe how we felt at losing so many mates, and the ship that for many of us had been our home for over 3 years. When morning came the* Petard, *which had been searching all night for survivors and was still in the danger area, put into a small bay on the coast of Turkey with the excuse that she had engine trouble. There we stayed until darkness fell and then we returned to Alexandria.*

Petard had rescued three officers, twenty-nine ratings, and ten soldiers, before having to clear the area.

Eclipse had been mined at about 0005 on the 24th. Some 20 minutes prior to this, her ship's company had been ordered to action stations and the army personnel instructed to prepare to embark ship aft. Amidships the troops were fallen in, a hundred to each side of the ship. They were receiving instructions for disembarkation into motor launches and other craft when the explosion occurred. It is thought that the heavy casualties among the troops, only forty-three survived, may have been partly caused by those on the port side becoming held fast against the guard-rail by shifting stores when *Eclipse's* crew were picked up, leaving about a hundred and twenty lost with the ship. Commodore Todd did not survive but Brigadiers Stayner and Davies did.

HMS *Rockwood*

Except by those who sailed in her HMS *Rockwood*, Lieutenant Samuel Lombard-Hobson, is a forgotten ship, a Type III Hunt, she was completed in November 1942. The following February she joined the 5th Destroyer Flotilla at Alexandria, remaining with the flotilla throughout her active service. On 10 November a large German force made landings at Kalymnos and Kos. That night *Rockwood*, *Petard*, and *Krakowiak* (Polish) bombarded the harbour of Kalymos. As the squadron withdrew in the early hours of the 11th, the *Rockwood* was hit in the gearing room by an Hs293 glider bomb which failed to explode. At the time, *Rockwood* was proceeding at 24 knots in company with *Petard* and *Krakowiak*, all endeavouring to clear the Aegean before daylight. The bomb struck *Rockwood* on the port side upper deck at the after end of the gearing room. A path of about 20 inches diameter was cut through *Rockwood* by the bomb. The bomb's passage through the switchboard bought the port turbo-generator and both steering motors off the board. The port and starboard diesel generators were put on load. One of the steering motors was restarted, but it stopped after a few minutes so hand-steering was connected. Meanwhile the emergency generator was started, leads coupled up, and steering gear subsequently run from this. In addition it also provided power to the fire–pump and lighting circuits aft. The emergency generator was directly responsible for *Rockwood* being saved, as without it she might not have reached Turkish waters by daylight and more than likely would have had to have been sunk. *Rockwood* took on an 8 degree list to starboard, found to be caused by the holing of No.3 oil fuel tank. The whaler was turned out on the port side and all depth charges jettisoned. This countered the list slightly and the flooding was brought under control. For a time she was conned by main engines but when the level of water in the gearing room was high enough to stop the forced lubrication pumps the engines had to be shut down. Under tow of *Petard* the *Rockwood* was just able to reach Turkish waters, air attacks being frequent throughout.

For five days *Rockwood* carried out repairs. A large hole in her starboard side was satisfactorily patched. She was taken in tow for Alexandria, arriving on 19 November after a 650 miles tow. Three months after the attack she arrived in England. In August 1946 she was taken out of reserve and broken up at Gateshead, she not being considered worth the expense of repair.

HMS *Dulverton*

Two days after *Rockwood* had been hit by the glider bomb one of her sister ships was hit by another of these weapons. The *Echo* and the Hunts *Belvoir* and *Dulverton* left Limasol in Cyprus on the morning of 12 December. The destroyers were proceeding at 22 knots towards the Aegean via the Rhodes Channel. Around 2300 a JU88 was sighted overhead. The bomber dropped a flare. It then shadowed the division on its progress along the Turkish coast. At 0330 Kiro Light was abeam. Twenty minutes later course was altered north so as to enter Kos Strait. In his account of events the captain of *Echo* states:

At 0401 a large splash as of a bomb was seen close up to the mainland of Cos through the night. At 0445 Dulverton *was hit forward by a glider bomb in position 36.50'N/27.30'E. The bomb gave no warning of approach and the noise of the rush through the air was only heard just before it struck.*

Dulverton was hit abreast the port Oerlikon, the bomb probably penetrating through the magazine. It is likely that the magazine exploded as all forward of the bridge was blown away. Lieutenant Anthony Evans was on *Dulverton's* bridge.

The bridge personnel were put out of action and many disappeared. Fires were started along the starboard side of the ship. The commanding officer, navigating officer, and principal control officer, were all on deck with various limbs broken. The coxswain, with great gallantry appeared out of the wreckage of the wheelhouse and endeavoured to save the commanding officer who was, however, unconscious and little could be done for him. He was placed on a floatnet but fell off and was not seen again.

As aircraft were still in the vicinity *Echo* and *Belvoir* circled the *Dulverton* before stopping to pick up survivors. The planes were engaged but they did not drop bombs. By 0320 109 survivors had been rescued. *Dulverton* was still afloat, though down at the head and burning from end to end. At 0333 *Belvoir* sank *Dulverton* with torpedoes. *Echo* and *Belvoir* then made towards Turkish territorial waters, 2 miles away. Both ships returned safely to harbour. Seventy-eight of *Dulverton's* crew, including her captain Commander Stuart Buss, had been lost.

Dulverton was the last destroyer to be lost in this phase of the Dodecanese campaign. A German invasion force began landing on Leros from 12 November. On the 16th Leros formally surrendered after tough fighting. Allied troops were withdrawn from other islands in the area. It would be almost a year before the Allies put together a force of sufficient strength to drive the Germans from the Dodecanese.

* * *

HMS *Tynedale*

For the next two destroyer losses the scene shifts from the Aegean to the Mediterranean and a KMS convoy. The KMS convoys between the United Kingdom and North Africa began in October 1942. On 12 December 1943 the *Tynedale* was hit by a torpedo while escorting KMS34 off the Algerian coast. Lieutenant-Commander John York, her captain, reports:

The signalled speed was 6 knots but the convoy was making good more than 7. Tynedale was zigzagging independently 60 degrees each side of the mean course at 12.5 knots. The orders were that the ship would not be steady for more than 5 minutes. It appears that shortly before 0700 the S/R key of the asdic set began to give trouble. It was found that some part needed replacement. While this was being fetched from the store the operator was ordered to keep listening watch. The ASCO was on watch at the time and I imagine his reason for not reporting this defect to me was that he knew that the set would be correctly again before the screen could be adjusted. He was an exceptionally good officer. At the moment of impact the ship had been on the port (northerly) leg of her zigzag for a full 5 minutes. The A/S operator heard nothing and the lookout saw nothing before the hit. The ship seems to have been hit beneath the funnel, possibly by a non-contact torpedo. She broke in half. The bow portion rolled to port and sank by the stern. A few men only escaped from the position; they are from such varied places as the galley flat, fore mess deck, cabin flat, asdic compartment, wheelhouse, and bridge. I myself swam off the bridge as it sank. The last I saw of the bows they were pointing skywards with the asdic dome well clear of the water. The stern portion floated better and many more men were able to escape from there. There was also time to unprime depth charges, which must have saved many lives. HMS Hyderabad *and HMS Rescue Tug* Hengist *came up fairly soon and picked up survivors. Both ships and the boats of HMS* Hyderabad *were very quick and efficient; at the time, however, it seemed a slow process.*

Tynedale had been hit at 0710 by U593. Sixty-six of the crew was lost. Lieutenant-Commander Yorke had been captain of the *Berkley* at Dieppe.

HMS *Holcombe*
During the search for U593 the *Holcombe* obtained a contact off her port bow. She had just turned to engage when a torpedo struck aft near her oil fuel tanks, which burst into flame. Her captain, Lieutenant-Commander Frank Graves, was on the bridge. Hearing a dull thud he immediately looked towards the stern, just in time to see a column of flame rise to 200 feet. This was accompanied by a 'terrific roar' which lasted 2 or 3 seconds. Graves had the impression that the flame was rising near the after mounting. *Holcombe* took on a list to port and began to go down by the stern. Graves walked down the starboard side and only pushed off the rescue craft when she was going down. Eighty-four of the crew died with the ship.

Kapitanleutnant Gerd Kelbling, who was twenty-eight, had sunk *Tynedale* and *Holcombe*. Both had been sunk by a gnat. He was about to attack another escort of KMS34, the *Calpe*, when himself was attacked by *Calpe* and the USS *Wainwright*. U593, badly damaged by depth charges, had to be abandoned. Kelbling and his crew were taken prisoners.

Tynedale and *Holcombe*, both Hunts, were the last of the 1943 sinkings in the Mediterranean.

HMS *Limbourne*
A few weeks prior to the loss of *Tynedale* and *Holcombe*, the Hunt class *Limbourne* met her end in Home Waters. She was lost in action with German naval forces. The engagement, on 23 October, took place 100 miles south of

Plymouth. The British ships, called Force 28, consisted of the cruiser *Charybdis*, the fleet destroyers *Grenville* and *Rocket*, and the Hunts *Limbourne*, *Talybont*, *Stevenstone*, and *Wensleydale*. The reason for the operation, one of a series known as Tunnel, was to intercept the German merchantman *Munsterland* as she made way between Brest and Cherbourg. She had a close escort of torpedo boats. At 1500 on 22 October the *Munsterland* sailed from Brest. A few hours later her outer escort of five TBs sailed for a position to the north of her route. At 1900 Force 28 left Plymouth.

Sub-Lieutenant Dudley Cunliff-Owen of *Limbourne:*

The squadron was in line ahead in the following order: Charybdis, Grenville, Rocket, Limbourne, Talybont, Stevenstone *and* Wensleydale. *At about 0030 on arrival in position 325 degrees, Les Heux 7 miles, course was altered without signal to 267 degrees and speed reduced to 13 knots. At about 0118 the first indication of the presence of the enemy was given by radio interception loud and clear. It was impossible to tell the relative position of the enemy, whose signals were, however, plainly received.*

Commander Walter Phipps, *Limbourne's* CO, signalled that the senior officer that the indications were that three enemy units were close. The signal appears not to have been understood in *Charybdis* and a repeat was asked for. At 0136, Force 28 was now 7 miles north of the Les Triago islands, *Charybdis* made radar contact with the enemy and signalled *Bearing 270 at 8,800 Yards*. During manoeuvres that took place over the next 15 minutes, events in the darkness were at times confused. Cunliff-Owen:

The senior officer was observed to alter course 40 degrees to starboard. No signal was received on Limbourne's *bridge and it was not clear whether a Red or Blue turn had been carried out.* Limbourne *followed in the wake of the next ahead. The other ships appear to have made a Blue turn and to be on a line of bearing. The following events appear to have developed.* Charybdis *increased speed and led round to port. She was heard to open fire on the enemy, whose position was not known in* Limbourne. Grenville *and* Rocket *did not immediately follow, but held their course, followed by* Limbourne. *This manoeuvre placed* Charybdis *on* Limbourne's *port bow, distance between 3,000 or 4,000 yards.* Charybdis *was picked up and assumed to be the enemy.* Limbourne *fired her rockets and clearly illuminated* Charybdis, *who was almost immediately struck by a torpedo. By this time* Grenville *and* Rocket *were leading round to port, crossing* Limbourne's *bows.* Limbourne's *wheel was put hard aport and two short blasts were sounded to avoid* Rocket. *While the ship was swinging to port, a torpedo attack was sighted on a relative bearing of Red 140 degrees. The wheel was put hard to starboard and the impression of officers was that the torpedo had missed ahead; however, there was a tremendous explosion forward. It appeared that the torpedo had struck the ship forward of the low power room, and in view of the damage done it is considered that the forward magazine blew up. The ship immediately took on a heavy but not frightening list to starboard and appeared to be sinking.*

It was then 0150.

The German ships, *Munsterland's* outer escort, were the torpedo boats T22, T23, T25, T26, and T27. At the moment of opening fire with torpedoes, the Germans were proceeding south of parallel to the British force. The T23 had been the first to fire torpedoes at *Charybdis*, scoring one hit. She was hit for a second time by a torpedo of T27. *Charybdis* sank at about 0230, 45 minutes after being hit. Still in line ahead, the German squadron cleared the area at speed. The attack had lasted 7 minutes, and with the exception of T25 all had fired a salvo of six torpedoes.

After *Limbourne* was torpedoed the position on her bridge was that Commander Phipps was concussed and incoherent, although he seemed to be taking an intelligent interest. The first lieutenant was much the same, but he appeared fit to assume command. Reports indicated that *Limbourne* was in no danger of sinking, although below the water-line she had been blown away from forward of the low power room and the forecastle deck from forward of the captain's cabin. She had steam on the engines and one steering motor was in action. However, hopes of steaming *Limbourne* stern-first for home was quickly dashed. Sub-Lieutenant Cunliffe-Owen:

Before any sternway had been made, steam was lost due to water in the oil fuel. I proceeded to the bridge to inform the first lieutenant of the situation. I found him incoherent and I considered him unfit to continue command. The command devolved on me and I left the first lieutenant on the bridge. A fire was reported in the low power room and a party was delighted to get this under control. The glare of the flames was showing through the damaged bow and giving the position of the ship away. In about half an hour the fire was extinguished. Steam had once more been regained and a further endeavour to the steam ship was made. Telephonic communication was established between the tiller flat and the searchlight platform. The emergency telegraphs in the engine room and the voice-pipe were used to communicate with the engine room. Things were well under control and it appeared that we had a good chance of steaming the ship away from the enemy coast, which was clearly in sight about 5 miles from distant. However, repeated efforts failed to steady the ship on a course either stern-first or bow-first and we succeeded only in turning in wide and uncontrollable circles which, if anything, seemed to be taking us nearer to the enemy coast.

It was decided to tow *Limbourne* stern-first. The wounded and all hands not required were transferred to *Talybont,* which was then to tow the ship. When the tow became taut, *Limbourne's* engines were put half astern together and the wheel amidships. *Limbourne* gathered stern-way and almost immediately took on a violent sheer which could not be checked, and the tow parted. Cunliffe-Owen concludes his narrative:

> *A conference of available officers was held on* Limbourne, *as a result of which I decided that in view of the adverse effect of wreckage forward, and the consequent impossibility of steering, that a successful towage in the circumstances was impossible. I informed* Talybont *of this and gave the order to prepare to abandon ship.* Talybont *once more came alongside and all hands boarded her. Considerable delay was caused due to extricating the seriously wounded from the WT office and bridge superstructure. In order to sink the ship the after magazine was flooded and I gave orders for the engine room running down valves to be opened. After the last of the wounded were aboard* Talybont *I left the ship.*

Limbourne was torpedoed and sunk by *Rocket.* By 1000 Force 28 had returned to harbour. Whenever details were known of a probable enemy shipping movement up Channel from Brest, a British force had been dispatched to intercept. The Germans became aware that the British always ran along the same patrol line in line ahead. Having discovered the pattern, they used the *Munsterland* to lure the British into a trap. German shore radar had followed Force 28, and the TBs had done the rest.

HMS *Worcester*
The penultimate destroyer loss of the year was the *Worcester,* though in fact she was a constructive total loss. On 23 December the *Worcester* was covering the seaward side of the Methil-Southend convoy FS8 when at 2252 a heavy underwater explosion was felt and a column of water about 60 feet high was seen around her stern abreast the after superstructure and mainly to port. She began to flood aft. Owing to the possibility of further damaging *Worcester,* her captain, Lieutenant Hamer, was advised not to move the main engines. The following morning at 0140 the *Quorn,* which had been sent to stand-by the ship, was ordered alongside to take off surplus ratings. Despite fine ship handling by *Quorn's* captain, this operation had to be abandoned owing to a strong wind and heavy swell. At this time it was thought *Worcester* was sinking, her upper deck at the stern being some 5 feet under water. The tug *Champion* arrived but was unable to get alongside to help with pumping. During the morning *Worcester* was taken under tow and by 1130 was brought to anchor off Yarmouth. A salvage tug was secured alongside and at once began pumping out. *Worcester* was not repaired for sea duty. From May 1944 she was used as an

accommodation ship. In June 1945 her name was changed to *Yeoman*. She was broken up in February 1947 after many years of loyal service.

HMS *Hurricane*

Along with the *Harvester, Havant, Havelock, Hesperus,* and *Highlander,* the *Hurricane* was laid down in 1939 for the Brazilian Navy. Launched as the *Japarua* she was taken over before completion and commissioned into the Royal Navy together with her five sister ships. Commander John Westmacott was her captain when she was sunk on Christmas Day.

The escort Group B1 of *Hurricane, Wanderer, Watchman,* and the frigate *Glenarm* sailed from Moville at 2200 in 17 December as a support group. Shortly after midday on the 22nd the group joined convoy ON216. At 1140 on the 23rd Commander Westmacott was ordered to leave ON126, providing the convoy was not threatened, to join and support OS62 (UK–Freetown). This convoy was contacted by radar at 0930 next morning.

Hurricane and *Glenarm* were sweeping ahead of the convoy when they received orders to proceed at best speed to position 45degreesN 22 degrees W where the US destroyer *Leary* had been torpedoed. The *Leary*, part of a US Task Group, had been hit and sunk by a gnat of U275. On approaching the area of the attack on *Leary*, Westmacott carried out a search based on the assumption that during daylight the U-boat would remain submerged and proceeding on a steady course of about 2 knots. At 1945 a radar contact was obtained at a range of more than 9,000 yards. As *Glenarm* was suitably positioned the range and bearing was passed to her with orders to investigate. *Glenarm* had in fact already picked up the echo. At 1951 the expected radar contact was made at 9,000 yards. Soon after this the U-boat dived. Asdic failed to pick her up.

The U451, Kapitanleutnant Kurt Neide, was having no such problems. The gnat he fired had no trouble finding *Hurricane*. The *Glenarm*, which had carried out an attack on another suspected U-boat contact, was ordered to join *Hurricane*. Westmacott warned *Glenarm* that she might have to take *Hurricane* in tow. Preparations for towing had already been put in hand when at 2214 a signal was received ordering *Hurricane* to be sunk if she was unable to steam. At 0945 on Christmas morning, the *Watchman* arrived. She was ordered to screen while *Hurricane's* crew transferred to *Glenarm*. The abandoned ship was then sunk.

Chapter Six

1944

On 22 January, under the command of Major-General John P. Lucas, United States Army, the Allied 6th Corps landed at Anzio in Operation Shingle. Taking part in Shingle were destroyers of the 14th Destroyer Flotilla. Two of the flotilla were sunk. At 0200 on the 22nd a German 6-inch gun was making things uncomfortable, so the *Jervis* and *Janus* were deployed northward along the coast to harass the gun. They pumped so many rounds into the position that they had to cease fire to allow their guns to cool. At dusk they moved seaward to sweep for U-boats and enemy shipping. Operation Shingle had taken the Germans by surprise, and the landings had proceeded against light resistance. By evening 90 per cent of the assault force was ashore with more than three thousand vehicles. Attacks by the Luftwaffe on the following evening accounted for the loss of *Janus* and heavy damage to *Jervis*.

HMS *Janus*
Signalman Raymond Freeman had joined the navy in July 1939, aged sixteen. On the bridge of *Janus* at the time of her loss, he recalls:

> *After seeing the troops ashore our duties then were to patrol up and down the coast giving them any gunnery protection possible. On the day of the 23rd we had been pestered by a German 88mm gun that had been taking pot-shots at us all day. At approximately 1730 we had it in our sights. Our skipper signalled 1730 we had it in our sights. Our skipper signalled to his senior officer, Captain D14 in Jervis:* Have Gun In My Sights. Request Permission To Close And Attack. *The reply came back:* Follow Me. *We did. Just the two of us in line ahead. Another signal came from Captain D:* Hoist Battle Ensign. *At that moment we were being attacked by enemy aircraft. After one or two short attacks all went quiet. We steamed closer to our target, bearing in mind we could only go so far because of minefields.*
>
> *We had all guns trained towards our target when at approximately 1750 in came another air attack, torpedo and dive-bombers. The number of aircraft I could not say. They came overland, as we were so well silhouetted with the sunset the*

other side of us. As they came nearer, one dropped two torpedoes quite close. I think everybody on the starboard side and on the bridge must have seen them. I reported: 'Torpedoes starboard side, sir', like a few others must have done. By now I reckon that the time would be 1753. Being so close to the minefield we had no alternative but to steam on, hoping the aircraft would miss us; but we just watched them get closer until with one flash it was all over. Janus *was blown in half. One torpedo hit the forward magazine and the other hit the boiler room. I had a clear idea of where they were going because we watched them close in. When I came to, I was at the back of the bridge. I had been blown from the front, where we had been standing at action stations, and over the director; I must have hit the rangefinder, which no doubt saved me from going right down to the upper deck. At this stage the remaining part of the bridge was under water with the stern above my head. I was waist-high in water with the ship slipping from under me. All I had to do was swim. What I remember after that was holding a hammock. Someone spoke to me, and then I lost consciousness again. The next thing I knew it was 0400 next morning. I woke up in bed in a large brick building with umpteen water bottles round me to get me warm. The only thing I salvaged was the red light off my lifebelt. Everything else was dumped because I was covered in horrible thick black oil. I learned that an American amphibious jeep (DUKW) had picked me out of the sea at 2200, so I had been there 4 hours. No wonder my body was cold. It had been snowing during the invasion. The captain was killed along with everybody else on the bridge, which could have been about twenty-five men. I have heard that there was only seven survivors forward of the funnel, and only me from the bridge. I lost too many friends to call it my lucky day.*

Lieutenant-Commander William Morrison, the captain of *Janus*, was the son of a brigadier. *Janus* was hit first command, his appointment dating from 16 June 1943.

* * *

The failure to strike out immediately from the Anzio beach-head led to the Allies being contained in the area for more than a month. During this period the cruisers *Spartan* and *Penelope* were sunk, *Spartan* by a glider bomb on 29 January and *Penelope* on 18 February by a U-boat. Then on 25 February the *Inglefield* was sunk by a glider bomb.

The Henschel 293 glider bomb was first used operationally on 27 August 1943 when aircraft attacked the 1st Group off Finisterre, badly damaging the Canadian destroyer *Athatbaskan*. These radio-controlled bombs had a wing-span of more than 10 feet. Two such bombs were slung beneath the wings of a Heinkel 117 or a Dornier 217. After its release from the parent aircraft, a liquid-fuel rocket-motor under the glider bomb's fuselage increased its speed to more than 350 mph. After 12 seconds the motor cut and the bomb glided in a shallow dive towards its target, guided by a small joy-stick in the parent aircraft.

HMS *Inglefield*

The *Inglefield*, Commander Christopher Churchill, was in the Anzio area when at about 1755 on 25 October a red warning was received. First degree of readiness was ordered. Around 1810 the sound of aircraft was heard. *Inglefield* increased from 11 to 20 knots and course altered to head towards the sound. An aircraft was sighted and then a glider bomb was observed approaching the ship, which was still gathering speed. The Oerlikons opened fire at the bomb, which hit the ship at 1812. A large hole was torn in her starboard side from the after superstructure to the foremost torpedo tubes. This hit was quickly by a second explosion, believed to be a near miss by another Hs 293. *Inglefield* took an immediate list to port and settled by the stern. The lights went out and communications failed. The searchlight platform, the forward depth charge throwers, and the after torpedo tubes, were blown over the side.

When Commander Churchill had sufficient reports to convince him that *Inglefield* could not move under her own steam, he ordered the boats and floats made ready, his intention being to clear the ship except for a towing party. But when the ship lost some of her list and settled further by the stern, he ordered her abandoned. It soon became evident that *Inglefield* had in fact sunk, her stern resting on the bottom. She remained in this manner for some time with her back slowly breaking. She finally disappeared between 1900 and 1930. Thirty-five of the crew had perished.

HMS *Laforey*

Under the command of Captain Henry Armstrong the *Laforey* was also involved in operations off Anzio. She was sunk towards the end of March in an attack by a U-boat. Gunner's Mate Robert Burns had been in the Navy ten years when he joined *Laforey* at the time of Operation Torch. The following is his account of the action which culminated in the sinking of *Laforey*.

'We are returning to Naples for a boiler clean and a well-earned break'. *The date was 28 March 1944; the scene, Anzio beach-head; the ship, HMS* Laforey, *flotilla leader extraordinary. The speaker, Lieutenant Boyer, RNR, Laforey's gunnery officer. 'Thank God', I murmered. At last there was the prospect of a break from the command that had kept us in action at sea for so long. We certainly needed it. The preceding 3 months had been exceeding demanding, a period in which the Royal Navy had experienced heavy losses.* Penelope, Royalist, Janus, *to mention a few 'chummy' ships, all lay on the bottom, after constant attacks from the air, by Jerry's 11-inch gun on the railway from Rome, and his radio-controlled bomb. My heart sang as we headed south to Naples. And in Naples harbour on the morning of 29 March Lieutenant Boyer and I were talking idly about our hopes for the days of peace to come when Jock Abernethy, a big raw-boned Scot, appeared to tell us that Captain 'Beaky' Armstrong, our new skipper, wanted us in his cabin. What would be his news? A recall to UK? Or perhaps a few days in Sorrento or Capri, just as Captain 'Tubby' Hutton had ordered the previous November when Naples had suffered a terrible typhus epidemic. No such luck. Our skipper's orders were that we were to proceed with full speed to an area west of Stromboli where a U-boat had been reported.*

After all our tremendous range of action in the Mediterranean, U-boat hunting was recognized by most as a 'piece of cake'. Had we not sunk the Italian submarine Ascianghi *off Sicily? And anyway, to operate in an area free from the Luftwaffe's attention would be a relief in itself. At noon, just before we arrived in the area where the U-boat had been sighted, we were joined by* Tumult, Blencathra, Quantock, *and* Lamerton. *And soon the metallic clang of the Asdics indicated we had located our quarry. Excitement ran high as an attack was mounted by Captain Armstrong, the senior officer of the flotilla. Most of us had visions of an early return to the Naples to continue our interrupted 'break', but this was not to be. Attack after attack failed to bring the U-boat to the surface but as darkness fell our asdic team was confident that, during the night, lack of air would bring her to the surface and then my gun teams would have the chance of delivering the coup de grace.*

Shortly before 0100.m next day, the message was passed to the transmitting station from the bridge that the U-boat was blowing her tanks and we were to prepare for starshell firing to illuminate our quarry. Captain Armstrong, for reasons best known to himself, decided not to sound off full action stations. The crew was therefore at defence stations, only half the armament manned, and many men were asleep in the mess decks. With hindsight one can say that many of the 179 men who lost their lives would have been saved had they been closed-up at action stations. The order came suddenly to open fire and within moments night became day as the starshell illuminated the area where the U-boat would break surface. 'Gunner's mate to the bridge!' Sub-Lieutenant Ticehurst, the youngest officer in the ship, for reasons that I was never to discover, made the call that was to save my life. When I got there I found the U-boat was clearly visible on the port bow. Our 4.7 armament was soon straddling the target, and when the gunnery officer arrived on the bridge, I jumped down over the bridge-screen to the Oerlikon, determined to ensure that the U-boat's deck was raked with fire in case resistance was offered. Then came the order to switch on the searchlight. It proved to be the opportunity the U-boat skipper needed, for suddenly there was a deafening explosion and I found myself hurtling upwards and then landing with a thud on the Oerlikon's safety rail. The U-boat had torpedoed us and I was conscious between bouts of blackness and pain that Laforey *was breaking up in her death throes. I tried to stand, but had no movement in my legs. Using my elbows I managed to propel my body to the ship's side.* Laforey *was almost V-shaped, as with a final effort I managed to slip down into the sea. Within seconds I was enveloped in the masthead rigging as* Laforey *started her final plunge. Frantically I tore myself free, and with arms working like pistons propelled myself as far from the inevitable whirlpool suction as possible. Suddenly, like a cork, I was whirled round and round, and drawn towards the vortex where our beloved ship had finally disappeared beneath the waves. Fortunately my half-inflated lifebelt kept me on the surface.*

Gradually the black silence was broken with the cries of shipmates dotted around the ocean. With the whistle always carried by a gunner's mate for turret drill, I began to signal in the hope of collecting the survivors in a more compact group. But unconsciousness intervened and when I came round again, it was to hear the groans of a young London AB clinging to driftwood and obviously in a bad way. At odd intervals shipmates would swim to us to offer words of comfort and encouragement, and then swim off to assist others. Two such gallant friends, Dave Barton, the PO Cook, and 'Knocker' White, the Yeoman of Signals, both uninjured but sadly not to survive, continued to help their more unfortunate shipmates.

After what appeared to be an eternity I spotted this darker shape of an approaching vessel. Suddenly there were cries of 'Swim you German bastards!' *Our would-be rescuers were convinced we were German survivors from the U-boat which* Tumult *and* Blencathra *had eventually sunk, unaware of the fact that* Laforey *had gone too. Cries of* 'Laforey! Laforey!' *came from the water, and soon the plop of oars was followed by* Tumult's *whaler appearing from nowhere. Within moments I was carefully and gently lifted from the sea and into the boat. Oil fuel fouled my mouth and eyes, and hid the tears of relief and gratitude for my rescuers. Soon I was hoisted aboard* Tumult.....

Laforey had been sunk by the U223. She had been steaming at 6 knots when at 0110 a torpedo had struck to port, just before the funnel. She sank within 2 minutes of being hit. Captain Armstrong was not a survivor. Oberleutnant zur See Peter Gerlach had been captain of U223 for less than 3 months. He did not survive.

HMS *Quail*

Events leading to the loss of *Quail* might be said to have begun 7 months prior to her actual sinking. At the beginning of November 1943 there were thirteen U-boats in the Mediterranean. On 11 November U453 laid mines off Bari. These mines were a new type: they ticked over for the passing of several ships before the mechanism activated. On 15 November, 1943, *Quail* and *Quilliam* were returning to Bari after night operations. *Quail* had turned into the same water passed through by *Quilliam* a few minutes earlier to enter harbour when a mine exploded under *Quail's* stern. Ninety minutes later, tugs had berthed her alongside at Bari. About twenty hands had perished. She remained at Bari for the next 7 months.

Around six in the evening of 16 June 1944 *Quail* left Bari under tow of the tug *Capotistria*. The trawler *Bream* and ML577 were in attendance for the 230 miles journey to Taranto, where *Quail* was expected to arrive at 0600 on the 18th for further repairs. She had on board a towing party of four seamen, an ERA, a shipwright, and a Lieutenant Gardner who was in charge. At 0410 on the 18th *Quail* was to the west of Gallipoli in the Gulf of Tarranto. Skipper Stanley Larner, RNR, of the *Bream* says,

I was stood on the bridge with the officer of the watch concentrating on the Quail *at the time and saw a huge flash and also heard a huge explosion. I tried to contact the tug but could not contact him, as he was signalling* Quail.

Skipper Henderson, RNR, of the *Capotistria* was on the bridge when he heard a noise.

The noise seemed to come from the stern. I immediately went to the side of the bridge and looked aft. I saw nothing. The Quail *seemed to be in her usual trim. I then tried to signal the* Quail *but the signalman could make nothing of the signals. I then heard shouting from the* Quail. *I could not make out what the shouting was.*

Suddenly *Quail's* stern disappeared below the surface, indicating that the after end was quickly flooded. *Capotistria* tried to slip but owing to the sudden up-ending of *Quail* a great strain was out on the tow. The *Capotistria* went full astern, which allowed her to release the tow. With the exception of the ERA, who disappeared, the towing party was rescued from the sea. *Quail* had gone down through striking a mine, probably under the engine room; this flooded and broke the forward bulkhead, which flooded the boiler room, and this sank the ship. The U453 had laid mines on 11 November.

HMS *Hardy*

Two destroyers were sunk while escorting Arctic convoys in 1944, bringing the total lost in such operations to six. On 26 January convoy JW56B of sixteen ships sailed from Loch Ewe. Comprised of the *Hardy, Inconstant, Offa, Venus, Vigilant, Virago,* and the Royal Norwegian Navy's *Stord,* the 26th Destroyer Flotilla sailed from Kola Inlet at 2100 in 28 January as a Support Group to JW56B. Captain D26 was Captain Geoffrey Robson, the CO of *Kandahar* when she was sunk in December 1941.

The first HF/DF bearing of a U-boat believed to be in contact with the convoy was received at 1745 on 29 January. Further such bearings indicated that U-boats were spread ahead of the convoy, which had not yet passed through the main concentration. Robson therefore decided to sweep the reverse route of the convoy with the whole flotilla in the hope of catching the enemy from the rear and disorganizing his arrangements by attacking from an unexpected direction. The support group and escorts were so successful in their defence of their convoy that all sixteen of its ships safely entered Kola Inlet on 1 February. *Hardy* was the only casualty among the warships.

At 0404 on 30 January *Hardy* had been hit a gnat fired by Kapitanleutnant Joachim Franze. About 3 minutes later another torpedo hit the ship. After the first explosion *Hardy* shook violently twice, then she trimmed by the stern and listed 5 to 10 degrees to starboard. On arrival in the engine room, the engineer officer found the starboard engine revolving at very high speed and making a loud rattling noise and the port engine stopped. As the regulating valves to both engines were shut, the starboard shaft was obviously broken. The engine room was free of water but the gearing room was found to be flooded to the upper platform and was evacuated. Shortly afterwards the second explosion occurred. The port engine was put out of action. *Hardy* was flooded up to the after engine room bulkhead, which was holding and not buckling visibly. No.2 boiler room was evacuated. Soon after this the order was passed for everyone to make for the fo'c'sle. No.1 boiler room was evacuated. After the initial list to starboard *Hardy* returned to upright, but finally listed from 5 to 10 degrees to port. At 0418 *Virago* was ordered by *Venus* to close and pick up survivors. *Virago* also went alongside *Hardy* and took off crewmen, as did *Venus*. And it was *Venus* which at 0551 sank *Hardy* with a torpedo. The son of an army officer, Captain (later Vice-Admiral Sir) Robson had in 1940 been awarded a DSO (Bar 1941) and in 1941 a DSC.

The convoy that followed JW56B (JW57) left Loch Ewe on 20 February. Three days later the convoy, around fifty ships, was sighted by a JU88 and was subsequently shadowed by a Kondor. Fourteen U-boats were deployed to intercept. On 24 February a Kondor established contact with JW57. Before it was beaten off by aircraft of the escort carrier *Chaser*, the Kondor homed four U-boats on to the convoy. One of these boats was sunk by *Keppel*. Throughout that day and the next, escorts fought off the U-boats, which by the evening of the 26th were no longer in touch. Another U-boat was sunk in the battle but in return the U990 had on the 25th sunk the *Mahratta* with a gnat.

HMS *Mahratta*

Leslie Bloodworth had joined the navy in 1942 when he was eighteen. He recalls:

At the end of my seaman's training I was picked out for a gunnery course, which I passed as an LRIIII (gunlayers). This was my job aboard Mahratta, *which I joined early in 1943. I was resting for my turn on the middle watch. At approximately 2045 a torpedo struck* Mahratta, *just as* La Paloma *was being played on the ship's radio. For some reason or other, I dressed into all my clothing and then turned back in! I was so tired I hadn't realized what had happened. Then the ship was hit again and she lurched to port. In the dark I made my way to the upper deck where, I suppose there were about fifty who had been killed by the explosions. When I arrived on deck there were about two hundred men there. As time went by, the captain informed us that a ship would come alongside to take us off. We were warned not to rush to the port side, as* Mahratta *was listing heavily to port. The ship took about 1.5 hours to sink, and no one came alongside to take us off. The list to port had grown steadily worse. Quite a few of the crew had become panicky and had dived into the sea. There was a bit of a swell, which caused a wave to take us into the water, which was 18 degrees below freezing.*

Once in the sea we seemed to split up into groups. Some went different ways. The water was icy cold. Nearly all of my group just stopped talking and slipped away. Suddenly, about a mile away, it's hard to judge in the dark, I saw a red and a green light come on. It was a ship making a search for us. As we had no red light on our lifebelts, the ship couldn't see us; so we had to get to her. The last person I was with Able Seaman McMillian, one of her messmates. 'Go on, Bristol. I can't make it', said Mac. I felt terrible about that. By the time I reached the ship, which was the destroyer Impulsive, *I had been in the sea about 45 minutes, and was very stiff. In fact I don't think I could have lasted much longer.*

Eighteen of *Mahratta's* crew were rescued by *Impulsive* although A petty officer died during the night. It is reported that *Mahratta* had at 2232 rolled slowly to port and sank by the stern. She was the only casualty of the escort, and none of the merchantmen had been sunk. Lieutenant-Commander Eric Drought, her captain, came from a seafaring family. He had entered Dartmouth in May 1925. Sadly, he did not survive the sinking.

Exactly 3 months to the day on which he had sunk *Mahratta*, Kapitanleutnant Hubert Nordheimer was sunk by a depth charge from an RAF aircraft. He and thirty-two of his crew were rescued, possibly the U276.

Mahratta was the last destroyer to be lost on the 'Russian Run'. Eighty-nine merchant ships and eighteen warships had been sunk on these convoys, and a total of 2,783 officers and men of the Royal Navy and the Merchant Navy had been lost.

HMS *Warwick*

Although she fought in two world wars the *Warwick*, Commander Denys Rayner, RNVR, is another of HM ships which nowadays is scarcely remembered. Her end came in February when U431 hit her with a torpedo. *Warwick* had sailed from Plymouth to rendezvous outside the Sound with *Scimitar* and *Saladin*. Having experienced engine trouble, *Saladin* failed to arrive from Portland. The ships were meant to conduct an A/S search between Pendeen Head and Trevose Head, a distance of some 50 miles, in response to the sighting of a U-boat reported to be in the area on a minelaying operation. The ships were disposed abeam and zigzagging broadly. On Sunday 20th at 0815 an asdic contact was obtained. One depth charge was dropped but this only brought some dead fish to the surface. Thereafter a large number of non-sub contacts of a 'fish' nature were received. After breakfast Commander John Heath, A/S officer to C-in-C Plymouth, discussed the desirability of changing the asdic amplifiers as he was not satisfied with them. At 1135 the HSD began to tune the asdic set. So, for a time the ship's asdic was out of action to enable adjustments to be made.

At about 1137 *Warwick*, zigzagging at 12 knots, turned 40 degrees to starboard. Eight minutes later a torpedo from U431, Kapitanleutnant Gustav Poel, struck the ship. *Warwick* was at this time on the southern leg of her patrol and 254 degrees/14.7 miles from Trevose Head. A column of smoke shot to a height of 150 feet. Commander Rayner, who at that moment was looking aft, disclosed later:

Everything turned red and there was a terrific blast of hot air, a violent explosion occurred in the after magazine which cut the ship in half abaft the bulkhead of the captain's cabin. The stern was blown clean away and floated separately. The ship remained on an even keel and was remarkably steady. A few seconds later another and minor explosion occurred which shook the hull more than the first much larger explosion. Even so, the ship remained on an even keel and it was considered there was every chance of saving the main hull.

Chief Yeoman of Signals William Spear had been 16 years in the navy and *Warwick* was his fifth destroyer. He recalls:

I left the bridge at about 1120 and went to the chief petty officers' mess, which was below the upper deck, the hatchway being on the starboard side near the break at the forecastle. The Warwick *was in position 50.26'42"N/05.22'47"W when at 1145 there was an explosion aft. I went up the ladder and looking along the upper deck I saw about 70 feet of our stern floating away. I immediately went up to the bridge to ensure the disposal of confidential material. On my coming down to the forecastle I encountered a seaman who in jumping down from B gun had broken his leg. He was being attended to by another seaman. I helped tie two lifebelts around the injured man before he went over the side. I heard later that he had survived. During this time the ship was gradually going over to port. I went down to the upper deck, which was at an angle of about 30 degrees. Most of the ship's company went over the port side but as I had come down the starboard ladders, and as time was getting short, I went over the starboard side. I clambered up the deck and onto the ship's side, which by then was at an angle of 45 degrees. I slipped and sat heavily on the stabilizer, injuring the bottom of my spine as a result. Taking off my shoes I went into the water and swam to a Denton raft, virtually a piece of cork about 18 ins x18 ins with ropes on each side, where, with two shipmates, I held on to one of the ropes. At the time of the sinking a number of fishing boats were some 10 miles distant of our starboard bow. The explosion attracted their attention and they were soon on their way to our assistance. After about 75 minutes and when frozen from the waist down, I was taken aboard the Belgian trawler* Christoforus Columbus *and placed next to the boilers to thaw out.*

Sixty-six of the crew did not survive. Exactly 6 months after sinking *Warwick*, the U413 was sunk by HM destroyers. Her captain, one of the few survivors, did not take another seagoing appointment. In 1947, after 10 years service, he left the navy.

*   *   *

HMCS *Athabaskan*

The Royal Canadian Navy lost twenty-four ships during the war. *Athabaskan* and *Skeena* were among the 1944 casualties. *Athabaskan*, one of the *Tribals*, took the name of the Athabaskan people, a linguistic family of about thirty-two tribes stretching across a vast area of Canada and the United States. *Athabaskan* was laid down in September 1940 at Vickers-Armstrong's High Walker yard at Newcastle. In February 1943 she was commissioned by Commander George Miles, RCN. After working-up at Scapa Flow she went operational with the Royal Navy. She had been in service about 7 months when she was damaged by a glider bomb. While she was under repair her captain left for another appointment. On 6 November 1943 Lieutenant-Commander John Stubbs, RCN, arrived from Canada to take command.

In February 1944 *Athabasken* and the Canadian destroyers *Haida* and *Huron* joined the newly-formed 10th Flotilla at Plymouth. Night sweeps against shipping in the Channel and Bay of Biscay followed. In the early hours of 26 April the cruiser *Black Prince* with *Athabaskan, Ashanti, Haida* and *Huron* engaged the German torpedo boats T24, T27, and T29, known to the Allies as Elbing class destroyers. During the action the T29 was sunk and the T24 and T27 damaged. T24 and T27 put in at Morlaix. Because they could be expected to make a run for Brest, a watch was kept on the area.

Haida, Commander Henry de Wolf, RCN, and *Athabaskan* left Plymouth to cover a minelaying force off the Ile de Bas. It was the evening of 28 April, 2 days since the action with the Elbings. Around midnight British shore radar picked up two contacts in the Channel on a westward heading. The T24 and T27 were making their 70 miles towards Brest. *Haida* and *Athabaskan* were ordered to intercept. At 0400 the Elbings were sighted off St Brieux. Twelve minutes later *Haida* fired starshell and ordered *Athabaskan* to do likewise. *Athabaskan* complied, and then followed with two broadsides before she herself was hit aft, probably by a torpedo from T24. The explosion caused the propeller shafts to snap, the pom-pom to be thrown into the air, and the whole of the after upper superstructure to be set on fire. Lieutenant-Commander Stubbs immediately signalled the C-in-C Plymouth that *Athabaskan* had been torpedoed, and at the same time let *Haida* know by RT. Seeing that the fire was spreading, Stubbs ordered the hands to their abandon ship stations. He then hurried to his cabin. No sooner had he returned to the bridge when there was another explosion. The after part of the ship sank at once, while the forward half rolled slowly over to port. As soon as the mast touched the water the after end began to sink. The bows lifted into the air and sank vertically. The approximate time between the first and last explosion was four minutes. The fact that the crew was at abandon ship stations when the second explosion occurred resulted in many casualties: many of those on the port side were killed, and those on the starboard side were badly burned or blown overboard.

The general opinion was that *Athabaskan* had been hit in the gearing room at 0417 by a torpedo and that the second explosion was the result of fire reaching the after magazine of Y mounting. While *Athabaskan* was abandoning ship the *Haida* went in pursuit of T24 and T27. When the Germans parted company with each other, *Haida* concentrated on T27. Badly damaged and on fire T27 ran aground on a rocky ledge of the Ile de Vierge. She blew up when fire reached her magazines.

Athabaskan had sunk at 0442. *Haida* arrived back in the vicinity at 0450. With daylight fast approaching and a hostile shore only 5 miles away, she had only a short while to rescue survivors. An empty lifeboat and a motorboat were lowered. Lifebuoys and Carley rafts were dropped into the sea and scrambling nets draped down the ship's side. Just over forty burned, injured, and oil-soaked survivors were taken on board before daylight made *Haida* vulnerable to aircraft attack and she had to leave.

At 0730 the T24 returned to the scene with two minesweepers. Between them they rescued eighty-three survivors. One hundred and twenty-eight of the crew perished. Canadian survivors felt that the British could have made an effort to rescue them with air support aiding the attempt. The Germans, even though fearing an air attack, had done what they could in the form of rescue.

A rather outspoken officer who did not suffer fools lightly, Lieutenant-Commander Stubbs had entered the RCN in September 1930. John Stubbs, who was thirty-one, did not survive the action. His body was washed ashore on the Breton Coast. He was buried at Plouescat.

HMCS *Skeena*

HMCS *Skeena* finished her war under very different circumstances to that of *Athabasken*. The *Qu'Appelle, St Laurent*, and *Skeena*, all RCN destroyers and all of the 11th Escort Group, had been directed to shelter for the night of 24/25 October. Accordingly the group was on a heading for Reykjavik. A force eight wind made for uncomfortable conditions on board ship. On approaching Reykjavik the destroyers were ordered to anchor independently to the east of Engey Island, just outside Reykjavik harbour. Lieutenant-Commander Patrick Russell of *Skeena* chose to anchor in the middle of the fairway rather than close under Engey, his reason being that the low elevation of the island afforded no better lee against the wind, and in addition the water was shallow near the island. Owing to the strong wind and poor holding ground he gave orders for a full anchor watch to be set.

On taking over watch keeping duties Lieutenant William Kidd was shown the lights in the vicinity by which *Skeena* had been fixed. Midnight came and went, as did several heavy hail flurries; but just prior to the last of the hail flurries Lieutenant Kidd checked the bearings and found them to be correct. During the last flurry, which lasted 3 or 4 minutes, no lights were visible. Just after the flurry ceased he noticed that the arc between two points was closing very rapidly. Kidd immediately ordered half-ahead on the engines and he called the captain. Seeing that half-ahead was insufficient he ordered an increase in speed. Just then the proximity of land was clearly defined and he ordered full speed ahead. Almost immediately afterwards *Skeena* touched bottom. Kidd explains:

During the period of no more than 5 minutes in which I estimate that it took us to go aground, the ship was jerked by a dragging anchor, and as lights were not visible during the flurry, there was no reason to suspect dragging.

When Lieutenant-Commander Russell arrived on the bridge, he found that *Skeena* had dragged astern onto the rocks of Videy Island and was bumping heavily. Though he suspected that the bumping would have damaged the propellers, one propeller had in fact been lost and the other had jammed, he rang for half-ahead both, and then full ahead. The crew was ordered on deck. To attract attention the searchlights were waved skyward and on to the shore. The trawler *Tritelia*, about 300 yards from *Skeena*, was also signalled.

Attempts by *Tritelia* to pass a tow to *Skeena* ended in failure. *Skeena* was hard-and-fast aground. She was flooded as far aft as the engine room, and was pounding heavily. High seas, mixed with oil fuel, was washing over the entire ship. Concerned that *Skeena* would break in two and capsize, Russell gave orders for all Carley rafts to be tailed at each end so as they could reach the shore and be capable of being hauled back to the ship. Three Carley rafts were launched. Half the hands embarked on these did not reach Videy Island, 50 yards away. This decided Russell that further attempts to abandon ship would only result in further loss of life, and so accepted the risk of keeping everyone on board.

Against a heavy sea and strong wind numerous and various unsuccessful efforts were made to get a line ashore to provide a means of escape should one be required. Personnel on shore were asked, and did, provide assistance from Videy. A party arrived on Videy after daylight. With the use of a Coston gun a line was fired across *Skeena's* fo'c'sle head. This encouraged Russell to land the greater part of her company. By 0900 *Skeena* had taken a heavy list. She was still pounding heavily and seas were sweeping over her upper deck, forecastle, and bridge. It was decided to abandon ship completely. The line from Videy was made fast to one end of a Carley raft and passed ashore. A second line was then made fast to the other end of the raft and made fast to the ship. Hands were hauled across to Videy by means of this line. All remaining hands were safely evacuated.

The grounding had taken the lives of fifteen men. *Skeena* was the last Canadian destroyer to be lost. The RCN played a major role in the war at sea. Loss of personnel was 1,797 officers and men. A further 319 were wounded. Ninety-five were taken prisoner.

* * *

Thursday 1 June. 'The long sobs of autumn's violins'. There was a momentary pause. Then again: 'The long sobs of autumn's violins'. This cryptic message, one of many being relayed that day from the BBC to the French underground movement, was the first line of Paul Verlaine's poem *Chanson d'Autome;* its significance was to signal to the Resistance that the Allied invasion of Normandy would take place within two weeks.

Monday 5 June. Together with other messages, at 2215 the second line of Verlaine's poem was broadcast: 'Wounding my heart with monotonous langour'. The Resistance could now expect the invasion to take place within 48 hours.

(Norwegian) RNN *Svenner*

Tuesday 6 June. D-day. The Royal Norwegian Navy's *Svenner*, which under the White Ensign would have been *Shark*, was a new ship and, at the time of her loss on D-day, had been in commission for only a few weeks. Her captain was Lieutenant-Commander Tore Holthe, R Nor N.

At the time of the invasion the *Svenner* and *Stord* were to assist in the escort of capital ships to a location off Ouistreham, situated at Sword Beach, the most easterly of the invasion beaches. At this point the force, termed the Eastern Bombardment Force, would, at the appointed hour, open fire on the area. *Svenner* and *Stord* were to move closer to the beach so as to engage the coastal guns with greater accuracy. The Eastern Bombardment Force, which included the battleships *Warspite* and *Ramillies*, sailed from the Clyde on 2 June. By the evening of the 5th it was to the south of the Isle of Wight. At 0530 on the 6th it dropped anchor off Sword Beach.

From the bridge of *Svenner* Lieutenant-Commander Holthe observed the enemy-held coast, visible in the grey dawn. Apart from German guns in the vicinity of Ouisstreham, the bombardment force was also in range of batteries at Le Havre, 7 miles to the east. To give the ships some protection from the Le Havre batteries, aircraft laid a smoke-screen to the east of the force. Minesweepers cleared a route for the destroyers to move closer inshore. It was while waiting for the sweepers to do their job that Holthe saw the wake of a torpedo heading towards *Svenner*. He at once ordered full ahead and full port rudder, though it is unlikely that he expected to get underway in time to avoid the torpedo. Fearing the worse he watched the distance between the torpedo and *Svenner* diminish at an alarming rate. He was surprised that the torpedo could somehow have passed right through the assembled ships without having hit any.

It had been around 0200 when Heinrich Hoffman received the news that six enemy ships had been sighted in the Bay of the Seine on a southerly heading. He sailed from Le Havre with three torpedo boats. When he first saw the smoke-screen that masked the bombardment force he mistook it for a bank of fog, but when he saw aircraft dropping smoke-flares he realized that the 'fog' was man-made. The TBs were without radar, and so they had no idea what lay beyond the screen. In line ahead they raced towards the smoke at 28 knots. Dawn was breaking as they emerged the other side. Although they had suspected that some kind of major operation was in progress they were not prepared for the daunting sight that greeted them: there were ships everywhere, and some of them looked very big indeed. The three TBs fired a total of seventeen torpedoes. This one that hit *Svenner* struck amidships. A fountain of oil shot upwards to fall like rain over the whole ship. *Svenner* visibly sagged. Holthe quickly perceived that she could not survive, and about 3 minutes after the explosion he ordered her abandoned. Her boats having been wrecked, Carley rafts were released into the sea and the crew jumped overboard.

Svenner broke in two. Her bow and stern rose high out of the water before sliding back until both sections touched the sea-bed so that the upper part of each remained above water. The stern section sank about 30 minutes later, but the bow remained visible for a considerable time. Thirty-year-old Holthe survived the sinking. Only thirty-four of his crew was rescued, including two Royal Navy liaison personnel.

All the Germans TBs escaped serious damage. They had certainly been very unfortunate in failing to hit anything other than *Svenner*. That they had been able to attack at all was due to the smoke-screen shielding their approach, and the Allied radar being confused by the presence of so many ships.

HMS *Wrestler*

Although she was not sunk, another destroyer casualty of D-day was HMS *Wrestler*, an old 'V and W' which had been completed in May 1918. She was off the Normandy beach-head when at 0637 on 6 June a mine exploded under her abreast the forward oil fuel tank, probably igniting the oil. The explosion blew a hole in her bottom about 12 feet long and 9 feet wide. Buckling and distortion of the hull plating extended for 50 feet. Immediate flooding occurred in two forward oil fuel tanks, the asdic compartment, the 4-inch magazine and shell room, and an oil fuel tank. The only remaining forward oil fuel tank was contaminated. Several fires broke out and a number of compartments were flooded. Shortly after the explosion Lieutenant Reginald Lacon, *Wrestler's* CO, ordered preparations for abandoning ship. All moveable gear and ready use ammunition forward was thrown overboard. Later the depth charges aft were jettisoned. This was to ease the strain on fractured and buckled deck plating near a bulkhead. Lieutenant Lacon states:

> *Although we appeared to be sinking and compartments next to the magazine were known to be on fire, all parties showed a complete disregard for personal safety. Their really fine work saved the ship.*

Following an examination of *Wrestler* in harbour, and taking into consideration her age, it was decided not to repair her. Two months later she was scrapped by Cashmores of Newport.

HMS *Boadicea*

A week after D-day the destroyer *Boadicea* was sunk with heavy loss of life. She had been escort to one of the convoys (EBC8) carrying vital provisions and war material to the troops ashore. EBC8 left Milford Haven on 12 June. It consisted of thirteen merchantmen escorted by *Boadicea* and the corvette *Bluebell*, and a few trawlers. Lieutenant-Commander Frederick Hawkins was the senior officer of escort and captain of *Boadicea*. At about 0440 the following morning, *Boadicea* was then about 248 degrees 12 miles Portland Bill, a JU88 attacked *Boadicea*. The aircraft, showing navigation lights, made its approach off the port bow. Nautical twilight had begun at 0406 so it was fairly light at the time. The bomber was seen to release two torpedoes, one of which broke surface several times before exploding 100 yards astern of *Boadicea*. The other torpedo hit the ship to starboard beneath the bridge. Within five seconds the fore magazine blew up with great violence, killing many of the crew outright.

Lieutenant A.K.MacKay, RNVR, was sleeping in the after lobby. All lower mess decks having been closed and battened down, officers and ratings were sleeping in spaces above the upper deck. Lieutenant MacKay was awakened by the explosion, which he at first thought was *Boadicea* running aground. The lights in the after lobby went out and MacKay roused several of his companions. They made towards the door leading on to the quarter-deck. Then three or four seconds after the torpedo hit, there came the heavy explosion of the magazine blowing up. MacKay says that:

The ship lurched to starboard and the stern rose out of the water at an angle of
some 45 degrees. We tried to open the door on to the quarter-deck; at this stage the
ship sank under us. Depth charges broke loose from their securings on the quarter-
deck and the trap, and, together and the force of gravity, forced the door back again
and threw us in confusion into the after lobby. By this time the ship had tilted up
to a greater angle. Water ran in, presumably from the lower spaces. I went down,
I should think about 15 feet, with the ship and, together with the force of air and
water from inside the lobby, the door was thrown open and I managed to be thrown
clear and come to the surface. On reaching the surface I observed that only a very
small part of the stern was sticking upright at an angle of 90 degrees to the water.
Two or three seconds later the ship sank completely, leaving a small number of
survivors in the water and a considerable amount of wreckage. I should think that
from the first warning we had until the ship actually sank was only a matter of
5 seconds, possibly 6 seconds.

A boat from the American merchantmen *Freeman Hatch* rescued eight men.
Another ship picked up four more. Two officers and ten ratings were the only
survivors.

Overhead visibility on the night of the sinking had been limited by low cloud,
at times the balloons secured to the merchant ships were scarcely visible. The
overcast sky had helped the attacking JU88, but also of considerable help was
that many Allied aircraft were returning to England from France, leaving those
in the ships with the feeling that any plane was almost certainly an Ally.

HMS *Fury*

Fury, Lieutenant-Commander Thomas Taylor, was mined off Normandy on
21 June. At 0935 on the 21st *Fury* weighed from her bombarding position in the
Sword area and proceeded west to the Juno area. An hour later, at 1038, she set
off a ground mine. The explosion threw a column of water over the bridge. Her
foremast snapped, carrying away the aerials. As the true extent of her damage
was unknown and as the wind was varying between strong and near gale force,
it was decided to tow *Fury* to the shelter of a Mulberry harbour. Two such
harbours existed: Mulberry A at the American Omaha beach and the British
Mulberry B 14 miles to its east at Arromanches, Gold beach. While waiting at
anchor for a tug to arrive *Fury* rolled heavily and took up a 6 degrees list to
starboard owing to the flooding of the after shell room and starboard gland
space. At 1325 the Dutch tug *Thames* took *Fury* in tow. Lieutenant-Commander
Taylor:

At 2114, while still in tow, Fury *collided with the stem of the SS* Berryden, *who*
was anchored outside the Mulberry, and sustained damage on the port side above
the water-line. At 2149 the tow parted across the bow of the Sea Salvor, *who was*

at anchor. Fury *collided with this ship, rebounded, and hit her again, inflicting damage above her water-line port side and damage to* Fury's *stem. After drifting clear, the port anchor was let go in a foul birth to prevent the ship drifting on to the* Phoenix[4]. *The tug* Thames *disappeared and was not seen again. The salvage ship* Lincoln Salvor, *who had been standing by since about 1400 waiting for an opportunity to place pumps on board, was called alongside and secured on* Fury's *port side as the anchor was dragging.*

At 2218 the tug Empire Winnie *got a wire secured on* Fury's *forecastle but it parted when she went ahead. The tug* Empire Jonathan *then got a wire in forward and, with the assistance of* Lincoln Salvor, Fury, *now inside the uncompleted part of the Mulberry, buoyed and slipped her port anchor and was got underway.* Lincoln Salvor *was then cast off, as she was a wooden-hulled ship receiving damage during crashing against* Fury.

At 2235 Empire Jonathan's *tow parted and* Fury *crashed amongst the shipping which was anchored close together inside the Mulberry. Tug* Danube IV *then got a tow onto* Fury *forward and progress was resumed, but the tow parted about 2310 and* Fury *once again crashed among the shipping. From now on, four separate tugs managed to get wires and/or hawsers secured to* Fury *ahead or astern, but they all parted in turn and* Fury *hit a number of ships including a floating crane (twice), a ship loaded with petrol, and another loaded with ammunition before grounding on the coast of Normandy about 2 miles west of Arromanches.*

Fury had grounded at 0130 on a falling tide. At about 0530 the ship's company walked ashore and made its way to Arromanches. Attempts to re-float *Fury* that same day were a failure. Not until two weeks later (5 July) was *Fury* re-floated. She returned to England under tow. Regarded as a constructive total loss, she was scrapped three months later.

HMS *Swift*

Three days after the mining of *Fury* the *Swift* was also mined off Normandy. Lieutenant-Commander John Gower, had been on commission only 6 months when she was sunk on the morning of 24 June. At the time of her loss *Swift* was about 5 miles northward of Ouistreham Lighthouse. She had left patrol at 0500 and at 9 knots was proceeding to the Sword area prior to going alongside the destroyer *Scourge* for ammunition. Lieutenant-Commander Gower:

At about 0710 a large explosion occurred, presumably from a mine, apparently under No.1 boiler room, which immediately broke the ship's back. The ship took a slight list to port and started swinging to port, and looked as if she might collide with an LCP which was steaming on a parallel course on my port bow. To check the ship's way I ordered the port anchor to be let go, and this brought the ship up.

The midship portion of the ship was soon under water to the height of the top of the funnel, while the bow and the stern remained above water at an angle of about 30 degrees, in which position she remained for some little time.

At the time of the explosion one watch of seaman was on deck standing by wires and fenders; the remaining hands were below at breakfast, having been called at 0700. The lower deck hatches were closed and the men already dressed as the ship had been at action stations throughout the night. Some of the men on the upper deck, and practically all the bridge personnel, were thrown into the sea, such was the force of the explosion.

The ship's company quickly mustered on the deck. Rafts and life-saving appliances were cleared away and launched. It was obvious to me that the ship would remain in her present position some little time, and so I ordered all men to remain on deck and not attempt to leave the ship in the rafts, although some had already jumped into the sea, as boats would soon be standing by. As it was, ML197 and the same LCP, together with boats lowered from ships in the vicinity (including HMS Venus, *HMS* Belfast, *HMS* Roberts, *HMCS* Sioux, and *HMS* Argonaut), *were soon on the scene. I was fortunate to land back on the bridge, from whence I was able to control operations. The ship was then abandoned in good order, the calmness of the sea and the number of boats greatly facilitating this. Having satisfied myself that both ends of the ship were evacuated I stepped into HMS* Venus' *motorboat. Survivors were then taken to ships in the immediate vicinity, and I proceeded on board HMS* Venus *to report to Commander J. S. M. Richardson, DSO, RN, under whose orders I was operating.*

As the bow and stern of the ship was still above water I returned to the ship with a working party from HMS Venus *and my chief boatswain's mate, in order to satisfy myself that there were no confidential books left on the bridge not finally desposed of. Having satisfied myself on these two points, and as the ship was gradually settling with the rising tide, I deemed it wise to finally leave the ship and return to HMS* Venus. *The ship completely disappeared about half an hour later in 10 fathoms of water, leaving only the top of the foremast visible.*

Eighteen of the crew had been lost with the ship. Lieutenant-Commander Gower was appointed to command *Orwell*. He retired from the navy, after thirty-six years, in 1962.

HMS *Isis*

Another destroyer mined off the Normandy coast was the *Isis*. On D-day she had been a bombardment ship in the Western Sector. Leading Seaman R. Real recalls:

During the night of 5/6 June 1944 we took over to the coast of France units of the Durham Light Infantry, who climbed the cliff and destroyed some guns. We then went to the beach-head proper, where the role of the destroyers moved out of the beach-head area and patrolled up and down providing an E-boat screen, returning to the beach-head at dawn to continue firing.

On 20 July we went to the patrol area at about 1800. We had already completed two legs when there was an almighty bang, and up she went. I managed to escape up the ammunition hoist and up onto the bridge, where the Buffer was cutting the Carley floats adrift. I joined one of these floats and began picking up men in the water. By dark I counted heads. There were forty-one of us. These floats when heavily loaded turn easily over. We had made a rota so that some of us were in the water hanging on to the sides of the float, thus making more room for those injured. Cyril Pearce, the cook, was very badly burnt, the salt water did him good though. We had an artillery-man on board as a liaison officer. He had two broken legs. Others had injuries of a lesser nature. Each time we turned over, so our number became fewer until, in the morning, only three of us were left: the cook, the army officer, and myself.

Petty Officer Ben Thomas was the torpedo gunner's mate. Of the mining he says

This could not have happened at a worse time as a high percentage of the ship's company was on the mess decks preparing or having their supper. The explosion took place just abaft the forecastle, breaking the ship's back. The forepart toppled over onto its side, trapping a very large number of the crew. The PO's mess was on the fo'c'sle. I got out and managed to scramble onto the after part of the ship.

Thomas then helped launch a Carley raft and rescue men in the water.
Charles Grey was another *Isis* survivor:

At 1700 on 20 July I was having a wash and getting ready to go on watch at 1800, the 'second dog'. I went on watch at the depth charges near Y gun. I was about a quarter of an hour early and I was checking the charges on the starboard side when BANG! I was flung backwards. When I got to my feet and looked towards the bridge, that and the whole of the forecastle had gone; it was sinking about 50 feet away. All the men, apart from the duty watch, were in their messes. They didn't stand a chance. I was dumbfounded and frightened. What was I to do? Another seaman came from the stern. We started to throw the cork nets overboard, and then helped to shove a Carley float over the side. There were people trying to get into boats and rafts. The noise of steam, the shouts, and the creaking of the ship, and the oil, was awful. The ship's cook, Cyril Pearce, and the torpedo gunner's mate, PO Ben Thomas, helped with the raft. They looked a mess. The cook had been scalded with hot oil in the galley, and his lip on the right was split down to his jaw. The TGM had a wound above his right ear. How he got out of the PO's mess I don't know. He looked very dazed. We got onto the float. I sat on the side with the TGM between my legs sitting in the float with the cook sitting beside him. The only officer, a sub-lieutenant I believe, and some more ratings were on, in, or hanging on the cords of the float. All this had happened in a matter of minutes. The ship had gone and there we were, floating about covered in oil, wet, and getting cold. The TGM was unconscious so I locked my hands under his chin to keep his head out of the water. The cook looked a mess but there was nothing that could be done to help. We just floated about the sea, so quiet and big. I don't know what the others were thinking but I was praying for someone to come to our rescue.

Around 0615 the next morning, some 12 hours after the explosion that sank *Isis*, an American cutter arrived in search of survivors. Whether *Isis* was mined or torpedoed seems to be a matter of opinion. If torpedoed, then it was in all probability by a German one-man craft known as a Neger. These craft consisted of two 21-inch electrically-propelled torpedoes, one clamped beneath the other with a 3 inch clearance. In the upper torpedo a tiny cockpit replaced the warhead. From their base on the Seine Bay, at Villiers-sur-Mer, the Negers went forth to attack shipping. A German claim is that a Neger attacked *Isis*. But it seems more probable that *Isis* had been mined. A survivor on deck at the time of the explosion stated that he felt a bump and heard a scraping noise which was followed a fraction of a second later by a big explosion. This was followed almost immediately by another two big explosions. *Isis* almost at once took on a heavy list to starboard and her deck became awash. About 20 minutes later she sank bow first, her stern remaining well out of the water from beginning to end. With the exception of one rating all survivors were certain that *Isis* had been mined. A large number of those who escape from the ship died from exposure during the night. Her captain, Lieutenant Henry Durell, was lost with the ship. A plaque in Portsmouth cathedral commemorates the nine officers and 144 ratings who did not survive.

HMS *Goathland*

Another mining off Normandy during this period was the Hunt class *Goathland*, Lieutenant Breon Bordes. In company with the *Quorn*, *Goathland* was, on the night of 23/34 July, patrolling north of the British sector. The patrol had begun at 2315 and was meant to end at first light. *Goathland* was proceeding at 11 knots when at 0423 what was undoubtedly a ground mine exploded under her stern. She appeared to give two distinct bounds before coming to rest. The mine was believed to have detonated directly beneath her as the upheaval of water parted equally to port and starboard. 'Stop Engines' was telegraphed at once, though in fact the engines were stopping even before the engine room artificer at the throttles closed the valve. *Quorn*, three cables astern, hauled clear. Within 3 minutes *Goathland* gave the appearance of settling a little at the stern. She also took on a few degrees list to starboard.

By 0500 preparations for towing were completed. *Quorn* then began to pass her emergency tow. At this stage the towline became entangled round *Quorn's* starboard screw. An attempt to pass a tow from *Goathland* to *Quorn* was successful and by about 0600 the tow was underway at a steady 7 knots, later increased to ten. With *Quorn* able to use one engine only, thus making steering very awkward, and *Goathland* unable to steer at all, the tow was not without problems. At one stage her starboard list was 11 degrees.

At 0928 *Goathland* was brought to anchor off the Juno area of Normandy. The salvage vessel *Sea Salvor* made an alongside. When a diver was sent down to examine *Goathland* it was discovered that a line of rivets on the starboard after fuel-tank had drawn, and that the plating under the after magazine was stove in, causing a leak into the magazine by the shaft tunnel. It was reported that the magazine had flooded almost to the deckhead. The magazine was pumped out and thereafter, with continuous pumping, the water-level in the compartment was kept low. By transferring oil fuel from one tank to another, the ship was brought to a 5 degree list. At 1730 that evening, she was taken in tow by tug for passage to England, arriving next morning after an uneventful passage.

No long term repairs were carried out on *Goathland*. By that stage of the war the urgent need for anything that could float was long past. After being laid up for a time, she was, in February 1945, placed in care and maintenance at Gareloch. About a year later she was scrapped.

HMS *Quorn*

Quorn was sunk with heavy loss of life just over a week after *Goathland* was mined. From July 1944 the *Quorn*, Lieutenant C. E. C. Dickens, operated from Arromanches, laying in harbour during the day and patrolling at night; but by way of a change, at dawn on 3 August she was to bombard Le Havre. Able Seaman Kenneth Hennessey was in charge of the asdic set. He recalls:

We went to first degree action stations in the early afternoon (2 August) as we had entered waters where anything could turn up, even though our 'shoot' wasn't scheduled till dawn. As it happened, nothing did turn up and midnight saw us cruising slowly eastwards along the French coast. There was a certain relaxation of tension when round midnight second degree of action stations was piped. This meant that a certain number of men could leave their action stations and get some rest. Having been cooped up for several hours in the tiny asdic compartment on the bridge listening for submarines, I sent my second operator down to the galley for some of that thick naval cocoa upon which British sailors everywhere depend on to see them through the night watches. My friend Paddy, who as ammunition loader was at his action station on the same deck, was joined by all the men who had been allowed below. Most of these immediately grabbed a place on the lockers and benches and were soon asleep. I don't know whether or not the long hours of underwater listening had made me more tired than I imagined, but at about 0100 I passed out. This had never happened to me before. The doctor was sent for and on his advice I went below decks for a rest before the balloon went up at dawn. On reaching the mess deck I could see that there no more room on the lockers and so I decided, luckily as it happened, to find my hammock and sleep in comfort. My hammock was on a rack with others. I slung it and was soon asleep.

Meanwhile Leading Seaman Roy Kissane was on duty at the forward twin 4-inch dual-purpose guns. From his position of 15 feet below the bridge he heard the asdic operator shout a torpedo warning. Then came an explosion and 'a great orange flash 25 feet high' in vicinity of the boiler room. *Quorn* at once broke in two. Leading Seaman Kissane:

The stern half sank immediately. The fo'c'sle went over to an angle of 45 degrees. I, dressed in sea-boots and duffle coat, was thrown backwards. I hit the guard-rails, did a back somersault, and then hit the water. The ready use ammunition lockers opened and 4-inch shells went plunk, plunk all round me. I did 100 yards in about 20 seconds, after getting off my sea-boots and duffle coat. Exhausted, I watched the saddest sight of all: a beautiful ship go down. After Quorn *had gone I thought, 'Is this what it's like to drown?' Suddenly my hands encountered a length of four-by-two timber, 8 feet long, that had floated off* Quorn. *Soon there were six of us holding on to this timber. Most of the others could not stand the cold and floated away. Eventually there were only two of us, myself and Lieutenant Dickens.*

At 0800, after five hours in the water, an MTB rescued Kissane and his captain. The explosion, at 0250, had destroyed the whole of the starboard side of the midship section abreast the funnel. *Quorn* had broken into two halves. The after portion had sunk very quickly, and the forward portion soon after, so that in about 4 minutes the whole of the ship had gone. The few who managed to clear the ship had very little time to do so. Able Seaman Hennessey, who had taken to his hammock, was helped by the bright moonlight to clear the ship:

As the front of the ship reared upwards all the men who had been asleep on the lockers and benches slid down the slope into a bottomless pit. Something stopped my friend Paddy's slide, but in doing so it mangled his legs to an awful mess. The ship steadied for a brief moment; this enabled Paddy to worm his way through the debris and towards a beam of moonlight that he could see. In this scramble he was joined by me. I had missed the confusion caused by the upending of the bows, my hammock simply swinging in a different position. In the brief moment the ship steadied, I jumped out of my hammock and was close behind Paddy when he reached the hole through which the moonlight was streaming. We were not a moment too soon, for, as we clambered through the hole, water was just beginning to pour in. We both must have thought of the suction which would be created as Quorn *went down, because in spite of his injured legs Paddy set off swimming madly, with myself in close attendance. As we reached a Carley float I looked back, and was just in time to see* Quorn *slide under. It had been a close call.*

It didn't feel too cold in the water, even though I had on neither clothes nor lifebelt. A shipmate allowed me to take a tight grip on his life-jacket, and this helped a lot in the exhausting business of trying to keep afloat. The Carley float was a bit of a menace in that it had been holed, and it in fact turned over more than once. As time passed optimism gradually died. We had been sure that we would be picked up fairly quickly, as other ships were about. But there was no sign of these now. Aircraft passed over us a few times. The first lieutenant told the lads who had lights on their life-jackets to douse them, he being afraid that Jerry would have a go at us in the water.

Dawn came to reveal a much depleted group round the float. All the badly wounded lads had gone, including Paddy, who had been extremely cheerful right to the end. Others had exhausted themselves by swimming around trying to find something better to hang on to. The stillness was broken only by the lapping of the water against the side of the float, all attempts at conversation by this time were quite clear. I remember having no fear of drowning, in fact during the latter stages the prospect seemed attractive. Neither did my past life flash in front of me as I had read it did when my men came close to dying. My entire thoughts were on home. I remember vowing to God that if He got me out of this, I would go to church every day, a vow which, alas, I did not keep. There was quite a swell running. I was surprised at the extent to which we went up and down with it. To crown it all I was seasick for the first time since joining my first ship. The coming of daylight brought a coldness which struck right through me. It was at this time that my impression that drowning seemed most attractive was at its strongest. This was my state of mind when I heard someone shout out something about seeing a ship.

The ship in question was HM trawler *Bressay* under Lieutenant John Wilmott, RNVR, a printer in more peaceful times. It was not by chance that Wilmott came upon *Quorn's* survivors. *Bressay* was one of a group of vessels which at this time spent periods of 10 days engaged in asdic duties off the Normandy coast. At night *Bressay* anchored on the outer defence line, then during the day she patrolled a mile and a half outside the defences. Richard Tinson was a telegraphist in *Bressay:*

Whilst on WT watch from midnight until 0400 on 3 August, I took a signal (around 0330) from the Flag Officer British Assault Area addressed to all ships in the area. This read: Quorn *Sunk In Position – Mine Or Human Torpedo Suspected. I duly passed the message to the officer of the watch, who commented that the position referred to was not far from us. I must explain that we were not allowed to leave our moored position until 0630 or later, if I remember rightly, and only then if visibility was good. Conditions were a little murky but by 0700 we were on the move to look for survivors.*

George Geraghty was instrumental in spotting the Carley floats to set up the rescue. In what seemed fairly good time we picked up some twenty-two of Quorn's *crew who were nearly all clinging to two Carley floats. Unfortunately four of them were dead. But the others, after being given a tot of 'neaters', cigarettes, and the warmth of the engine casing, were soon very much alive and expressing their reaction to the ordeal. Right up until lunch-time our boys applied artificial respiration unceasingly to the four who did not survive, and who were pronounced dead by a surgeon officer who had been brought aboard. During the afternoon a padre and a bugler from the Marines came aboard. We left the anchorage for a spot in the Channel where we buried the four deceased.*

A hundred and thirty of the crew were lost. The survivors, there were about twenty-six, were landed in France. After some leave they were dispersed to other ships and naval establishment. Able Seaman Hennessey joined a minesweeper at Malta, and spent the remainder of his service in sweepers. Leading Seaman Kissane, who had lost a brother in *Glowworm* and another brother in the submarine *Stonehenge*, served at Portsmouth Barracks until leaving the navy in late 1945.

Some credence is given to the notion that *Quorn* had been the victim of a German Linsen explosive motor-boat, but if that was a craft of the Small Battle Unit then it was in all probability one of the Marders, an almost identical craft to the Neger.

HMS *Rockingham*

Rockingham was one of the Lease-Lend destroyers, the ex-USN *Swasey*. Her loss on 27 September was an unfortunate affair. She sailed from Rosyth at 1535 on 25 September for duty as a safety ship for the rescue of aircrew. *Rockingham* arrived on station at 2210. She remained on patrol until ordered at 2008 on the 26th to return to harbour. Since leaving Rosyth her navigation had been wholly by dead reckoning. By the time of her ordered return, weather conditions had made *Rockingham's* dead reckoning position unreliable. A sunsight had been taken during the forenoon, but the ship's violent motion nullified its accuracy. A position line possibly indicated that she was to the northward of her dead reckoning position. A heavy rainstorm prevented the taking of starsight, and by the time the moon became visible it was also setting.

It was the intention of *Rockingham's* captain, Lieutenant-Commander John Cooper, RNVR, to use transmissions from the Redhead Radio Beacon, situated about 6 miles south of Montrose, to provide navigational aid for his return to harbour through a gap (Gap A) in a minefield designated QZX604. In response to *Rockingham's* signal of 2059 a transmission was arranged from 2130. While on her way back to harbour, *Rockingham* struck a mine in the early hours of the 27th. Lieutenant-Commander Cooper:

> *Having been on the bridge most of the night, I went to my sea-cabin at about 0345 to warm, the ship then being on a course of 259 degrees. At 0404 I was struck on the head by a piece of radar gear. I rushed onto the bridge and ordered 'Stop engines'. Investigation by the first lieutenant showed that Rockingham had been mined aft on the port side and her back had apparently broken just forward of the after superstructure. The tiller flat was flooded and the after mess decks were filling rapidly. Hands at the after gun's crew, and on the after mess deck, were injured. The engineer officer's inspection suggested that the port propeller had been blown off and that water was entering the after engine room at a steady rate through the bulkhead glands and couplings. This leakage was greatly reduced by the use of wooden wedges and the tightening of the glands. All available fire and bilge pumps were started and in addition the 70 tons portable pumps and mains circulator were brought into use. The water was thus kept well below the platform plates. Fuel oil was pumped overboard to bring up the stern and calm the sea.*
>
> *All but one of the WT aerials had been carried away, but this was quickly restored and the following signal made to Commander-in-Chief: Am Mined In Position 56.47'N/01.31'W. Situation Serious. And later: Help Needed Urgently. Distress signals by searchlight, signal projector fireworks, and Oerlikon tracer were also made. At about 0500 the starboard anchor was let go in about 35 fathoms in an attempt to bring the ship head-to-wind to ease the pounding on the damaged structure aft, but with no result. The motor-boat and whaler had also been turned out for lowering, the former being lost shortly afterwards. In the meantime the injured had received treatment and had been placed in the whaler. One rating, Stoker R. Grant, was missing and had apparently been blown over the ship's side. The remainder of the ship's company not employed on damage control were ordered to prepare to abandon ship.*

At 0445 the destroyer *Lancaster* was escorting a convoy when she received *Rockingham's* signal reporting the mining. Ten minutes later she picked up *Rockingham's* Help Needed Urgently signal. Within minutes she was on a heading for *Rockingham's* reported position. At 0552, by which time it was estimated that *Rockingham* should be 10 nautical miles distant, *Lancaster* requested *Rockingham* to fire Oerlikon tracer skyward. This was done. The expectation had been that *Rockingham* would be sighted on a bearing of 105 degrees, but her tracer was observed at 138 degrees and at a distance which made it probable that she was in a minefield QZX604. A subsequent radar plot confirmed this to be so. *Rockingham*, signalled that she was unable to steam or to steer and that she was at anchor. She was asked by *Lancaster* to slip her cable and drift out to starboard. When *Lancaster* came to a stop to leeward of *Rockingham*, it was realized that the drift was considerable. A Dan buoy was dropped about a mile clear of QZX604, and a position maintained close to the buoy. *Rockingham's* drift was plotted by radar as 2 knots.

On the night in question the destroyer *Vanity* was acting as AA guard ship and emergency destroyer at Methill. Ordered to provide assistance to *Rockingham*, she was, by 0925, proceeding through Gap A with the trawlers *Strephon, Robert Stroud,* and *Harry Melling.* The group sighted the two destroyers at 1310.

By 1417, a line having been passed, *Lancaster* was able to start towing. *Rockingham* slowly came round into the wind. As she did so, the after part of the ship started to work heavily. The wind had risen to force nine and at 1635 the tow parted. At this stage *Rockingham* transferred eight casualties and forty-seven non-essential personnel to two of the trawlers, this being made possible by the skilful handling of the trawlers in the heavy seas, and the assistance of *Vanity* in pumping oil onto the sea.

For two hours *Vanity* tried to pass another tow to *Rockingham*. Then at 1915 the *Robert Stroud* passed a 3 inch wire, but she seemingly did not have the power to bring the ship round into the wind. The tow parted soon afterwards. In view of the weather and the likelihood of no improvement, and the onset of darkness, Lieutenant-Commander Cooper, also having in mind the increase in working of the after part of the ship, reluctantly decided to abandon ship. All hands mustered on the forecastle. With *Lancaster* and *Vanity* illuminating *Rockingham*, the trawlers tried to make an alongside, but none could do so. At 2000 Cooper reported that *Rockingham* was sinking. Risking damage to herself, *Vanity* closed from leeward and took off the remaining hands. Within minutes of her moving away, *Rockingham*, at 2038, sank stern first.

In an assessment of how *Rockingham* came to find herself on the north-east corner of minefield QZ1604 the Redhead Beacon featured prominently. Doubts were cast on the reliability of the beacon in certain circumstances. *Vanity's* captain stated that when he passed through Gap A with the trawlers, he was, '*navigating entirely by direction finding as the Redhead Beacon was considered unreliable*'. And later, '*Redhead Beacon was being received with considerable interference during the dark hours; it was fluctuating 6 degrees between bearings, and comparisons of bearings between Lancaster and Vanity were unsatisfactory. I considered my dead reckoning positions were very accurate*'. *Lancaster* also reported that during darkness Redhead's signals were very weak. Tests showed that the more experienced the operator receiving the Redhead signals, the more reliable was the bearing.

Lieutenant-Commander Cooper had been *Rockingham's* captain for only a month. Although one of the eight L class destroyers in commission at the outbreak of war, by the end of hostilities the class had suffered heavily, four having been sunk and three regarded as a constructive total loss, *Lookout* being the only one to survive intact. Launched in October 1941 the *Loyal* was the last of the Ls to enter service. She almost came to grief off Anzio in February 1944 when a shell from a shore battery burst on the upper deck. Though her starboard main engine and a steering motor were put out of action *Loyal* was able to return to harbour. She was out of action for six weeks.

On 12 October *Loyal* was involved in an engagement off Italy's Adriatic coast. Her captain, Commander Godfrey Ransome, had been in command since the previous August. *Loyal*, in company with *Lookout*, was bombarding positions in the Cesenatico area, a few miles north of Rimini. After firing off 850 shells *Loyal* was returning southward at 20 knots with *Lookout* three cables astern when at 1607 she exploded a mine in position 037 degrees, Pesaro 2.8 miles. The mine detonated to starboard approximately 10 yards from the ship. Depth of water was 7.5 fathoms. The explosion shook *Loyal* considerably and threw up a column of water 200 feet in height. Main engines were put out of action. Oil fuel flooding caused the ship to take on a 7 degrees list to port. A line was passed between *Lookout* and *Loyal* and at 1700 the tow was got underway. Course was set for Ancona, 35 miles south of Pesaro. No difficulty was experienced in towing at 6 knots, and speed could have been increased if necessary. After little more than 6 hours, the destroyers arrived at Ancona at 2315 without further incident. As a result of the mining *Loyal* was eventually reduced to care and maintenance. In August 1948 she was sold for scrapping at Milford Haven.

HMS *Wensleydale*

HMS *Wensleydale*, one of the Hunts, saw much action in her 2 years service, which for the greater part was spent with the 15th Destroyer Flotilla at Plymouth. Two highlights of her career took place in 1944 when in August she had a hand in the sinking of U671 and U413. But a few weeks prior to these triumphs she was involved in the first of two collisions that year. On 3 July *Wensleydale* was in collision with a tug. In this she suffered damage port side forward in the form of a gash in her side about 2.5 feet in length. Then on 21 November she was involved in a much more serious accident when she collided with a Landing Ship Tank (LST367), *Wensleydale's* engine room and gearing room becoming flooded and open to the sea. Though it was not seen to be the case at the time, this collision ended her active service career and led eventually to her being scrapped. Within a month of the collision she was placed in category C Reserve, which meant that it was unlikely that she would be re-commissioned. Two months later she was upgraded to category B Reserve, an indication that she would be fully repaired with the possibility of her entering Royal Navy service, or being loaned or sold to another navy. But this hopeful sign came to nothing, as in June 1946 *Wensleydale* was sold for scrapping. She has been awarded four Battle Honours.

HMS *Aldenham*

The Adriatic in mid-December was the scene of the *Aldenham's* loss. She had been in commission only a few weeks when in March 1942 with *Grove, Leamington,* and *Volunteer* she took part in the sinking of U587. The following May she joined the 5th Flotilla at Alexandria. *Aldenham,* one of the Hunt class, spent the remainder of her service in the Mediterranean. *Aldenham* was sunk among the islands of northern Yugoslavia.

By the autumn of 1944 more than half of Yugoslavia had been cleared of German troops, mostly by Tito's partisans. Britain had played an active part in arming and helping them. *Aldenham* was lost giving support to partisan activity against Pag Island, a narrow 35-mile-long stretch of land close to the Yugoslavian coast and opposite the town of Karlobag. A little to the south of Pag Island, and part of the island group known as the Dalmation Islands, is the harbour of Salinska, part of which forms the peninsula of Veli Rat. It was from there that *Aldenham* sailed on her final operation. Her captain, Commander James Farrant, had been approached as regards to bombarding strong points in Pag town and four 105mm guns to the south of Karlobag prior to a direct attack by land to capture Pag. Commander Farrant decided to give the maximum support with the forces under his command.

At 0900 on 14 December *Aldenham* and her sister ship *Atherstone* opened a bombardment of enemy positions. During the next 2 hours 20 minutes they fired between them approximately one thousand rounds. That afternoon Commander Farrant was informed that the partisan commander required a bombardment by destroyers of enemy strong points in Pag town between 1400 and 1500. This request was complied with, both ships firing two salvos a minute throughout the hour. Commander Farrant:

Aldenham *and* Atherstone *weighed on completion of the bombardment; I increased speed to 20 knots as I wished to save daylight and return to Veli Rat to re-ammunition. Course was set to pass about 1 mile north of Skerda Island, which was a reverse pf the route by which I had come that morning. At approximately 1545, when the north-western edge of Planik Island bore 176 degrees,* Aldenham *altered course to 176 degrees so as to pass between Planik and Olie. The ship was still under wheel when there was an explosion amidships by the funnel and the ship broke in two, both halves settling in a few minutes.* Atherstone *passed* Aldenham *and on anchoring to leeward lowered her whaler and life-saving apparatus to pick up survivors, being assisted later by Mls and LCG12. In all, five officers and sixty-two ratings were picked up. The regrettably heavy loss of life was undoubtedly due to the fact that the forepart of the ship capsized at once and the after part sank virtually within a minute. The survivors were taken to Zara.*

Lieutenant Eric Pilditch, the captain of *Atherstone*, states:

At the time of the explosion Atherstone *was two cables astern of* Aldenham, *speed 20 knots. The explosion seemed to occur abreast of the funnels. The ship was completely enveloped in smoke and spray, and when it subsided she was seen to be broken in half. The fore-end capsized at once and sank in 10 minutes. The after end disappeared within 1 minute. It is considered that the mine was a moored magnetic. Both ships had passed over already close to the position when entering Slatina Bay. The sea was moderate to rough, and it was found that* Atherstone *drifted down wind (force 6) much faster than the survivors and it was necessary to let go both anchors in 40 fathoms to leeward of the wreck and to collect survivors by boat and lines as they drifted past. Men in the water stand far more chance of being rescued if they can keep together in groups supported by their lifebelts and holding on to some sort of float. The sea was too cold and rough for individual swimmers to last for more than a few minutes and those not wearing lifebelts were drowned at once.* Atherstone *left the area shortly before dark, when no more survivors could be found, and proceeded to Zara.*

The mining had taken place within a few minutes of 1530. There were only sixty-seven survivors. Commander Farrant, who later took command of the Hunt *Beaufort*, suffered a broken leg.

Aldenham was the last Royal Navy destroyer to be sunk in the Second World War.

Chapter Seven

1945

At the dawn of the new year, the defeat of Nazi Germany was little more than 4 months away, while the war with Japan would continue a further 4 months beyond Germany's surrender. Although no Royal Navy destroyers were sunk in the remaining months of the war, HMS *Walpole* and *Pathfinder* were written off and two British destroyers were sunk while on loan to foreign navies.

Walpole and the frigate *Rutherford* arrived at their patrol billet off the Dutch coast around 1820 on 5 January. The patrol was uneventful until 0740 the following morning when *Walpole's* OOW, Lieutenant Alan Kingdon, sighted an object floating on the surface about 40 yards ahead of the ship. Although the streak of dawn was perceptible, sunrise was 70 minutes off, it was still fairly dark. Raising his binoculars, Kingdon recognized the object as a mine. He ordered starboard 30 degrees but before the rudder had taken full effect there was a very heavy explosion, which killed two stokers. It was presumed that *Walpole* had struck the sighted mine.

At the time of the explosion *Walpole's* captain was passing through the plot on his way to the bridge. On reaching the bridge he saw that it was a complete shambles and that the ship was already taking on a starboard list. All watertight doors were ordered closed. An emergency signal was passed to *Rutherford* by VS, and a similar signal was originated for transmission by WT, though this was not sent as all power had failed and the wireless emergency batteries had been shattered. No.1 boiler room flooded quickly, and all steam-pressure was lost. The list to starboard stopped at about 12 degrees. Orders were given to lighten ship and to transfer upper deck weights to the port side. These measures gradually reduced the list by half.

An examination of the damage disclosed that the bulkhead between the forward and after boiler room was distorted. While this bulkhead was being shored, *Rutherford* was ordered to take *Walpole* in tow. Towing began at 0930. Because the rudder had jammed with 30 degrees of starboard wheel (it was 2 hours before the rudder was freed) towing at first was a difficult affair. All steering from the wheelhouse had been blown away, so when the steam was eventually obtained *Walpole* had to be steered from aft. At 1615 she anchored off the East Tongue Towers, her captain not wishing to risk a tow through the Edinburgh Channel at night in visibility that was rapidly deteriorating. *Rutherford* had towed her for 37 miles. Sheerness tugs took up the tow. Almost 32 hours after being mined, *Walpole* was secured to a buoy at 1452. Completed in August 1918, *Walpole's* 25 years were against her. With the end of the war only months away she was sold a short time after the mining, but was not broken up until September 1946.

In common with many destroyers featured in this history, the *Pathfinder* had an eventful career, serving in the Atlantic, Mediterranean, and Indian Ocean. In January and February 1945 she was in operations against the Japanese in Burma. It was during this period that *Pathfinder* was involved in the fierce fighting at Ramree Island, just a mile off the Burmese coast and 60 miles from Akyab. In this engagement the ship was badly damaged. The action is described in a report by her captain, Lieutenant-Commander Thomas Halifax:

> *During Operation Block in the Mingaung Chaung and Paikseik Taungmaw and Kaleindaung rivers to the east of Ramree Island on Sunday 11 February 1945, HMS* Pathfinder *had occasion to leave her berth at the head of the Paikseik Taungmaw river to replenish fuel, ammunition and provisions from HMAS* Nepal. *On passage back to my station, I received information that parties of Japanese were suspected at two points close to it so I swept the first with pom-pom and Oerlikon fire at close range in passing at 1653, and the second with 4-inch fire immediately after anchoring in my station at 1705.*
>
> *At 1732 and 1746 I received an urgent request from FOB No.1 to call off four Spitfires which he stated were strafing our troops to the southward. At 1756 single-engine aircraft were sighted at about 12,000 yards and 5,000 feet over the Kaleindaung river and at 1757 some of these were seen diving on HMS* Paladin *anchored at the entrance of the Paikseik Taungmaw river. The armament had been in LA control and so was immediately switched to HA. The target was indicated to the director on a bearing of approximately Red 50 and preparation made to engage.*
>
> *At 1758 two aircraft were sighted right ahead at a range of about 2,000 yards diving straight at the ship at an angle of sight of about 40 degrees. At 1758 degrees, before the forward 4-inch guns could bear and while the close range weapons were still wooded, the leading aircraft released its bomb, followed closely by the second from about 150 feet directly over the ship. The first bombs entered the water at a point 50 feet from No.81 station to starboard and must have exploded on or near the river bottom. The second fell some 100 yards astern and does not appear to have damaged the ship. A great column of water at least 100 feet high was thrown into the air and fell over practically the whole ship. The ship herself was lifted by the stern in two distinct kicks which at the time it was difficult to believe had not broken her back.*

It was reported that the ship's structure was generally distorted and buckled from the after end of the gearing room to just forward of the steering compartment. *Pathfinder* sagged about 10 inches and there was a whipping buckle down the side-plating abreast the bulkhead between the engine room and the boiler room. The after magazine was flooded to the water-line. Owing to the weakened condition of the structure, the after guns could only have been fired in an emergency. The degree of damage which resulted from two small bombs, each of about 68 kg, was surprising, especially when it is considered that one bomb had dropped 17 yards to starboard and the other had exploded 100 yards astern, and thus was unlikely to have caused any damage. The shallowness of the river, it was about 5 fathoms, may well have contributed to the severity of the damage.

The next morning, with her port propeller smashed and a hole in her stern, *Pathfinder* proceeded at 7 knots to Kyaubpyu. Ten iron-girders were welded to her upper deck. The *Paladin* then escorted harbour flying a Japanese flag, a gift from the Royal Garhwal Rifles whom *Pathfinder* had been supporting with her guns. It was several months before she was ready to journey to the United Kingdom.

The extensive repairs needed to make *Pathfinder* fully operational were not implemented. At one stage she was used for target trials. In November 1948 she arrived at Howells, Milford Haven, to be broken up.

The first of the two destroyers to be lost while on loan to a foreign navy was the *Deiatelnyi*. She was one of the ex-American destroyers, in this case the USN *Herndon*. In her Royal Navy colours she was the *Churchill*.

There is no real certainty as to whether *Deiatelnyi* set off a mine or was torpedoed by a U-boat; if the latter was the case then the attack would appear to have been made by Oberleutnant zur See Willi Dietrich of U286 in what was probably his one and only sinking. If Dietrich did make the attack it was in the evening of 16 January while the *Deiatelnyi* was doing duty as escort to the Kola Fiord-White Sea convoy KB1. At the time of the sinking, *Dieatelnyi* was in the reported position 68.56'N/36.31'E, in the White Sea. Three months after the sinking, the U286 herself was depth charged and sunk by Royal Navy frigates off Murmansk.

The final British destroyer to be sunk in the Second World War, the *La Combattante,* was on loan to the Free French Navy. Her captain, Lieutenant-Commander Jacques Pepin Lehalleur, says:

I was sent to La Combattante *in October 1944, at Sheerness. Her previous COs were Lieutenant-Commanders Bocesgine and Patou. She was a Hunt class destroyer Mark III built in a Glasgow shipyard in 1942. She was first named HMS* Haldon *and was transferred and commissioned by the Free French Navy of 15 December 1942. In March 1943 she was in the 1st Destroyer Flotilla based in Portsmouth. From that day onwards she operated relentlessly in the Channel-convoy work, night patrols, and fighting against German units. On D-Day she was off Courseulles in Normandy and fired on German shore-batteries, going so close she grounded.*

During her 2 years and 2 months with the French, *La Combattante* steamed 53,620 miles. Then came the night of 23/24 February 1945. Liaison Petty Officer John Tuttlebee was serving in the ship. He recalls:

We were on patrol off the mouth of the Humber with MTB770 saw an underwater explosion, which blew the ship in two, just abaft the midships of La Combattante. *The forward part rolled about 60 degrees but regained an even keel fairly quickly. The after part sank rapidly. A lookout on the MTB reported that he had sighted a periscope, but the periscope was not sighted by any other crew member and it is officially considered that a mine caused the explosion. When the explosion occurred I was asleep in my hammock in the Liaison Staff Mess, which was on the port side of the lower deck of the forward part of the ship. As far as I can remember, my first thought was that we had been hit by a torpedo. However, the immediate reaction was to get out fast. Everywhere was in darkness. By holding on to stanchions, pipes, and any other metal supports we could find, we made our way to the escape ladder on the midships bulkhead. Fortunately the bulkhead was undamaged and the watertight doors to the seamen's deck and the deck above that were still open. When we arrived on deck the forward half was afloat on an even-keel. The after part was starting to slide into the sea. At this point I think my main worry was as to how long our part of the ship was going to stay afloat, as the MTBs could not come too close to the forepart in case they sustained damage. In the event, it remained afloat for 2 hours.*

There were more than 120 survivors to rescue. Several men were clad only in singlet and shorts, and were minus a lifebelt. To get to the MTBs involved a swim in icy-water for some thirty yards, followed by a scramble onto a float as to be pulled into the MTBs. A number of our shipmates were lost at this stage owing to exhaustion and the cold. The mining of La Combattante *was a sad end to a good ship. She had sailed some 50,000 nautical miles, had escorted many convoys in the Atlantic and in Home Waters, and had been in the forefront at the invasion of Normandy, and had sunk four ships in Channel engagements.*

In his report of 25 February to the Flag Officer in Charge (Humber), Lieutenant-Commander Pepin Lehalleur, set down details of his ship's loss as follows:

FS La Combattante *was on No.1 patrol (that is between buoy 59A and latitude 53.12'N, just two miles SE of No.58 buoy) in company with HM MTBs 763 and*

770, during the night of the 23rd/24th February, 1945, when at 2335 (BST) there was a powerful explosion amidships and the ship over to starboard developing a 60 degree list within a few seconds. No distress signal by WT was made. Distress rockets, however were fired. The ship's position was then 030 degrees 1.5 miles from East Dudgeon Buoy, course 140 degrees speed 12 knots. Weather conditions: sea calm, visibility good with slight haze, cloudless sky, wind WNW 1, full moon bearing south, altitude about 60 degrees. Tide running 330 degrees, 1 knot.

Immediately after the explosion, I rushed from my cabin to the bridge, and I could observe the following: the ship had broken in two amidships, the rear part was sinking rapidly and the forepart consisting of the fo'c'sle and the bridge was reeling over to the starboard and in about 15 seconds had developed a list of 60 degrees, which almost immediately amplified to 110 degrees approximately, and remained floating. Together with about 50 men, I managed to stay on the port side of the bows, which were awash. A number of men had taken to the sea either in rafts or clinging to pieces of wreckage. A certain amount of fuel oil was spread over the surface of the sea. Both MTBs immediately started picking up survivors which were scattered over a wide area. It was not before 0145 hours that MTB763 was able to come alongside the wreck and pick us up. I was the last to leave the ship at 0200 approximately. Both MTBs made for Immingham to land the survivors. Another MTB unit had joined us and remained on the spot.

I am of the opinion that the loss of La Combattante was due to her hitting a mine because:

(i) No HE was observed by the A/S operator although listening conditions were excellent.
(ii) No wake was observed. No radar echo.
(iii) The concussion seemed to come from underneath the ship and seemed too powerful for a torpedo explosion.

Losses: three French officers, sixty-two French petty officers and ratings. Two British liaison ratings are missing. One French petty officer died while on board MTB770. There are 1117 survivors. The total complement was 184 officers and men.

The fact that it was alleged that a periscope had been observed by an MTB had led to speculation as to the exact cause of *La Combattante's* loss. Rear-Admiral Jacques Pepin Lehalleur states:

It had been reported in various accounts of the sinking of La Combattante *that she was torpedoed by a German pocket submarine. In fact there has been confusion with another event which happened in the same area but as a different hour. It is definitely established that* La Combattante *was sunk by a mine laid in shallow water, the result being that the degaussing system although working well and having been tested on Portsmouth loop a few days before, cannot be incriminated.*

It is certain that mines had been laid in the area of the sinking; these mines had been laid by E-boats on the night of 17/18 February. There is, however, a claim that a small German submarine known as Seehund (Seal) had torpedoed *La Combattante*. These midget submarines had a two-man crew. It is now believed that one of the Seehunds (KU330) fired a single torpedo at *La Combattante* from a range of about 850 yards. The Seehund KU330 was commanded by Leutnant zur See Klaus Sparbrodt.

For His Majesty's destroyers it had been a long, a hard, and a costly war; a war on which some 8,000 destroyer men did not survive. It should be born in mind that for every destroyer that was sunk, two more were damaged in action or by mines.

Index